DADA AND BEYOND

AVANT-GARDE
CRITICAL STUDIES

27

Editor

Klaus Beekman

Associate Editors

Sophie Berrebi, Ben Rebel,
Jan de Vries, Willem G. Weststeijn

International Advisory Board

Henri Béhar, Hubert van den Berg,
Peter Bürger, Ralf Grüttemeier,
Hilde Heinen, Leigh Landy

Founding Editor

Fernand Drijkoningen†

DADA AND BEYOND

VOLUME 2:
DADA AND ITS LEGACIES

Edited by
Elza Adamowicz and Eric Robertson

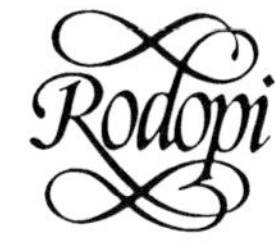

Amsterdam - New York, NY 2012

Cover design: Aart Jan Bergshoeff

All titles in the Avant-Garde Critical Studies series (from 1999 onwards)
are available to download from the Ingenta website http://www.ingenta.com

The paper on which this book is printed meets the requirements of "ISO
9706: 1994, Information and documentation - Paper for documents -
Requirements for permanence".

ISBN: 978-90-420-3589-8
E-Book ISBN: 978-94-012-0864-2
Editions Rodopi B.V., Amsterdam - New York, NY 2012
Printed in The Netherlands

Contents

List of Illustrations

Preface

Elza Adamowicz and Eric Robertson

As the chapters in the first volume of the book demonstrated, performance was one of the most fundamental aspects of Dada's originality. This idea is developed further in the opening essay of the present volume. In her detailed study of Sophie Taeuber's contribution to Zurich Dada, Jill Fell explores one of the defining yet still under-researched areas of Dada performance, namely dance. Through a detailed examination of Taeuber's training with the Laban school and her interaction with her fellow Dadaists, Fell corrects a lingering misconception of Dada dance as an unstructured improvisation, revealing it to be a much more consciously created entity. Fell suggests possible areas of interaction and cross-fertilisation between dance and other creative forms of expression, and reveals the extent to which Dada dance anticipates later forms of twentieth-century experimentation.

As Catherine Dufour argues in her essay, "L'Acte Dada", the performative dimension of Dada plays a key role in the alternative history of twentieth-century art. Studying the relationship of Dada's actions with the pre-war avant-gardes in Italy, Russia and Czechoslovakia, Dufour argues that Dada action stemmed from the need to transcend the traditional parameters of artistic expression. As Dufour explains, Dada action differs according to the context in which it is produced, but two essential characteristics emerge from it: while on the one hand it enacts a cathartic, physical celebration of our existence, its tendency to provoke a strong response from the public endows it with a political character. If the former trait is evident in later forms of performance such as body art, action art and even punk music, Dada's political dimension re-emerges in the work of the Situationists and the Russian ultra avant-garde. While an empty ritualistic form of Dada reappeared in some neo-Dada work of the 1960s, Dufour argues that the world crises of the new millennium have given rise to a "third age" of Dada in the work of artists such as Wem Delvoye and Jose Castro.

Starting with Tzara's famous declaration that "Dada is a state of mind", Kerstin Sommer considers the ongoing relevance of Dada to artistic practices in the late twentieth and early twenty-first centuries. She explores its legacy in the work of three diverse artists: the action painting of Jackson Pollock, the *Atta*-art of German performance artist Christoph Schlingensief and the work of contemporary British artist Richard Layzell. As Sommer observes, Pollock's action-paintings are considered as a form of Dada performance, sharing the Dadaists' preoccupation with chance, whereas Schilingensief's art is indebted to the politically-charged activities of Berlin Dada, and Layzell's installations and events show the unmistakable influence of Schwitters in their subversion of audience expectations while undermining notions of social order. In their various ways, these successors of the original Dada revolution keep its flame alive.

In "Dada and Cinema", Jennifer Wild turns her attention to the role of cinema as a decisive influence on Francis Picabia's paintings of the period 1913–15, a full decade before he ventured into filmmaking. As the essay reveals, the visits Picabia made to New York not only familiarised him with popular American cinema, but may have offered the impetus for his famous mechanomorphic style. In particular, Wild argues, Picabia's encounter with the famous dancer-turned-film star Stacia Napierkowska in January 1913 would prove to be decisive for the development of his mechanomorphic paintings, many of which conflate the theme of woman with a cinematographically inflected evocation of the US experience.

Man Ray's films are widely acknowledged as vital contributions to both Dada and Surrealist cinema, yet most studies omit to separate and evaluate the respective roles of the two movements, or the degree to which they interact in his cinematographic œuvre. In her essay, Kim Knowles examines Man Ray's *Emak Bakia* (1926) in detail, and argues that it occupies a unique space on the borderline between Dada and Surrealism. The use of automatic techniques, and the co-existence of subjective and objective vision and abstract and figurative forms, are all revealed to be of key importance to the film's particular status within his repertoire.

Ramona Fotiade examines Man Ray's experimental films in an essay where parallels are drawn between early twentieth-century avant-garde film and the post-modernist aesthetic of New Wave cinema. Man Ray's innovative techniques – his radical montage techniques, the creation of optical illusion, and the self-referentiality of his films – impact on film-makers Chris Marker and Jean-Luc Godard, whose disruptive strategies – concerning the role of montage and photography, or the relationship between montage and soundtrack – subvert conventions of cinematic realism.

In the section "Dada Cultures", attempting to locate Dada culture, Dafydd Jones highlights the very difficulty of establishing any singular definition of Dada, given that its very basis lies in the rejection of categories and straightforward definitions. As Jones points out, it is as difficult to impose a chronological starting point or a moment of closure on the movement as it is to attempt to ascribe it any single, coherent ideological stance. Reconsidering Dada's position from the perspective of poststructuralist theory, Jones argues compellingly that we must remove Dada from the implicitly oppositional – and ultimately redundant – conceptual framework of an "avant-garde" in order to think of it instead as a phenomenon in flux, constantly reconstituting and redefining itself.

Given the etymology of "culture" as something that has grown, it is appropriate that Nadia Ghanem should focus on the birthplace of Dada, the Cabaret Voltaire in Zurich's Spiegelgasse. Highlighting its status as a haven amidst the devastation of the First World War, Ghanem considers the Cabaret as a necessary abstraction from the real world in which the Dada group could create their own universe. In some key respects, the Cabaret's closed micro-utopian space foreshadows recent works such as Maurizio Cattelan's *6th Caribbean Biennial* (2001) which, echoing Zurich Dada, appropriates the practices of the official art world only in order to subvert them.

Extending the etymological definition of culture as a product of the earth, Patrick Suter examines Dada from an environmental point of view. Taking as his first exemplary instance Duchamp's *Fountain*, Suter contends that amongst its most radical achievements are the emphasis it places on the act of naming, and its exposure of the cleft that traditionally separates the art work from the real world in the mind of the spectator. The "recycled" collages of Kurt Schwitters, too, pose questions of an environmental nature, while his Merzbau creations undermine the institutionalisation of art by removing it from the museum and integrating it into a living space. Similarly, Dada textual practices of cutting and pasting random words from newspapers erode the divisions between "artistic" practices and everyday life. By emphasising notions of assemblage, collecting and recycling, Dada underlined and indeed anticipated the disjuncture that still exists today between the institutions of art and an ever-more threatened ecology.

The next section, "Dada Legacies", begins, appropriately, with a discussion of three figures who, while not Dadaists themselves, were all indebted to the influence of Dada. As Nathalie Roelens's essay sets out to prove, Jean Dubuffet, Pierre Alechinsky and Henri Michaux are all, in different yet related ways, children of the Dada revolution. Their rejection of formal artistic institutions, and their rejection of Paris in favour of more peripheral French-speaking areas, go hand in hand with their privileging of "primitive" and marginal artistic practices such as Dubuffet's crude scrawls, Alechinsky's left-handed paintings and Michaux's indeterminate watercolour stains. These and other experiments would ensure that Dada's legacy continued into the second half of the twentieth century.

Paul Cooke examines the reception history of the Surrealist writer René Crevel, whose creative legacy has tended to be either neglected or overshadowed by accounts of his suicide. Basing his research on extensive bibliographical data, Cooke reveals significant disparities in the reception of Crevel's work in the Anglo-American context and in Europe. As his study reveals, research in recent years has helped to generate a renewed interest in, and to shed new critical perspectives on, Crevel's creative work, moving away from the Romantic myth of the suffering artist instigated by Crevel's suicide to more recent studies where Crevel is a point of reference for writings on gay studies, colonialism, illness and the body.

Andrea Oberhuber explores the work of Dada women artists and their legacy among their "spiritual daughters" in Surrealism. The legacy of Baroness Elsa von Freytag-Loringhoven, embodying Dada's spirit of provocation in her excentric behaviour on the streets of Manhattan; of Emmy Hennings and Sophie Taueber's dances and recitals in Zurich Dada evenings; or of Berlin Dadaist Hannah Höch's subversive and ironic montages of mass media images, can be traced in the work of Surrealist women artists such as Unica Zürn's multiple fictional identities or Claude Cahun's theatrical representations of the self. Oberhuber argues that the overt theatrical display of Dada women artists contrasts with the decentred introspection of Surrealist women artists.

Completing this section, John Goodby's essay brings Dada beyond the confines of continental Europe and into a UK context, exploring a fascinating but hitherto under-researched connection between Dylan Thomas, Dada and Surrealism.

"Beyond Dada", the book's final section, engages with Dada's ongoing legacy throughout Europe and beyond. Alfred Thomas explores the influence of Dada on postwar Czech cinema. Unlike Czech Surrealism, which existed in the interwar years and flourished in the postwar period, Dada had no significant group identity in Czechoslovakia. As Thomas argues, however, Dada exerted a subversive influence in Communist Czechoslovakia long after its popularity had waned in the West. Against the background of tight state control over art, Dada's oppositional stance made it an ideal subversive voice, and this is especially evident in Věra Chytilová's provocative experimental film *Daisies* (1969). Not only does it contain clear echoes of Dada's iconoclastic and confrontational strategies, but it captures the mood of political disaffection in Czechoslovakia in the wake of the failed Prague Spring of 1968.

The focus of Olivier Salazer-Ferrer's essay is Benjamin Fondane's musical film *Tararira* (1936). Shot in Buenos Aires with the participation of the Cuarteto Aguilar, it was never distributed and considered lost until the recent rediscovery of the film stock, the musical score and still photographs from the set. The essay documents the genesis and thematic interest of the film, considering it in relation to Fondane's writings on cinema, to Dada and Surrealism. Finally, it advances an interpretation of its message that relates it to the growing political and racial tensions affecting Europe in the 1930s.

Closing this volume, Stephen Forcer's essay focuses on one of the founders of Dada, Tristan Tzara, and reassesses his contribution to the movement from the perspective of the new millennium. While much of Tzara's early poetry is dismissed as "nonsense", or as a mere adjunct to his Dada manifestos, Forcer contends that it deserves to be removed from this specific context and read on its own terms as polysemic text. By understanding Dada in similar terms, we are better able to appreciate that beneath its ludic surface is a culturally critical phenomenon of direct relevance to the major preoccupations of the twenty-first century.

DADA PERFORMANCE

Chapter 1

Zurich Dada Dance Performance and the Role of Sophie Taeuber

Jill Fell

When he came to chronicle the record of how Zurich Dada began, Hugo Ball recalls their discovery of the strange power of masks to impel them to dance. The Dada creed demanded no dancing skill from the performers, but the physical proximity of the Cabaret Voltaire's premises to the winter premises of the school run by Rudolf Laban, the so-called Father of Modern Dance, combined with the romantic ties of the Dadaists with his dancers, could not help but result in a cross-pollination of skills and ideas between the two groups. The principal figure in this subtle transference, and the only dancer truly to have had a foot in both camps from Dada's very beginning, was the artist Sophie Taeuber.

The difficulty in isolating Taeuber's individual contribution to the Dada group effort is that the concept of uplifting the individual over a combined effort ran contrary to her personal philosophy as an artist. She kept no written record of her own for this period and her choreographic role in Zurich Dada dance performance, although registered in the programmes, is not filled out in detail. I am therefore going to pull together some of the existing published records on her actual performances. It is also instructive to see how today's Laban scholars view the excursions of the first Laban dancers into Dada territory and whether Laban scholarship in general throws any light on the scene.

Between 1914 and 1919 Taeuber worked alongside two particularly strong artistic personalities, of which the first was Rudolf Laban. Hungarian by nationality, he had set up his summer school as a nature-focused artistic cult in the mountains at Ascona by Lake Maggiore in Switzerland. The second was Hans Arp, with her, one of the founding figures of Dada and with whom she remained for the rest of her life. We can begin to delineate the boundaries between Taeuber's work within the Laban School and her performances for Zurich Dada with the help of Tristan Tzara's telling review of a Laban performance in 1917, and also later reviews devoted to Mary Wigman, Laban's lead dancer and assistant. Laban and indeed Taeuber were interested in harmony; Dada was dedicated to disruption. Under Taeuber's guidance, and drawn as much by the anti-materialist, spiritual aims of Dada as by romance, the Laban dancers themselves lent their expertise more and more to the Dada cause. The savage ideals of Dada could theoretically be accepted within the context of Laban's striving towards the primitive. When the Laban School took up its winter quarters in Zurich, a mutual awareness and an interchange of ideas between the two groups, first through the partnership of Taeuber and Arp, then others, became inevitable.

It is important to remember that each of the individuals who came together under the Dada banner had a pre-Dada life and brought their own particular ingredient to it. In Taeuber's case, she brought the abstract forms of her vertical and horizontal compositions, her love of costume-making and her newly acquired dance philosophy – in those early days, not yet a proper philosophy, according to Wigman, but in her words "a wilderness, an exciting and fascinating hunting ground, where discoveries were made day after day" (Sorell 1973a: 35–6). Although Laban had started his experiments a year earlier, and his aims could be construed as almost diametrically opposed to those of Dada, in terms of a striving towards harmony, as against deliberate disharmony, both groups were experimenting and took close note of each other's experiments. Within the talented Dada group, Taeuber possessed the unique combination of choreographic practice and innovative artistic composition; of rhythm and what is known in the lexicon of dance as "flow". From her Laban experience she was practised in analysing different types of movement and in joining them together; as an artist she was interested in the visual effects that could be produced by light and shadow and geometric shapes. She would have been used to dancing to Laban's so-called movement scales, an abstract structural underpinning to movement, which consisted of five different swinging movements leading in a spiral line from downward to upward, dictating, like musical scales, the most natural succession of one movement after another. Taeuber's mental guideline in the dance performance process would have been Laban's 3-dimensional model of the icosehedron, inside which he envisioned the dancer, and which dictated the dancer's relationship to the intersecting horizontal and vertical planes and corners that constituted a series of repeatable relationships to space, i.e. the scales themselves (Prevots 1985: 5).

It is perhaps only because of Taeuber's premature death, aged 54, from the fumes of a paraffin heater, a suspected but unproven act of suicide, that we possess a more substantial handful of firsthand accounts of her dancing and choreography than might otherwise have been the case. In the absence of her own voice, in the form of letters from this period, these records are important material but must be used with the caveat that they were written some twenty-three years after she stopped dancing and also bear the gloss of affectionate memorials from close friends of her grief-stricken husband.

Taeuber was born in Davos, Switzerland in 1889 to a Swiss mother. Her German father, a pharmacist, came from Mogilno, now in Poland. He died of tuberculosis when she was two years old, leaving three other daughters and a son. Davos having no school, the enterprising Frau Taeuber, an embroidery teacher, photographer and painter, taught the children herself till Sophie was seven. She then moved to the larger town of Trogen, Appenzell, where she designed and built a large student hostel, in which the five children were brought up in a free and easy atmosphere, but presumably helped with the domestic chores.

When her secondary education finished, Taeuber embarked on further training in textile design at three different schools in St Gallen, Hamburg and Munich. No dance training is mentioned and it is only at the late age of 26, after moving in with her Zurich-based sister to help her with her children in 1914, that she joined Laban's summer school on Monte Verità, a session interrupted by the outbreak of the First World War with the dancers fleeing home. The school had operated for one previous season, but this year Laban changed its name from the Schule für Kunst [School of Art] to the Schule für Tanz-Ton-Wort [School of Dance, Sound and Word]. As he had been organising Carnival entertainments in Munich for the two previous years and a 1913 photo shows Taeuber at a fancy dress ball there, it is probable that she had already come across him. For Taeuber, dancing may have begun through her enjoyment in making costumes and taking part in these carnival balls, but then become more serious as an adjunct to a semi-spiritual or psycho-physical project, begun with Laban and stretched to an extreme form of expression by the early Dada experiments. The rigorous and constantly repeated exercises with the Laban group had given her physical abilities of turning, twisting and leaping that she was able to adapt to disharmonious Dada principles. Both groups were trying to tune into ancient rhythms, but by different methods and towards different ends. A central tenet of Laban's beliefs was that dance gave access to what he called "the land of silence" and that the dancer, possessing extra-sensory, visionary powers, was a messenger from this hidden world – the portrayer of the forms and shapes of its realities. Indeed Arp credited Taeuber with these visionary powers. He was convinced that she possessed a special gift for giving visual form to natural rhythms both in her art and in her dancing. Hence his profound artistic reliance on her, to which she acceded. Her physical dance career effectively ended at the age of 31 when she moved with him to Cologne at the end of the war, but the patterns of dance would re-emerge in her work, particularly her late drawings.

The Taeuber-Arp artistic partnership had begun with Arp's *coup de foudre* on seeing her abstract vertical and horizontal compositions at the Galerie Tanner in November 1915. Without her particular affinity to Arp's work and willingness to work with him, it is unlikely that Taeuber would have taken part in the Dada experiments at all. For Hugo Ball's partner, the charismatic diseuse, Emmy Hennings, the packed, smoke-filled and noisy Cabaret Voltaire was a natural element. Not so for Taeuber. Making the transition to this tiny, unruly space from the peaceful open air lakeside dancing at Ascona must have been a challenge. Even the idea of an audience would have been inimical. Could she possibly transport the "land of silence" to the café? This was certainly not the philosophy behind the provocative Dada performances.

Marcel Janco's primitivist cardboard masks, daubed with blood-red paint, proved to be a dynamic catalyst towards the Cabaret Voltaire's first performance. When in February 1916 he arrived carrying the masks, no one wasted any time in putting one on. We do not know what other materials were to hand. Ball's account states that everyone felt impelled to add more and more to their costume; he writes of them all walking round festooned with "impossible objects", each trying to outdo the other in inventiveness. So whereas the Laban

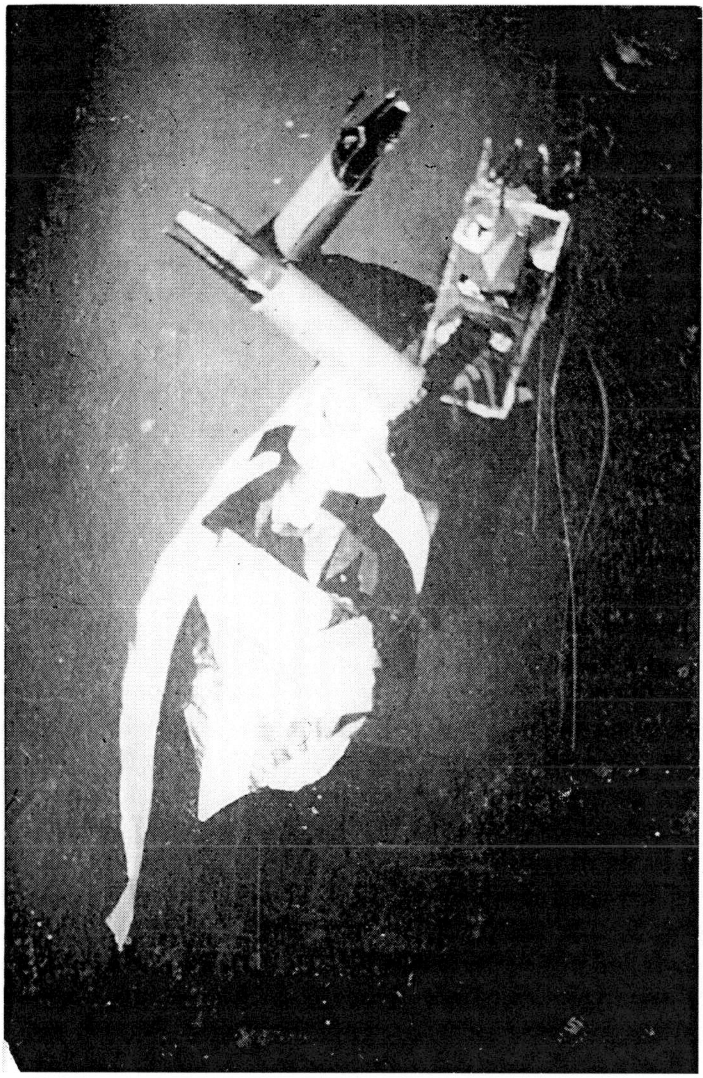

Figure 1. Sophie Taeuber dancing at the Cabaret Voltaire, Zurich (1916).

group had been casting their clothes to the wind so that they could dance with the sun on their skin, admittedly in summer, the Dada group began by collecting an armory of masking material, to immure themselves in chrysalises of strange disguise. How much time passed between this cataclysmic experience and the actual performance is uncertain. The speed with which the performers apparently chose their masks and spontaneously began dancing is in direct opposition to the procedure described by Wigman for herself and her co-dancers, when masks were used. For the big group dance, *Dance of Death*, she specified that the dancer must know his mask better than he knows himself, imposing a minimum of two evenings of meditation; on the first each dancer gazed at the mask in their lap to a gentle background of gong beats; this was continued on the second, when they were finally allowed to put on the masks but had to bring their own mirrors finally to immerse themselves in the character of the mask (Sorell 1973b: 120). This practice was in direct oppostion to the spontaneous, reactive method of the Dadaists. Ball writes that he immediately sat down at the piano and composed three pieces of music for three of the masks. The three dances were each then given a special name: *Fliegenfangen* [Catching Flies], *Cauchemar* and *Festliche Verzweiflung* [Solemn or Ceremonial Despair]. Taeuber's dance may have been either *Festliche Verzweiflung* or *Cauchemar*. The latter dance was assigned to the mask described as having a broad displaced nose and a wide-open mouth. If this is the mask in the well-known picture [figure 1], it would seem to depict the stock fairytale figure of an evil, if not mad king with beard and crown. Ball nonetheless writes of a female performer wearing the *Cauchemar* mask, who, if not Taeuber, could only have been Hennings, as no Laban dancers apart from Taeuber were participating in the Dada activities at this stage.

It is worth pausing for a moment on the word "festlich" in the title of the final dance, *Festliche Verzweiflung* and its root "Fest" meaning feast or ceremony, as the notion of ceremony binds Laban and Dada and tells us more than the other two titles. For all its surface noise and agitation, Dada believed it had a holy mission. In composing his subsequent *Lautgedichte* [Sound Poems], and *Verse ohne Worte* or *Poèmes des mots inconnus*, to which Taeuber was to dance, Ball was seeking the sacred core of language, the magical power inherent in recitation itself, so potent in liturgy, ballads and nursery rhymes. In this, the influence on Ball of Wassily Kandinsky's

Das Geistige in der Kunst [On the Spiritual in Art] and his prior work *Klänge* [Sounds] should not be forgotten. "We must return to the innermost alchemy of the word", Ball wrote. "We must even give up the word too, to keep for poetry its last and holiest refuge" (Ball 1995: 71). Both Ball and Arp were assiduous in their studies of what Ball called "wonderfully plaintive words that no human mind can resist" from the so-called "language of Paradise" of the seventeenth-century visionary, Jacob Boehme, to the "lost language of the soul", fragments published by the Swabian poet, Justines Kerner, in 1829 (Melzer 1994: 40). Laban also made the dancers experiment to the rhythms of poetry or to poems made up by the dancers themselves, and included these in his end of year performance of 27 June 1917. Dancing to words was therefore not an unusual exercise for Taeuber (Manning 1993: 55). Although there is no record of Laban's actual participation in any of the Dada events, Ball (1995: 102) records that he at least came to watch Taeuber's solo performance of the Abstract Dances on 29 March 1917.

The title *Festliche Verzweiflung* surely refers to ancient rituals of mourning connected to funerals: contortions of grief; wailing; tearing of clothes and hair; smearing with dirt. These are the signs of abject apology, that those left behind must demonstrate to the dead person's spirit for staying alive, or risk attracting their wrath, and that are so removed from the measured, quiet comportment and genteel, smart costume demanded at the Western European funerals of then and now. Ball's description of the repetitive movements of *Festliche Verzweiflung* is the only one so precise that it can be reconstructed: "The figure turns several times to left and right, then revolves slowly and ends by suddenly collapsing into a heap before slowly returning to the first position and starting again" (Ball 1995: 64). We do not know who performed this dance, but it seems to have less in common with the joyous irreverence of Dada than with the Laban repertoire; the organic continuity of its endlessly repeated movements, denoting the bewilderment of bereavement and collapse of despair, is suggestive of Laban and evokes the death dances of Mary Wigman. Although, as one of the only two females in the group, it is the *Cauchemar* dance that is normally attributed to Taeuber, she was probably the only Dada performer capable of executing this kind of fluid movement sequence.

In his account of Taeuber's later dance to his poems, *Seepferdchen und Flugfischen* [Sea Horses and Flying Fish], at the opening of the Galerie Dada in March 1917, Ball describes the kind of movements that the body produces in response to sudden pain, such as might be inflicted by a whiplash, writing that "a gong beat is enough to stimulate the dancer's body to make the most fantastic movements" (Ball 1995: 102). Given that the primitive culture that had inspired Taeuber's decoration of her own room in her early teens was that of the North American Hopi Indians, we can speculate whether she might have been projecting herself into the initiation ceremony undergone by their children, introducing them to the supernaturals, known as the Kachinas, and in which a ceremonial "father" or masked "scare-kachina" flogs the child with a yucca-fibre whip (Turner 1979: 89). Hennings asserted that the mask for Taeuber's dance was necessary to cover the deep convulsions of the face (Ball-Hennings 1960: 10). Hennings's account, given in her memorial, lends weight to the words "délirante" and "démence", used of her dancing by Tzara in his review of the end of year Laban School performance in June 1917 (Tzara 1975: 558).

The single photograph of Taeuber's dancing in a mask shows the rectangular masked head at a peculiar angle to her body, while the tubular arms form a skewed right-angular figure adjacent to it. Richard Huelsenbeck's *Dada Almanach* records "cubist dances" for both May and July 1916. Rather than referring to the cubist aesthetics of Picasso, listed as he was as a Dada collaborator, the rectilinearity of the mask and arm position could just as well reflect Arp's and Taeuber's current idealisation of the rectangular form as the supreme vehicle for conveying a spiritual dimension free of any vestiges of the material world (Robertson 2006: 44). Because of uncertainty about the date of this photograph, opinions differ as to whether the mask was Janco's or Arp's. The exaggerated tilting of the rectangular shapes could even be said to evoke Arp's *Elementary Composition (According to the Laws of Chance)*.

The aesthetics of Cubism do, however, seem to influence Ball's description of Taeuber's 1917 Galerie Dada dance. "The lines of her body broke up", he writes, "each gesture decomposed into a hundred precise angular movements" (Ball 1995: xxxi). Certainly the cardboard costumes made by Janco and Arp for Ball and Taeuber point forward to the costumes designed by Picasso for Jean Cocteau's *Parade* the same year, although much less sumptuous. The photograph of Ball in his rigid blue cylinder seems to show him wearing the same arm casings as those worn by Taeuber, evoking the prostheses of war amputees, who were filtering back into the civilian world.

Both Ball and Tzara's admiring accounts of Taeuber's dances of 1917, although referring to different performances, in different contexts, evoke an innovative and striking sequence of fast, angular, vibrating movements, which look forward to André Breton's 1934 notion of *beauté convulsive* and *explosante-fixe* (Fell 1999: 277). Writing of the unskilled male Dadaists and basing her analysis on Ball's description of the Cabaret Voltaire's earlier masked dances, Laban's biographer, Valerie Preston-Dunlop (1998: 44) speaks deprecatingly of "clumsy snatches and isolated actions", as against what she describes as "the passionate, dynamic force of a Wigman work". Having worked closely with Wigman, Taeuber possessed the strength, agility and training to provide precisely the passion and continuity of movement, of which Preston-Dunlop bemoans the lack. In her analysis of the Abstract Dances, Monika Kroepfli (1995: 51) classifies them into different "strands". She points out that Taueber had to respond to two different "sound strands": the gong beats and the words of the poems. We do not even know how the gong beater and the reciter related to each other. "Space", writes Kroepfli, "can be created by sounds coming from different sources". Taeuber would have had to identify and adapt her movements to the "space" created by the two.

The Taeuber dance that Tzara describes, reviewed with one of Wigman's, almost definitely relates to the end of year Laban performance of 27 June 1917 at the Grosse Saal zur Kaufleuten. On this occasion she wears no hand-concealing cardboard tubes. Tzara writes: "Mlle. S. Taeuber: bizarrerie délirante dans l'araignée de la main vibre rythme rapidement ascendant vers le paroxysme d'une démence goguenarde capricieusement belle" (Tzara 1975: 558). This is distinguished from the dance of Wigman described as "finesse grandléger créatrice d'abstraites notions d'expression sans musique – pures", and whose dances usually possessed a dark or supernatural character, as in her *Witch Dances*. This character is absent from Taeuber's dances, which elicit a vocabulary evoking brightness, drollness and irony, just like the bold colours she preferred for her costumes. Yet the two dancers do seem to have some features in common, for five years later we find this review of Wigman in *The Hannoversches Tagesblatt*:

> And what trembled and flamed in her whirling feet: this burning, passionate sensitivity, that flows through the **uninterrupted** movement right down into the fingertips of her **vibrating** hands, that manifest a life of their own. [my emboldening] [1]

The importance of an "uninterrupted composition of line" is a notion that Wassily Kandinsky used in relation to dance.[2] He stipulated that the linear composition of the dance movement must reach down to the very fingertips – something that Laban instilled in all his dancers. As we know from Tzara, the vibration of the hand mentioned in the Wigman review is also a Taeuber signature, one can see her hand moving in the otherwise static photograph of her and her sister showing off Hopi-style costumes and abstract masks of her design [figure 2]. Here the geometric shapes and symbols supplant human features, while the human head itself, usually represented as spherical, becomes a more threatening rectangle.

Kandinsky had withdrawn to Lake Constance to formulate his ideas at the beginning of the First World War at the same time as Laban too was trying to formulate his notation for dance. Ball was more interested in the stimuli to movement than its recording, and especially aural stimuli. Although he claimed to be in charge of the rehearsals of his *Negertanz* using Laban dancers, it was probably left to Taeuber to register and record the dances and to carry them from their embryonic improvised stage into the later rehearsed group performances.

Preston-Dunlop (1998: 49) states that Taeuber and Kaethe Wulff are known to have used a different notation to Laban's for some of the Dada dances, confirming speculation that Taeuber developed her own. Hans Richter (1965: 71), however, asserts that they used Laban's notation for the final Dada display of dancing, titled *Noir Kakadu*, at the Saal zur Kaufleuten for their grand Soirée on 9 April 1919. Taeuber took over the role of choreographer and director for this performance. There was no question of it being unrehearsed. It is not recorded whether these include any of the five dancers, of whom Ball (1995: 104) had written two years earlier in April 1917: "I am rehearsing a new dance with five Laban-ladies in long black caftans and face masks". There is no photograph of this dance in the public domain but Ball's description recalls Wigman's known costumes.

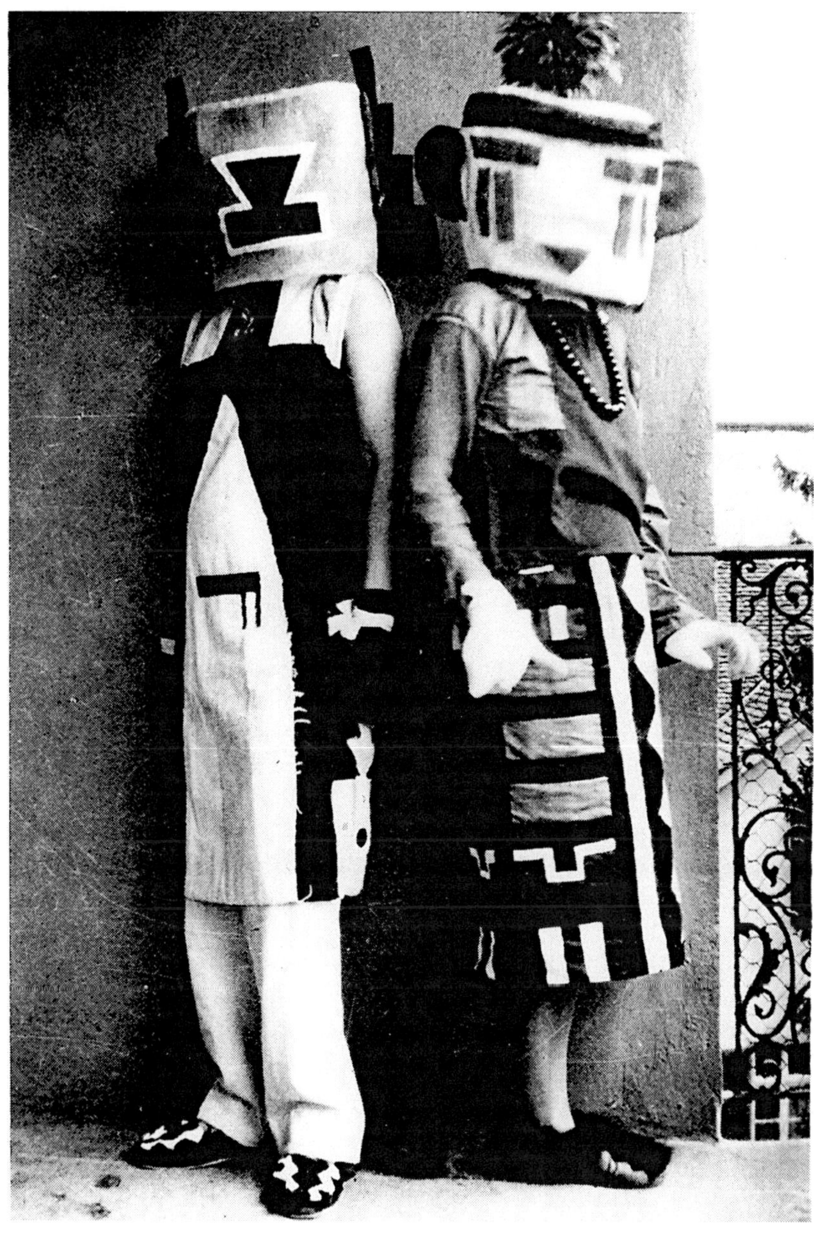

Figure 2. Sophie Taeuber and Erika Schlegel in Hopi costumes (1918-1920)

Noir Kakadu, a title that refers more to Arp's backdrop of giant black cucumbers than to the dances, seems to have consisted of two separate dances with different costumes. The dancers had been drilled by Taeuber and were led by Wulff who, unlike Taeuber, had taken on a vocal role in Dada, entering fully into its destructive, iconoclastic ethos, reciting poetry as well as shouting at the audience. The first dance consisted of five dancers in tubular costumes: "les tuyaux dansent la rénovation des pythécanthropes sans tête", records Tzara (1975: 567–8), a description which recalls the photograph of Ball reciting his *Sound Poems*, his oracular voice emanating from a long white tube placed over his head with a hat on top of it; the second had six dancers in masks that he describes as "énormes et éblouissants". Richter (1965: 78–9) refers to these as "Negro masks" and attributes them to Janco, describing the dancers' costumes as "all enveloping" and "abstract" in conception. He seems to be out of tune with Ball's aesthetic of "studied, deformed ugliness", deploring the fact that "the beautiful faces of the dancers were made ugly and the curves of their shapely bodies hidden". As Richter also describes them as "fluttering like Ensor's butterflies", it seems more likely that they were wearing coloured caftans rather than the earlier black ones described by Ball, and that he had perhaps confused them with Odilon Redon's butterflies. A photograph of Wigman in a 1916 *Witch Dance* shows her in a costume not designed to flatter, which demonstrates the gender neutrality that Taeuber also espoused [figure 3]. The "fluttering" helped by wide costumes may have been a Wigman-inspired technique, for when commenting on her later dance, *Pastoral*, she refers to "a rhythmic vibration [...] a transparency in everything physical in which eroticism fluttered like a butterfly", and revels in the rippling of the costume, caused by the fast rhythmic movements of the feet (Wigman 1966: 53). In Ball's case "vibration" was an important notion, to which he had been alerted by Kandinsky, applying to works of art, and felt the need to experience physically:

> One day the problem of vibration came up. We found the answer to it by sitting on a sofa the whole night, with the springs helping us to bounce back. Then on our feet without any outward help, the demands of momentum carried us gradually further until the repetition of the movement finally broke down any mental opposition and vibration became a true experience for us. (Melzer 1994: 99)

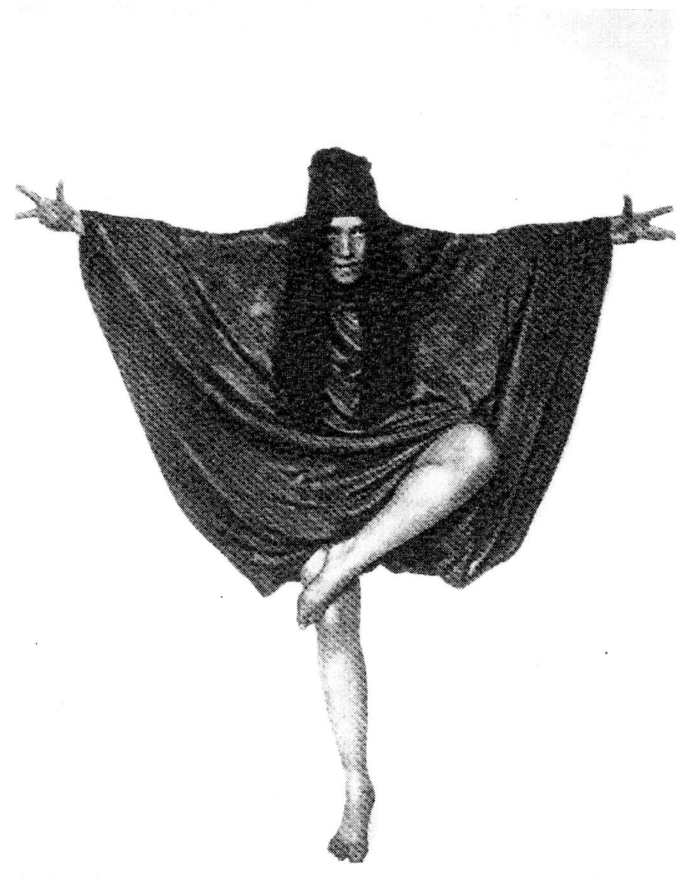

Figure 3. Mary Wigman performing a "Witch Dance" (1916).

It is unlikely that this group of sofa-bouncers would have included Taeuber. We can discern a considerable difference between the male performers' exercise of a single gymnastic movement endlessly repeated and the "hundred-jointed" movement that Ball ascribes to her dancing.

Laban's Zurich winter premises for his school were in Seegartenstrasse. Melzer (1994: 89) refers to Laban's studio as Dada's celestial headquarters as opposed to what she calls the terrestrial base at the Café Odeon. Following her, Preston-Dunlop (1998: 45) describes Seegartenstrasse as "the celestial headquarters" of the dancers, but rather implies that Bahnhofstrasse no. 19, home to the Galerie Dada, was its infernal equivalent. It is noticeable that Laban scholarship attempts to distance the Laban dancers from the disorderly Dada context, while Dada scholarship downplays the introduction of skilled dancers and notions of harmony into the raw materials of the Dada experimental crucible. Huelsenbeck's *Almanach* nonetheless records increasing participation by the dancers and even by Wigman in a New Year's Eve party performance of 1918, with Wigman, Taeuber, Chrusecz and Otto Flake in cardboard legs. This was probably the occasion on which Wigman, in a letter to Sorell dated 1931, recalls herself and Taeuber sewing each other into their costumes so firmly that they could not get out of them for the whole evening (Sorell 1973a: 141). By now we can plot clear cross-fertilization between the two groups, with Laban offering a musical composition at one moment and Wigman offering a dance at another, there being only a thin borderline between formal programmed performance in front of an audience and Wigman's fancy dress parties with dancing to which the Dadaists were invited (Bolliger 1985: 44).

Wigman and Wulff went on to make their careers as dancers. For Taeuber, the Laban and Dada years had been a fascinating five-year kinetic experiment in creating and manipulating different geometric forms. It was an experiment that she absorbed into her art and her designs for marionettes, but which she kept in a rear compartment of her mind. Her late pencil drawings after the outbreak of the Second World War, when materials for painting were difficult to obtain, finally record the choreographic inspiration of these years (Lulinska 1989: 114).

The academic analysis of dance has increased in a way that is often invidious to dancers and would have appeared ridiculous to the Dada performers. Sophie Taeuber's five-year dedication to Laban dance performance and her humorous transposition of Laban principles to Zurich Dada performance, combined with her own instinctive rhythmic inspiration, left an echo of her peculiar gift for abstract expression in the memories of all the artists connected with that explosive experiment – one which her own visual art contains for posterity.

Notes

[1] Signed A.H. "Städtisches Oper und Schauspielhaus: Tanzabend von Mary Wigman" in *Hannoversches Tagesblatt,* 22 September 1922 (MWA Berlin). Cited in Reynolds (1999: 301).

[2] "In the dance, the whole body – and in the new dance, every finger – draws lines with very clear expression. The 'modern" dancer moves about the stage on exact lines, which he introduces in the composition of his dance as a significant element (Sacharoff). The entire body of the dancer, right down to his finger tips, is at every moment an uninterrupted composition of lines (Palucca)" (Kandinsky 1979: 100).

Bibliography

Ball, Hugo. 1995. *Flight out of Time* (ed. J. Elderfield). Berkeley, Los Angeles and London: University of California Press.

Ball-Hennings, Emmy. 1960. "Zur Erinnerung an Sophie Taeuber-Arp" in E. Scheidegger (ed.). *Zweiklang. Sophie Taeuber-Arp, Hans Arp.* Zurich: Verlag der Arche.

Bolliger, Hans, Guido Magnaguagno and Raimund Meyer (eds). 1985. *Dada in Zurich.* Zurich: Arche Verlag.

Fell, Jill. 1999. "Sophie Täuber: The Masked Dada Dancer" in *Forum for Modern Language Studies* 35(3): 270–85.

Kandinsky, Wassily. 1979. *Point and Line to Plane* [1926] (tr. H. Dearstyne and H. von Rebay). New York: Dover Publications.

Kroepfli, Monika. 1995. *The Role of Movement and Dance in Dada Zurich.* M.A. thesis. London: Laban Centre.

Lulinska, Agnieska. 1989. "Sous le signe de la ligne" in *Sophie Taeuber.* Paris: Musée d'Art Moderne de la Ville de Paris and Lausanne: Musée Cantonal des Beaux Arts de Lausanne.

Manning, Susan A. 1993. *Ecstasy and the Demon. Feminism and Nationalism in the Dances of Mary Wigman.* Los Angeles and London: University of California Press.

Melzer, Annabelle. 1994. *Dada and Surrealist Performance.* Baltimore and London: Johns Hopkins University Press.

Preston-Dunlop, Valerie. 1998. *Rudolf Laban: An Extraordinary Life.* London: Dance Books.

Prevots, Naima. 1985. "Zurich Dada and Dance: Formative Ferment" in *Dance Research Journal,* 17(1): 2 –8.

Reynolds, Dee. 1999. "Dancing as a Woman: Mary Wigman and 'Absolute Dance' " in *Forum for Modern Language Studies* 35(3): 297–310.

Richter, Hans. 1965. *Dada: Art and Anti-Art.* London: Thames & Hudson.

Robertson, Eric. 2006. *Arp.* New Haven and London: Yale University Press.

Sorell, Walter. 1973a. *The Mary Wigman Book.* Middletown, Connecticut: Wesleyan University Press.

——. 1973b. *The Other Face. The Mask in the Arts.* London: Thames & Hudson.

Turner, Geoffrey. 1979. *Indians of North America.* Poole: Blandford Press.

Tzara, Tristan. 1975. *Œuvres complètes I* (ed. H.Béhar). Paris: Flammarion.

Wigman, Mary. 1966. *The Language of Dance.* Middletown, Connecticut: Wesleyan University Press and London: Macdonald & Evans.

Chapter 2

L'Acte Dada

Catherine Dufour

Dada entre catharsis et politique

Dans les premières pages de son *Dada art et anti-art*, Hans Richter (1965: 11) citait Erostrate comme modèle du Dadaïste, "au même titre que ceux de Paris ou Berlin", pour avoir "brûlé le temple d'Artémis à Ephèse, afin de secouer la torpeur de ses concitoyens et d'attirer leur attention sur sa propre personne". Cet exemple a le mérite de rappeler que si Dada a produit des œuvres, des objets et du texte, il est avant tout action, performance, scandale.

Bien avant le début des activités Dada à Zurich en 1916, l'excentrique Frank Wedekind, digne précurseur du mouvement, n'hésitait devant aucune provocation de nature à menacer le pouvoir ou la morale publique sur la scène du cabaret munichois (Goldberg 2001: 50–1). Tzara et ses amis poussèrent un peu plus loin ses pitreries, contorsions et insultes au public lors des soirées zurichoises de 1915 à 1919:

> [O]n crie dans la salle, on se bat [...] on proteste, on crie, on casse les vitres, on se tue, on démolit, on se bat, la police interruption. [1916]
>
> des chaises arrachées, projectiles, craquements, effet attendu atroce et instinctif [...] folie progressive sauvage [...] la salle oublia les frontières de l'éducation, des préjugés. [1919] (Huelsenbeck 1980: 13, 26–7)

La salle de spectacle était ce "champ de bataille" préconisé par Marinetti dès 1910 et Dada cette "gifle au goût public" à laquelle les futuristes russes consacrent un manifeste dès 1912.[1] A en croire Huelsenbeck, dans sa première allocution à Berlin en février 1918, les manifestes Dadaïstes ne devaient pas être "seulement lus", mais "prononcés avec défi et un maximum d'intensité vocale" dans un "désir de contact direct" pour "secouer [l'] adversaire pour l'inciter à l'opposition et, si nécessaire, [se] créer d'autres ennemis" (Richter 1965: 102). Les Dadaïstes zurichois cherchaient à renouer avec leurs pulsions primitives, au rythme des roulements de tambours, à se débarrasser des oripeaux de la civilisation, sortir d'eux-mêmes leur propre nègre, à la manière de Rimbaud qui clamait: "Je suis une bête, un nègre. [...] Faim, soif, cris, danse, danse, danse, danse!" (Rimbaud 1964: 123–4). Tzara ne cessera jusqu'à sa mort, dans ses nombreux essais critiques, d'assimiler Dada aux primitifs, dont il définit l'art comme "efficacité" (Tzara 1980: 315) et importance primordiale accordée aux actions. Pas plus que le primitif Dada ne se distinguait des gestes qui le reliaient au monde:

> Nous ne prêchions pas nos idées, mais nous les vivions nous-mêmes, un peu à la manière d'Héraclite dont la dialectique impliquait qu'il fît lui-même partie de sa démonstration comme objet et sujet à la fois de sa conception du monde. (Tzara 1982: 67)

Sur la scène zurichoise le corps était mis à contribution: transe liturgique de Ball, non dénuée de réminiscences expressionnistes, hystérie de Huelsenbeck zébrant l'air de coups de fouet (comme Wedekind, surgissant sur les planches en dompteur de ménagerie), déhanchements frénétiques de Tzara, sarcasmes du diabolique Dr. Serner. Du côté du spectateur se libérait quelque chose de profond, propre à faire vaciller ses défenses psychiques. Cette secousse émotionnelle[2] se reproduisit dans diverses manifestations européennes, donnant raison à la célèbre formule de Schwitters, dans une lettre à Hausmann du 29 mars 1947: "chacun a à passer à travers son propre Dada" (Hausmann 2004: 122). Un petit extrait d'une lettre de Hausmann à Schwitters (datée du 14 novembre 1946), relatant la soirée d'Utrecht du 29 janvier 1923, illustre combien Dada, avant des œuvres, était un moyen d'action sur soi et sur le public:

> A Utrecht, ils sont montés sur scène, m'ont offert un bouquet de fleurs séchées et des os sanguinolents et ils se sont mis à lire à notre place mais Doesburg les jeta dans la fosse, là où se tient généralement l'orchestre, et tout le public fit Dada. C'était comme si l'esprit Dadaïstique avait gagné des centaines de gens qui remarquaient soudainement qu'ils étaient des êtres humains. Nelly alluma une cigarette et cria au public que, puisque le public était devenu complètement Dada, nous étions maintenant le public. Nous nous assîmes et regardâmes nos fleurs et nos jolis os. (Schwitters et Hausmann 1962: 13)

Les happenings des années 70 se souviendront que Dada était avant tout une pratique, une réhabilitation de l'expérience. Le public devait s'y sentir impliqué.

Mais cette dimension cathartique, existentielle, de l'acte Dada ne doit pas en faire oublier une autre, plus sociale, promue par Marinetti qui, le premier, pour secouer le public et ouvrir la voie de la provocation généralisée, se fit propagandiste dans les rues de Berlin en février 1912, diffusant ses manifestes en voiture décapotable (Richard 1998: 64). C'est aux futuristes italiens que Dada a emprunté d'abord le style de l'agitation portée sur la scène publique pour déloger l'artiste des espaces confinés de la littérature et des musées. Mais des signes avant-coureurs de cet état d'esprit existaient déjà un peu partout en Europe bien avant la guerre de 1914. Dada ici et là grimaçait sous les traits de quelques écrivains infréquentables, auteurs des premiers happenings comme le tchèque Jaroslav Hašek, poète-voyou et alcoolique, anarchiste et mystificateur, bien connu pour ses très anti-patriotiques *Aventures du brave soldat Chvéïk*, Dadas avant la lettre, ébauchées dès 1911.[3]

A Zurich l'antinationalisme se déchaîna sur la scène du Cabaret, parodie du cirque tragique dont l'Europe était alors la piste, contaminée peut-être par le voisinage de Lénine (qui habitait dans la Spielgasse de Zurich, à quelques numéros du Cabaret Voltaire, et fréquentait les mêmes cafés que les Dadaïstes) ou les textes de Bakounine que connaissait Hugo Ball. A Berlin Dada descend dans la rue et participe directement à la Révolution, la vraie. L'acte se fait "geste", voire épopée, quand Hausmann et Baader déplacent la troupe avec de fausses nouvelles adressées à la presse, que Baader pose sa candidature à la présidence de la République par des tracts lancés dans une assemblée officielle et interrompt un sermon par des propos blasphématoires en pleine cathédrale de Berlin en 1918 (Hausmann 2004: 69–83). Ou mieux encore, quand Franz Jung en 1920 détourne un cargo vers Moscou (Jung 2007).

Les mouvements héritiers de Dada n'ont cessé d'osciller entre ces deux pôles, cathartique et politique. C'est dans la tradition cathartique que s'est inscrit le "body art", mise en scène exhibitionniste susceptible de lever le voile sur des pans entiers de l'inconscient collectif. Chez les actionnistes viennois le corps devint matériau, lieu d'une sexualité violente, objet de mutilations. Pendant des années l'Autrichien Rudolf Schwartzkogler exposa des morceaux de son sexe, jusqu'à sa mort en 1969. Cette même année eut lieu la *Messe pour un corps* de Michel Journiac, distribuant sous forme d'une hostie faite de boudin cuisiné avec son sang un concentré des énergies subversives propres à l'acte Dada. En 1989, Greil Marcus dans le prologue de *Lipstick Traces* comparait le "grondement sismique ricanant", le "hurlement d'outre-tombe" du chanteur punk Johnny Rotten, qui avait fait scandale au Royaume-Uni une dizaine d'années auparavant, avec les gesticulations agressives des Dadaïstes de Berlin ou Zurich (Marcus 2004: 9). Autant de symptômes des secousses d'une "histoire secrète du 20e siècle".

Parallèlement aux délires du corps, de nombreuses performances politiques ont commémoré les pratiques insurrectionnelles de Dada. Parmi celles-ci la *Ceremony of US* de Anna Halprin organisée à Los Angeles en 1969 en réaction contre les émeutes raciales meurtrières de Watts d'août 1965, qui valut à son auteur de sérieux problèmes avec l'administration Reagan. Ou cette autre, relatée par Richter en 1971, qui fut très controversée: une femme nue, recouverte du sang et des tripes d'un cochon tué sur place, sur laquelle ensuite son mari pissa et déféqua, fut exhibée pour protester contre la guerre du Vietnam (Sers 1997: 193). Plus récemment, on a pu assister aux actions de l'ultra avant-garde russe des années 1990, réincarnation vivante de Dada avec ses happenings réactivés par les turbulences de l'Histoire. Sur la place Rouge, du haut de l'échafaud des exécutions médiévales, le poète-performiste Alexandre Brener défia en caleçon et gants de boxe le président Boris Eltsine, protégé par les murailles du Kremlin, et arrosa de bouteilles de ketchup l'ambassade de Biélorussie. En 1999, le peintre Avdeï Ter-Oganian fut poursuivi par la justice pour avoir au cours d'un happening fendu à coups de hache des icônes orthodoxes (Koudriavstev 2005: 416).

Tuer l'art ?

Cathartique, anti-social, l'acte Dada, dès ses origines, fut investi d'une fonction majeure: subvertir les formes traditionnelles de l'art. C'est dans cet esprit que le poète-boxeur Arthur Cravan organisa à Paris de 1913 à 1915 de burlesques conférence-spectacles et à Barcelone le 29 avril 1916 un mémorable combat de boxe contre le champion du monde Jack Johnson, qui le mit KO au premier round (Béhar et Dufour 2005: 46–55). A New York en 1917, Cravan fut arrêté par la police lors d'une prestation publique qui tournait au strip-tease. La même année Jacques Vaché menaçait la foule, revolver au poing, à la première des *Mamelles de Tirésias* (Breton 1988: 200). Autant d'actes pour dire le dégoût de l'art et l'impossibilité de se satisfaire de "la littérature". Dada voulait en finir avec l'univers de la représentation, remplacée par des actions susceptibles de subvertir le statut des œuvres en même temps que les mécanismes sous-jacents des pouvoirs politiques, institutionnels ou marchands. L'urinoir de Duchamp en témoigne, comme ses ready-made ou ce geste fameux: ayant payé son dentiste avec un chèque fictif dessiné par ses soins, l'artiste le lui racheta longtemps après pour sa collection personnelle.

Rien d'étonnant à ce que l'acte de naissance du néo-Dada ait été inauguré en 1953 par Rauschenberg demandant à De Kooning de lui donner un de ses dessins pour l'effacer. Car l'idée de destruction était inscrite au cœur de la redéfinition de l'art par Dada. L'injonction de changer la vie (Rimbaud) avait été relayée par la nécessité de "tuer l'art" (Vaché, Breton), d' "humilier l'art et la poésie" (Tzara 1982: 353). L'art devint anti-art, voire a-art. Duchamp se retira de la peinture pour se consacrer aux échecs en vertu de cette supposée fin de l'art à laquelle, jusqu'aux situationnistes, toutes les avant-gardes se sont référées par la suite.[4]

A moins qu'il ne faille entendre par "meurtre" quelque visée créatrice plus subtile… Car si la négation Dada était aux antipodes de la modernité positive fondée sur de nouvelles valeurs artistiques – ce fut le projet de Breton contre Tzara en 1922 lors du "Congrès pour la détermination des directives et la défense de l'Esprit Moderne" – elle se distinguait aussi du nihilisme par un jeu de balancier dialectique entre négation et création. Des "gestes" innovants ont émergé de l'acte destructeur: déchirer / recoller des papiers jetés au hasard (Arp), couper / coller des bribes de journaux pour faire un poème (Tzara), découper / monter des photos (Hausmann, Höch), décoller / recoller des affiches (Hausmann, Baader), assembler l'hétéroclite (Schwitters). Les lettristes des années 40, les néo-Dada des années 60, Hains, Villeglé (grand admirateur et exégète de Baader (Béhar et Dufour 2005: 225–9) ont réinterprété à leur manière les gestes de leurs aînés: décoller, déchirer, lacérer des affiches, "ciseler" des pellicules. La violence était au rendez-vous du projet cinématographique d'Isidore Isou énoncé dans son film *Traité de bave et d'éternité* (1951):

J'annonce la destruction du cinéma [...]. Je ferai foutre la pellicule en l'air avec des rayons de soleil [...], je prendrai des chutes d'anciens films et je les rayerai,

> les écorcherai pour que des beautés inconnues paraissent à la lumière. (Ciret
> 2004: 152)

Le film de Guy Debord, *Hurlements en faveur de Sade*, diffusé l'année de sa rupture avec la première génération lettriste en 1952, doit encore beaucoup à ce romantisme noir de la destruction. Quelques grands insurgés (Sade, Rimbaud, Lautréamont) en sont les inspirateurs, passés maîtres dans les stratégies de provocation et de subversion. Mais l'acte Dada remonte plus loin encore. Il se rattache à un courant de la parodie, de la dérision, du grotesque qui renvoie à Aristophane et rencontre Rabelais. Il croise l'Absurde de l'écrivain roumain Urmuz – précurseur de Dada et ancêtre de Ionesco – que Tzara connut peut-être à Bucarest. Nietzsche en est une des figures tutélaires dans l'introduction de l'*Almanach Dada* (1920) de Huelsenbeck, qui assimile les Dadaïstes aux "pitres de Dieu" évoqués par le philosophe dans *Par-delà le bien et le mal* (Huelsenbeck 1980: 169). Le meurtre de l'art s'inscrit aussi dans le sillage de l'acte gratuit selon Jarry, qui connut son apogée avec la fascination exercée sur Breton par le revolver de Vaché[5] et sur les surréalistes en général par quelques grands criminels comme Violette Nozière ou les sœurs Papin.

Au chapitre "La Poésie révoltée" de *L'Homme révolté*, Camus écrivait en 1951: "La théorie de l'acte gratuit couronne la revendication de la liberté absolue". Ce libertinage philosophique est incarné par une célèbre phrase de Jarry: "Lorsque j'aurai pris toute la phynance, je tuerai tout le monde et je m'en irai", que Camus commente ainsi: "Que signifie en effet cette apologie du meurtre, sinon que, dans un monde sans signification et sans honneur, seul le désir d'être, sous toutes ses formes, est légitime?" (Camus 1951: 124). Dans ses entretiens avec Philippe Sers en 1971 Richter revient sur la figure d'Erostrate "avide de brûler les temples, les endroits saints", de se "libérer" de tous les "dieux". N'est-ce pas ce même Libre Esprit qui poussa Michel Mourre le jour de Pâques 1950 à renouveler l'exploit de Johannes Baader: prendre d'assaut Notre-Dame de Paris pendant la messe de Pâques et y prononcer un sermon blasphématoire?[6]

Hélas, l'acte Dada n'a pas toujours échappé au fétichisme répétitif, dénoncé dès 1920 par Breton, qui en 1952 qualifiait de misérables "ruses de baraque foraine" (Breton 1999: 467) certaines des manifestations Dada conçues par Tzara. Dans les années d'après 1945, les lettristes, prétendant détrôner Dada, reproduisirent systématiquement sa méthodologie du scandale. Mais ils firent souvent des bides, comme Gabriel Pomerand qui, tirant au pistolet à amorces sur le public lors d'une soirée en 1947, ne récolta que l'ironie des journalistes: "Mais seules quelques jouvencelles, non habituées aux manifestations de ce genre prirent peur. On s'injuria mais sans fureur" (Descargues 1947). C'était, il est vrai, la énième mouture du "coup de revolver", numéro imaginé par Vaché, vanté par Huelsenbeck et Breton, et finalement remis en question par Tzara après la seconde guerre mondiale, à cause d'un célèbre "coup de revolver contre la culture" de sinistre mémoire.[7]

Les mises en scène des néo-Dadas dans les années 60 n'ont pas toujours su éviter la ritualisation d'une avant-garde de pacotille inféodée à la société de consommation. L'acte Dada était devenu avec le temps action labellisée, dans le bric-à-brac de la "société du spectacle". C'est pourquoi, après s'être acharné contre les lettristes, Hausmann condamna sans indulgence les actes-simulacres de ce néo-Dada, anticipant sur les diatribes de Debord (1963: 22) contre la "canaille néo-Dadaïste". Richter dans ses mémoires et entretiens ne s'en priva pas non plus:

> Exposer des voitures compressées et des garde-boue tordues et repeints, prendre une fille nue, bien faite, la tremper dans de la couleur et la rouler sur une toile, placer un cadavre artificiel dans une voiture d'enfant, donner un concert où le pianiste reste dix minutes devant son piano sans jouer, montrer une pièce de théâtre où il n'y a pas de pièce à jouer, nourrir un ours en peluche de blanc d'œuf battu en neige, suspendre une pomme de terre à une vieille chaîne de w.c.. (Richter 1965: 195–6)

> Pourquoi ne pas creuser un fossé au Sahara ou emballer la côte australienne dans du plastique. (Richter 1997: 93)

Pour Richter (1965: 195), ces actes étaient les symptômes d'une grave crise de société: "Un vide qui cherche à s'extérioriser, et le besoin de se prouver sa propre existence par l'objet, parce que le sujet, l'homme lui-même, s'est perdu". Mais "Dada resurgit toujours, d'une manière ou d'une autre, chaque fois que s'accumule trop de bêtise", écrivait Schwitters (1990: 121) en 1924.

Il ne faut jamais désespérer. 1947, c'est l'apogée des pitreries lettristes, mais c'est aussi la date de la Conférence d'Artaud au Vieux Colombier ! Un vrai geste Dada ! Et si Richter (1965: 195) croit voir le "diable" au sein du Pop Art, il épargne Kaprow, Tinguely, "ce mélange d'homme d'affaires, de clown et de génie", Johns, Higgins, Rauschenberg, César et quelques autres.

D'authentiques actes émergent de l'accumulation des performances. Le 26 novembre 1965, à la galerie Schmela de Düsseldorf, Beuys, la tête enduite de miel et couverte de feuilles d'or, visite une exposition de ses œuvres avec un lièvre mort dans les bras, à qui il fait toucher des pattes les tableaux. "[M]ême dans la mort, un lièvre a plus de sensibilité et de compréhension instinctive que certains hommes avec leur rationalité obstinée" (Goldberg 2001: 149–50). Puis il s'assied un peu à l'écart et commence à exposer à l'animal le sens de ses œuvres. Voilà du pur Dada, dont l'artiste lui-même nous livre la clé:

> Nous devons révolutionner la pensée humaine. La révolution a lieu, avant tout, en l'homme. Et quand l'homme sera devenu un être réellement libre et créatif, capable de produire quelque chose de nouveau et d'original, il pourra révolutionner son époque. (Goldberg 2001: 149)

En France, les situationnistes furent les maîtres d'œuvre du "dépassement de l'art" et du "tuer l'art" indissociable des nouvelles utopies du vivre théorisées par Henri Lefebvre. Ils prétendaient que la vie était plus importante que l'art. Cette affirmation, qui concluait déjà le *Manifeste Dada 1918* de Tzara, fait écho également à sa Conférence de dissolution du mouvement à Weimar en 1922: "Ce qui intéresse un Dadaïste est sa propre façon de vivre" (Tzara 1975: 424). Pour Debord et ses amis, la création de situations devait permettre un usage passionnant de la vie. Le Dadaïsme allemand, qui avait concilié contexte insurrectionnel et critique des formes, en incarnait la forme idéale (Debord 1962: 23), qui inspira les "enragés" de mai 68. Pour Debord le soulèvement du Congo en 1960 était un acte Dada, une mise en œuvre du détournement du "langage extérieur des maîtres comme poésie, et mode d'action" (Debord 1962: 23). En 1963, il résumait ainsi sa pensée: "Il ne s'agit pas de mettre la poésie au service de la révolution, mais bien de mettre la révolution au service de la poésie" (Debord 1963: 31).

Dada est ce moment où on se dit, comme Greil Marcus (2002: 10), "ça se passe pour de vrai". A la suite du premier Dadaïsme, issu du cataclysme de la guerre, puis du second, contemporain de la colonisation de la pensée par la société de consommation, un "troisième Dadaïsme" est apparu, celui des années 2000, favorisé par de nouvelles maladies de civilisation. Ce n'est plus l'heure du "merdre" primordial du père Ubu, mais celle des gigantesques machines à fabriquer de la merde, les *Cloaca* de Delvoye, ou des cages surchauffées de Jota Castro sur le modèle de Guantánamo, que l'on peut interpréter, avec Philippe Dagen (2005: 39) comme autant d'actes de dérision Dada pour autant de "raisons de désespérer".

Notes

[1] Marinetti, "Lettre circulaire aux journaux" (Lista 1973: 90); *Une gifle au goût public*, manifeste signé par Alexeï Kroutchenykh, Velimir Khlebnikov, Vladimir Maïakovski et David Bourliouk (Robel 1971: 13–15).

[2] Elle est bien illustrée par le récit que fait Richter en 1971 de certaines soirées Dada (Sers 1997: 87–9; Richter 1997: 87–9).

[3] Paru dans une première esquisse, *Dobrý voják Švejk a jiné podivné historky* [Le brave soldat Chvéïk et autres histoires curieuses], cet ouvrage de renommée internationale fut achevé en 1920. Piscator le mit en scène en 1928 à Berlin, accompagné de caricatures du Dadaïste George Grosz. Il a été publié en français sous le titre *Le brave soldat Chvéïk* (Paris: Gallimard. Folio, 2002).

[4] Le silence de Duchamp est en effet en grande partie mythologique, comme l'a démontré Aurélie Verdier (2006).

[5] On se souvient de la célèbre phrase de Breton (1988: 783): "L'acte surréaliste le plus simple consiste, revolvers aux poings, à descendre dans la rue et à tirer au hasard, tant qu'on peut, dans la foule".

[6] Sur les soubassements existentiels et philosophiques qui ont inspiré Michel Mourre, du Libre Esprit médiéval jusqu'à Dada et les situationnistes, on pourra se référer au brillant chapitre de Greil Marcus, "L'assaut sur Notre-Dame de Paris" (2002: 344–97).

[7] En 1920 Huelsenbeck (2000: 13) voulait "faire de la littérature, le revolver en poche". En 1950 Tzara (1982: 577) cite cette phrase et la rapproche de Goebbels, tout en se défendant de vouloir faire de son ex-comparse Dadaïste un nazi!

Bibliographie

Ball, Hugo. 1993. *La Fuite hors du temps. Journal 1913–1921* (tr. S. Wolf). Monaco: Éditions du Rocher.

Bargues, Cécile. 2004. "Les Lendemains de Dada" in *Lunapark*. Nouvelle série. Paris: Transédition.

Breton, André. 1988. *Œuvres complètes I*. Paris: Gallimard (Collection La Pléiade).

——. 1999. *Œuvres complètes III*. Paris: Gallimard (Collection La Pléiade).

Camus, Albert. 1951. *L'Homme révolté*. Paris: Gallimard (Collection Folio Essais).

Ciret, Yan. 2004. "Hurlements en faveur de Sade, Guy-Ernest Debord lettriste 1951–1952" in *Figures de la négation*. Saint-Étienne: Musée d'Art Moderne.

Dagen, Philippe. 2005. "L'Esprit de catastrophe" in *Le Magazine littéraire* 446: 37–9.

Debord, Guy. 1962. "Communication prioritaire" in *Internationale Situationniste* 7: 20–4.

Debord, Guy. 1963. "All the King's Men" in *Internationale Situationniste* 8: 29–33.

Descargues, Pierre. 1947. "Les Lettristes en liberté" in *Arts* (18 avril).

Goldberg, RoseLee. 2001. *La Performance, du futurisme à nos jours.* Paris: Thames & Hudson.

Hausmann, Raoul. 1962. *PIN and the Story of PIN.* Londres: Gaberbocchus.

Hausmann, Raoul. 2004. *Courrier Dada.* Paris: Allia.

Huelsenbeck, Richard (ed.). 1980. *Dada Almanach.* Paris: Champ Libre.

Huelsenbeck, Richard. 2000. *En avant Dada* (tr. S. Wolf). Dijon: Les presses du réel.

Jung, Franz. 2007. *Le Chemin vers le bas.* Marseille: Agone.

Koudriavstev, Sergueï. 2005. "Les héritiers de Dada ou la révolte de l'indétermination" in H. Béhar et C. Dufour (eds). *Dada circuit total.* Paris: L'Age d'homme (Dossiers H): 409–17.

Lista, Giovanni. 1973. *Futurisme. Manifestes, Documents, Proclamations.* Paris: L'Age d'Homme.

Marcus, Greil. 2002. *Lipstick Traces. Une histoire secrète du vingtième siècle* (tr. G. Godard). Paris: Gallimard (Collection Folio).

Richard, Lionel. 1998. *D'une apocalypse à l'autre.* Paris: Somogy.

Richter, Hans. 1965. *Dada art et anti-art.* Bruxelles: Éditions de la Connaissance.

Rimbaud, Arthur. 1964. *Une Saison en enfer.* Paris: Flammarion.

Robel, Léon. 1971. *Manifestes futuristes russes.* Paris: Les Éditeurs français réunis.

Schwitters, Kurt. 1990. *Kurt Schwitters Merz* (ed. M. Dachy). Paris: Champ Libre.

Sers, Philippe. 1997. *Sur Dada.* Nîmes: J. Chambon.

Tzara, Tristan. 1980. *Œuvres complètes IV* (ed. H. Béhar). Paris: Flammarion.

Tzara, Tristan. 1982. *Œuvres complètes V* (ed. H. Béhar). Paris: Flammarion.

Verdier, Aurélie. 2006. "La Fabrique du silence, Mythologie et mise en scène chez Marcel Duchamp" in *Les Cahiers du Mnam* 95: 31–44.

Chapter 3

'Dada is Dead – Long Live Dada': The Influence of Dadaism on Contemporary Performance Art

Kerstin Sommer

"Dada is a state of mind. You can be happy, sad, melancholy or Dada", wrote Tristan Tzara (1998: 16). Dada was more than just an artistic movement, it was a way of life, a frame of mind. So while the movement has blown over, the state of mind can still continue to exist and can still inspire artists' work. While it may be impossible to pinpoint a contemporary form of Dadaism, it is possible to see an influence of Dadaism in various manifestations of contemporary art and performance.

While Dada was an international movement, founded by a multi-national group of artists and later spreading out across several countries, it took different forms, adapting to the special circumstances within the countries it entered, thus creating special "national" forms of Dadaism. "Dada is a state of mind. This is why it changes according to races and events", Tzara rightly declared (1998: 21). Berlin Dada, with its political stance, for example, was the German form, adapting to German culture. This special form of Dadaism would not have worked in France or the USA, because it would have met different circumstances there. The work of German performer and filmmaker Christian Schlingensief is equally specific: he addresses German culture, history and topics, issues which are known to people immersed in life in Germany, but which are not easily understood to outsiders of the culture.

Schlingensief is known for his provocative statements: during a presentation about modern art at the 1997 *Documenta*, he demanded that the German chancellor Helmut Kohl be assassinated in an event called *Tötet Helmut Kohl* [Kill Helmut Kohl]. This earned him a lot of controversial press and led to his imprisonment. Just like the Dadaists, he appears to delight in causing controversy and public outcries, and uses performances and public appearances in the same way as the Dadaists used their manifestos. In Berlin, Dadaist Johannes Baader caused a scandal of similar scope in 1918 when he interrupted a political speech and declared himself to be the president of the globe; or when he distributed a Dadaist newspaper to a similar effect in February 1919 during a National Assembly at Weimar (Riha 2003: 104). Schlingensief follows in Dadaism's footsteps in causing disturbances in the political realm.

Schlingensief's work goes against rational sequences, against conceivable order and expectations: he presents a

> theatre of addresses and presentations of single acts, which always creates the impression that some decisive moment is just about to arrive, that what is just being presented could be the one essential message which would explain everything. The worst point, however, is that nothing happens. (Löhndorf 1998: 94)

This, in my opinion, is close to Dada's nihilism and enjoyment of paradoxes. Tzara, for example, presented his audiences with a barrage of nonsense and manifestos, and rigorously refused to provide any relief or sense. His *Première Aventure Céléste de M.Antipyrine* (Tzara 1975: 75–84), for example, consists of meaningless and unintelligible monologues between the characters. "This play is a boxing match with words", says Tzara (Melzer 1994: 73), which is then interrupted by a manifesto read by a character called Tristan Tzara, which makes more sense than the rest of the play, but does nothing to explain it. So an audience would expect Tzara's appearance and monologue to provide some sort of framework in order to make sense of the rest of the play, but this never happens.

Schlingensief uses the same tactics in his work: he aims to irritate and confuse his audiences, bombarding them with his work, but never offering any form of explanation. He states that "there is no clear message" in art. His own work is experimental, and none of his performances are like the previous one: "the result of an experiment is never certain", writes Marion Löhndorf (1998: 94). Nothing in his work is certain, nothing is simple, and there are many paradoxes. This is an important legacy of Dadaism, which was a movement full of contradictions and paradoxes: speaking out against art, and yet creating art.

"What else can art do?" asks Schlingensief. "It can attempt to interfere, but it has not been involved for a long time. But still: Schlingensief does not resign. He produces fear and suspicion and disgust", comments Löhndorf (1998: 91). Schlingensief creates art without pretensions. He realises that he cannot change the world by creating art, but he knows how to use it to get a reaction out of the witnesses of his work. The experimental, often spontaneous, dimension of his work is also reminiscent of the Dadaist predilection for chance.

In 2003, Schlingensief attempted to create a new type of art, a new style, which was developed in a series of performances and films, titled *Atta Atta – Die Kunst ist ausgebrochen* [Atta Atta – Art has escaped]. *Atta* art, his new and primitive artform, which has been continued and used for further performances and films, has various stylistic similarities to Dada. Just like Dadaist anti-art, *Atta* art is art for everybody, and made by everybody. There is no pretence in *Atta*, and it has no intellectual background. Judging from Schlingensief's enthusiastic report about the work done in a performance space, it appears that, at least for him, a sort of re-birth of the arts has taken place:

> And so, it was an overwhelming experience FOR ALL OF US. We would not have expected anything like this. It was like a trance. We painted! Can you imagine that? With colours and sonic waves! I can hardly describe it. Suddenly, everything was gone. No obstacles, no review of past art-forms, but a private escape. (www.schlingensief.com)

This ecstatic review of the performance is reminiscent of Hugo Ball's experience of the first Dada evenings at the Cabaret Voltaire: "Everyone has been seized by an indefinable intoxication. The little cabaret is about to come apart at the seams and is getting to be a playground for crazy emotions" (Ball 1996: 51-2). *Atta*, just like Dada, appears to be a return to simplicity, to ritualistic and primitive art. The name *atta* also appears to belong to the same family as Dada: it is a simple word, reminiscent of baby-language, and can mean anything at all. Whether or not Schlingensief is conscious of this proximity perceived between Dadaism and his artistic creation is impossible to know. While there appears to be no attempt on his part to start a movement like Dada, the spirit visible in his *atta*-works is clearly similar to that of early Dada works. Schlingensief, the German phenomenon, seems to be happy to remain just this: a national source of artistic interference. It has to be noted, however, that the new *atta* art has been used and developed further in films and related performance projects. It remains to be seen how or even if he develops the experiment.

As previously established, the Dada performer is the "personal actor" (Melzer 1994: 60–1), always recognisable in his performances. This appears to be equally true for Schlingensief, who can be construed to be following the Dadaist tradition in this respect. While he was absent from his films, he has been present and identifiable in all of his pieces since he moved to the stage:

> Chaos and contradictions of his pieces come to a point in his (stage) persona [...] They have face now, a figure, an aura [...] He does not only emerge from his work, but becomes an integral part thereof. This is what causes the appeal of his theatre, this is Schlingensief's real achievement. [...] "The piece of art will shine the most if it is very closely related to the artist's personality", he says. (Löhndorf 1998: 94–101)

Therefore, we can say that Schlingensief presents Schlingensief, just like the Dada artists and performers before him presented themselves. He builds on his own personality to support his work and make it "shine", just like the Dadaists who valued individuality highly, and believed that all of an artist's work should be related to his own individual experiences and personality. Each of the Dadaists produced and presented their own unique form of Dadaism, and while there is no evidence that Schlingensief's work is actively influenced by Dadaism, there can be no doubt that certain similarities can be traced back to Dadaist performance.

Just like Schlingensief, British artist Richard Layzell can be seen as a "personal actor" and the influence of Dadaism can be seen in his work as well. Layzell, like many of the Dada artists, originally came from a fine art background and then moved to performance. While still a student at the Slade School of Fine Art (Layzell 1998: 5), he already began to develop a certain style: creating installations and performances within them. He was strongly influenced by contemporary art (1969), witnessing the advent of what was soon to be called "performance art": events, sit-ins, and happenings. This led to his first experiments with installations and performance:

> The theatre project was straight-forward and open-ended. But what an opportunity. Do what you like with this space and we'll have a performance at the end of the week with lights and all. This project contributed to my complete change of direction. (Layzell 1998: 6)

The type of artistic expression known as a happening is reminiscent of Dadaist performances: these performances were often created by artists, displaying their own personal views, creating and presenting their art in ways which bear more resemblance to Dadaist than traditional theatrical performances. However, unlike the Dadaists, these artists were only united by the term happening, whereas the Dadaists shared a disgust with the time they lived in and began an anarchistic rebellion. Happenings, though similar in form, did not stem from a common belief.

> None of the artists ever agreed on the term, and despite the desire of many of them for clarification, no "happening" group was formed, no collective manifestos, magazines or propaganda issued [...] It covered this wide range of activity, however much it failed to distinguish between the different intentions of the work. (Goldberg 2001: 132)

Layzell, who counts the Dadaists among his influences, began his artistic career by combining his artwork with performances, and has continued along this path ever since, finding new forms of expression, integrating personal experiences and circumstances into his work. Layzell conducts it in the form of performance experiments.

In contrast to Schlingensief and the Dadaists, Layzell is not an aggressive performer. I consider his work to be an artistic interference with everyday life, but he neither aims to offend nor to shock. He moved away from his early performance-based work for a while and concentrated on installation-pieces, returning to performance to "activate an installation, to create a more direct relationship with an audience" (Layzell 1998: 18). Layzell explores himself in relation to the spectators, and attempts to engage them in a dialogue, as the *Guardian* reviewer comments:

> [T]his can be a bit like watching someone with a severe personality disorder [...] He also has enough physical discipline to make those insane gestures conjure up something disturbing and Surrealistic. But what exactly? In the end, we who crave for meanings are left floundering in a sea of ambiguity. (Layzell 1998: 60)

Layzell's work is personal, and, in my view, feels unthreatening in comparison with Dadaist performances and manifestations. He refers to the *Merz*-Dadaist Kurt Schwitters as one of his heroes, thereby linking himself and his work to the works of Schwitters. In his piece *Here One Minute,* which was "a performance/lecture which claimed to be a history of live art/performance art" (Layzell 1998: 74), he dressed up in a costume of cardboard tubes similar to the one Hugo Ball wore at the Cabaret Voltaire to recite some of his sound-poems:

> I had made myself a special costume [...] My legs were in a cylinder of shiny blue cardboard, which came up to my hips so that I looked like an obelisk. Over it I wore a huge collar cut out of cardboard [...] I also wore a high, blue-and-white-striped witch doctor's hat [...] I could not walk in the cylinder so I was carried onto the stage. (Ball 1996: 70)

Layzell (1998: 74) chose a sound-poem by Kurt Schwitters to read, and explains that, after some insecurity about performing the piece, he "grew passionate about this experience", and considered it to be "a tribute, not a rip-off".

His next work, *Mentations* (1994–95), a collection of short pieces, included the recital of Schwitters' poem:

> The working title was "Shorts". This format would allow for many forms of presentation from pseudo-lecture to anecdote, physical action and visual narrative. And the freedom to target the audiences through the chosen units: leave this one out for the gig in Eastbourne, include these two for the Hammersmith Palais. And a random element, like choosing playing cards from a pack [...] At the start of every performance there would be a random selection of cards, each one a different mentation. Pull out a few and that would be it. (Layzell 1998: 75)

This work, which includes an element of chance, is reminiscent of the Dadaists' experiments: the random selection and combination of these "mentations" is akin to Tzara's method for writing Dada poetry by combining words randomly picked from a bag. The effect of his performance would be like looking at a Dadaist collage: a piece made up of unrelated, differing elements united to form a whole.

While Richard Layzell's work can take quasi-Dadaist forms, and even use Dadaist techniques like chance and a collage-like style, he differs greatly from most of the Dadaists. He does not really protest against or attempt to subvert or revolutionise art, he merely creates his installations and performance pieces around his personal aesthetics and his view of the world. In this respect, he is very close to his hero Kurt Schwitters. This is rather fitting, since I can see parallels between Layzell's work and Schwitters' work.

Kurt Schwitters was a one-man Dadaist movement. Rejected by the Berlin Dada circle around Huelsenbeck, he called his art *Merz* and continued to produce collages, sculptures and poetry in a Dadaistic style. He created art out of scraps and objects he found (thus exploiting chance), and writing sound-poetry as well as nonsensical poetry. Schwitters created, performed and lived *Merz*, but he always remained a singular figure. His brand of Dadaism was a peaceful, a-political one, which, while it was closer to Paris Dada than to Berlin Dada, remained non-confrontational. It was an artistic exploration and development of Dadaist ethics. *Merz* was Schwitters, Schwitters was *Merz*.

His most famous piece of work, a poem called "Anna Blume" (Riha and Schäfer 1994: 160), deconstructs the conventions of ordinary love poems, and thereby both exposes and ridicules them. Layzell, in some of his pieces, appears to be working in a related way. His pieces entitled *Definitions* and *Re-Definitions* (1985–87) examine what it means to be a performance artist at that time:

> I had a lot to say about stereotyping as an artist in no small measure. To call yourself a performance artists in 1985 was an issue in itself. It still is. I could expose this in the performance as well as issues of male identity. It could demonstrate the desire to break out, risk-take and confound people's expectations. (Layzell 1998: 44)

Through his monologue he hoped to escape being pigeon-holed, while displaying a desire for order by calling everything by a name in order to be able to feel in control of it:

> Is this what I do for a living?...When people ask me, what I usually say is: "Well, you know, it is a bit like acting and a bit like art [...] It's as if they want it to be categorised. [...] John would want to hear something he'll be comfortable with, so he can pigeon-hole me. [...] But now that I've seen them once I'm OK, I can give'em a name. (Layzell 1998: 44)

In the next section, he addressed what the audience might have been thinking, thereby making them feel exposed. Finally, he expresses the desire to "fit in", illustrating the problems and the self-doubt his position as a performance artist causes. In this way, Layzell's performance works in a way similar to Schwitters' poem: he exposes society's desire for order, expresses his disagreement with it, then subverts what he has established, first exposing himself, then the audience, and ridiculing the whole issue in the end, just as Schwitters does in his poem.

Richard Layzell's body of work borrows techniques and ideas from Dadaism, which he counts as one of the artistic directions which influence him and which he incorporates into his work.

Dadaism is also directly linked to what has become known as "action painting": painting as performance. American artist Jackson Pollock is maybe the most prominent example here. While he had no overt political stance, and pre-dated *Fluxus* and *Happenings,* his work seems to embody the element of chance and spontaneity the Dadaists were looking for through their work. Pollock himself was aware of, and influenced by, Surrealism, Dadaism's offspring, and his work is often seen as relating to the Surrealists' experiments in automatism. Jackson Pollock's interest in Surrealism was also fuelled by his own experiences with psychoanalysis and the concept of the unconscious mind. During his treatment for alcoholism and depression, he discovered Jung's theories of the unconscious, which then began to influence his work and finally led to his experiments in action painting: dripping and splashing paint onto canvases in random fashion, thus both letting his unconscious take over and at the same time exploring the Surrealist concept of automatism (Taylor 2003).

It should not be overlooked, however, that the Dadaists had already begun this exploration of the subconscious mind. Their experiments with chance and spontaneous actions led them in a very similar direction. Hans Richter (2002: 57) wrote:

> Chance appeared to us a magical procedure by which one could transcend the barriers of causality and of conscious volition, and by which the inner eye and ear became more acute, so that new sequences of thoughts and experiences made their appearance. For us, chance was the "unconscious mind" which Freud had discovered in 1900.

Interestingly, Pollock, the alcoholic, only worked on his pictures when he was sober, and therefore fully aware – maybe to keep his "inner eye and ear" as acute as possible to help him create. When talking about his pictures, it is quite clear that he allowed himself the utmost freedom:

> When I am in my painting, I'm not aware of what I'm doing. It's only after a sort of "get acquainted" period that I see what I have been about. I have no fears about making changes, destroying the image, etc., because the painting has a life of its own. (O'Connor 1967: 39–40)

In his work, I see the Dadaists' credo embodied, an "absolute and incontestable belief in every god that is the immediate product of spontaneity", according to Tzara (1998: 60). Unlike the Surrealists, who concerned themselves with psychology and dream imagery in most of their work, here we have an artist who does not question or analyse his creations. He appears to have achieved something the Dadaists longed for, and something the Surrealists abandoned in favour of an artistic exploration of dreams and unconscious thought processes: he has succeeded "to restore to the work of art its primeval magic power, and to find the way back to the immediacy it had lost" (Richter 2002: 59).

"Action painting" can be seen as a performance. It is both the action of painting and painting as a performative action: it is both performance and production of art. Pollock himself becomes a spectator to his actions, simply letting the picture happen. The action is more important than the result – the act of dripping and splashing paint more important than the painting which is being created. "In Action Painting the canvas is the arena in which the artist acts". Just like Dadaism, action painting combines art and performance. While Dadaist soirées, artworks and literature became a canvas for the individual artists to express their feelings and opinions, here the canvas becomes the stage on which the individual acts out his own emotions. "The action of painting becomes a moment in the biography of the artist – the canvas becomes the index (record) of the event" (www.artlex.com/ArtLex/a/actionpainting.html). The random splashes of paint on the canvas are the record of an artist's spontaneous creation, maybe even a manifestation of his unconscious thoughts at the time of creating the image. Since they have been created by chance, no two pictures by the same artist will ever be the same. Every individual would produce different results, thereby linking the images to their unique personality. This once again brings me back to Tristan Tzara's experiments with chance poetry (Motherwell 1981: 92). He states that a cut-out poem will reflect its creator's individuality, because a different individual would not come to the same result. This is an idea which I would like to apply to action painting, or more specifically, Jackson Pollock's pictures created by dripping and splashing paint onto canvases. While technically this method of producing art is easily copied and imitated, I believe that the results would differ greatly from person to person.

Pollock's work is as unique to him as every Dadaist's work was to them. In his case, the link to Dada (via Surrealism) is quite obvious:

it can be seen as a continuation of the experiments with chance and the unconscious begun by the Dadaists which then found their way into Pollock's work. However, there is slightly more to Pollock's work than this. While Dadaists like Hans Richter were wondering what chance is, and where it originates (Richter 2002: 56), Pollock's explanation is both simple and significant. "I am nature", he declared (Madoff 1999: 97). This statement links him to Dadaism: it was an "identification with nature" like Pollock's which the Dadaists claimed in their struggle against the mechanisation of everyday life. "Dada", they declared, "is without a meaning, as nature is" (Richter 1997: 37). The action paintings produced by Jackson Pollock, as products of "nature", in my view, can be considered to be a more contemporary manifestation of Dadaist art.

Traces of Dadaist influences can be found in the most unlikely places: *Trio*, an Austrian pop-band of the 1980s, landed an international hit with their song *Da Da Da*, which is probably not directly connected to Dada, and maybe not even influenced by the movement. However, it fits in nicely with Kurt Schwitters' famous *Merz* poem "Anna Blume", discussed earlier, and with the Dadaists' enjoyment of paradoxes and nonsense.

The lyrics to the song consist solely of the words "Da Da Da I don't love you you don't love me aha aha aha". This can be seen as a direct attack on popular love songs, and since it managed to enter the charts, it can almost be seen as an ironic attack upon German pop culture as well as upon the world created by and presented in popular love songs. Like Kurt Schwitters, they use a common form in order to pastiche it. While Schwitters' *Merz* poem "Anna Blume" uses the form and phrases of a classical love poem, they used the form of a standard pop-song for theirs. It was created by improvisation, and was meant to be nothing but a joke yet had surprising success.

Looking back to the beginnings of Dadaism, Hugo Ball's statement proves to have been prophetic: "From its beginnings in poetry and visual art, the Dada revolution was carried into architecture, the film, music, typography and articles of everyday use" (Richter 1997: 49). The results of this revolution are still visible today.

Bibliography

Ball, Hugo. 1996. *Flight out of Time* (ed. J. Elderfield). Berkeley, Los Angeles and London: University of California Press.

Goldberg, RoseLee. 2001. *Performance Art.* London: Thames & Hudson.

Layzell, Richard. 1998. *Enhanced Performance.* Colchester: Firstsite.

Löhndorf, Marion. 1998 "Lieblingziel Totalirritation" in *Kunstforum* 142(10): 94–101.

Madoff, Steven Henry. 1999. "Creative Chaos" in *Time* 154(21): 97–9.

Melzer, Annabelle. 1994. *Dada and Surrealist Performance.* London: Johns Hopkins University Press.

Motherwell, Robert (ed.). 1981. *The Dada Painters and Poets, An Anthology.* London: Belknap Press of Harvard University Press.

O'Connor, Francis V. 1967. *Jackson Pollock.* New York: Museum of Modern Art.

Richter, Hans. 2002. *Art and Anti-Art.* London: Thames & Hudson.

Riha, Karl (ed.). 2003. *Dada 113 Gedichte.* Berlin: Verlag Klaus Wagenbach.

—— and Jörgen Schäfer. 1994. *Dada Total.* Stuttgart: Phillip Reclam jun. GmbH & Co.

Taylor, Sue. 2003. "The Artist and the Analyst" in *American Art* 17(3): 52–72.

Tzara, Tristan. 1975. *Œuvres complètes I* (ed. H. Béhar). Paris: Flammarion.

——. 1998 *Sieben Dada Manifeste.* Hamburg: Verlag Lutz Schulenberg, Edition Nautilus.

Internet sources:

http://www.artlex.com/ArtLex/a/actionpainting.html

http://www.stephan-remmler.de/Trio

http://www.beatmuseum.org/pollock/jacksonpollock.html

http://www.schlingensief.com

DADA AND CINEMA

Chapter 4

Francis Picabia, Stacia Napierkowska, and the Cinema: The Circuits of Perception

Jennifer Wild

Francis Picabia's pre-Dada period between 1913 and 1915 is filled with *jeunes filles* and dancers in near to fully blossomed mechanomorphic forms or depicted upon richly coloured canvases that delight the eye as a "sensorsium" of colour, movement and music (Pierre 2001: 58–81). In studies of these works – which were produced in the context of Picabia's sojourns between Paris and New York with Gabrielle Buffet-Picabia (20 January–10 April 1913; June–December 1915) – there stands one, prominent and telling figure: Stacia Napierkowska. Her name first appears as "Npierkowska" on the bottom of *Mechanical Expression Seen Through Our Own Mechanical Expression (Npierkowska)* [figure 4] that Willard Bohn (1985: 676) believes was made between 28 March and 9 April 9 1913 in New York. As is now well known, the Picabias and Napierkowska were both traveling to New York upon the transatlantic liner the Lorraine in January 1913 – the former for the 17 February opening of the Armory Show, the latter for her 24 March début of *The Captive* at the Palace Theater and a tour performing on the American music-hall circuit.[1]

William Camfield (1966: 313) was the first to turn to Gabrielle Buffet Picabia's recollections of her and Picabia's voyage upon the Lorraine in order to pinpoint the identity of "Npierkowska" and, subsequently, the source for Picabia's works such as *Udnie, jeune fille américaine Danse* (1913), *Danseuse étoile sur un transatlantique* (1913), *Danseuse étoile et son école de* danse (1913), *Je revois en souvenir ma chère Udnie* (1914) (Gabrielle Buffet-Picabia 1956: 35).[2] Camfield (1979: 62) writes that "the brassy forms and extroverted rhythms of *Udnie* may be presented as plastic-psychological equivalents for Picabia's impressions of young American girls, dance and, perhaps, New York and Napierkowska".

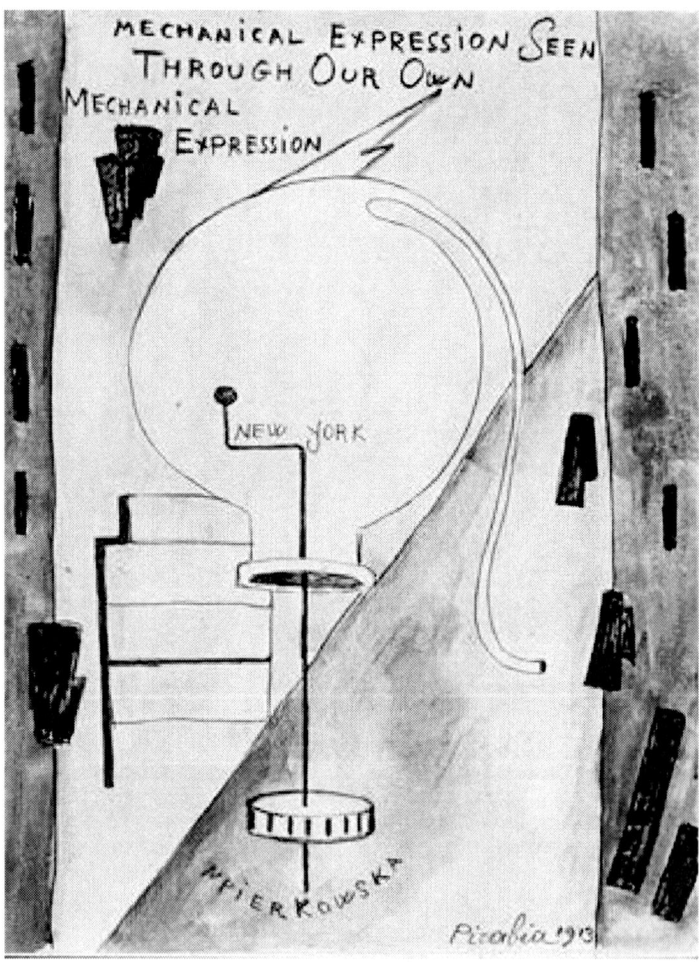

Figure 4. Francis Picabia, *Mechanical Expression Seen Through Our Own Mechanical Expression (Npierkowska)* (1913).

It has become essential to the Picabia-Napierkowska legacy that the dancer was served a summons to appear in court following her performance of "The Dance of the Bee" – or "a sort of hoochi koochi" as one prosecutor called it ("Napierkowska May Dance", *New York Times*, 29 March 1913).[3] Although Napierkowska was dismissed of charges that included "a danger to morals", Bohn (1985: 676) argues that this is the historical event that "led Picabia to create his first mechanomorphic work", a claim that has in turn rerouted our understanding of *Mechanical Expression*'s importance to Picabia's development of machine portraiture. Bohn describes this event's significance with particular attention to the light bulb-like form that dominates *Mechanical Expression*:

> At best, the light bulb might suggest the luminary quality of Napierkowska's dancing or the bright lights of Broadway. In fact, Picabia has chosen to depict Napierkowska as a radiometer which allows him to allude both to her profession and to a particular incident [...] But the functional analogy at the heart of this work is more complex and more precise. Not only does Picabia's radiometer evoke her radiant personality, but it refers to her dancing. Like the radiometer which is fond of sunlight, Napierkowska loves to bathe in the limelight. Just as it revolves in response to solar radiation, she pirouettes furiously before the footlights. Among other things, the object-portrait is a humorous commentary on her profession. Picabia posits a cause and effect relationship between the technical effects and her dance, as if the simple flick of a light switch were enough to set her in motion [...] As *Mechanical Expression* makes clear, the authorities had effectively "pulled the plug" on Napierkowska's act. (Bohn 1985: 675–6)

In this constellation of chance meetings, transatlantic voyages, brushes with the law and yet other contemporary machine forms or scientific discourses that historians have used to analyze *Mechanical Expression*, there lies a layer of history *in absentia* that I would like to address here.[4] This history is of the popular cinema in Paris and New York that are the contexts both before and after Picabia's mythic encounter with Napierkowska. First, this history unmasks Stacia Napierkowska's full identity as not simply a music-hall dancer, but as a rising and highly visible film star; second, it uncovers Francis Picabia's position as an historical film spectator and cinéphile – a position that provides a window into his potential psychic activity of both fascination and identification with Napierkowska especially as he found his own "instant celebrity" upon entering New York art and social worlds (Camfield 1979: 41). Finally, the cinema history imbedded here generates anther perspective of the figuration found in

Picabia's work between 1913 and 1915 as well as sheds light upon his later Dada works such as *Américaine* (reproduced in *391*, 6, 1 July 1917), or *Entr'Acte*, his 1924 post-Dada film made with René Clair in which we find a quite note-worthy, pirouetting "female" dancer. The cinema history surrounding Picabia and Napierkowska succinctly transforms *Mechanical Expression* into a map that codes Picabia's arrival into the electric city and cinema culture of New York, and it also suggests a more precisely cinematographic animus within Picabia's broader passage into the mechanomorphic style.

La Napierkowska, *l'étoile*

By focusing solely on her identity as a dancer, Camfield has defined our art historical understanding of both Napierkowska and her contribution to Picabia's works. As Camfield's research implies, the Picabias may have read the 1912 reviews about Napierkowska in *Comœdia*, the most important cultural and arts magazine of the period that incidentally began running daily film criticism in 1913 and advertising film programs several years earlier (Camfield 1979: 41).[5] It is highly likely that the Picabias would have also been aware of Napierkowska's publicity that appeared in a vast array of other sources: not only was she the subject of a feature cover-article in the specialized cinema magazine, *Le Cinéma* (15 March 1912), between 1911 and 1914 she was the subject of a spate of popular and trade press iconography, articles and advertisements in magazines such as *Femina* and *La Rampe*.[6] Her rise from the *corps du ballet de l'Opéra* to her more central role at the Opéra-Comique is punctuated by significant runs in music-halls such as l'Olympia, Aux Ambassadeurs, Le Gaîté-Lyrique or the Folies-Bergère where, in 1909, she danced "en son rôle de Smirlin dans *Romi Tchave,* le brillant ballet de Richepin".[7] From a 1913 magazine soap advertisement featuring her face in a full-page close-up ("Mlle Napierkowska, de l'Opéra Comique, dit: 'les effets remarquablement adoucissants du Savon Cadum font de lui le meilleur savon de toilette' "), to her body's full image on the cover of a 1913 issue of the popular woman's magazine *Femina*, to yet other magazine spreads for fashionable hats, Napierkowska was everywhere, including the cinema.[8] Between April 1912 and January 1913 alone, Napierkowska appeared in at least eleven films made and released by the company Pathé Frères.[9]

Like her contemporaries Mistinguett, Sarah Bernhardt and Francesca Bertini ("La Bertini"), Napierkowska's carreer on the stage was concomitant with the circulation of her mechanically reproduced moving image. As early as 1908, companies such as Pathé and its Films d'art production unit or Films d'Arte Italiana (an Italian production company linked to Pathé) had turned to stage actresses to attract more theatrically-minded spectators to the moving pictures as well as to raise the "moral" and artistic status and reputation of their cinematographic productions.[10] Mistinguett's and Bernhardt's film personae were always preceded and/or sustained by their theatrical and music-hall aura, but it seems that Napierkowska's fame as a dancer grew explicitly with the rise of the cinema and the birth of the star system. All three, however, signal the extent to which early cinema stardom often grew out of a performer's popularity in the performing arts. The author of the cover article in *Le Cinéma* (29 March 1912) paints Napierkowska not simply as *une danseuse étoile* for L'Opéra Comique (by 1900), but as a multi-faceted performer whose simultaneous reign on both stage and screen had no precedents in theatre history and had furthermore transformed her into her own competitor. On any given night, spectators including Picabia could choose to see Napierkowska "live and in the flesh" or as a projected image:

> Partout, des manifestations exaltées naissaient spontanément sur son passage. C'est alors que l'on vit cette chose unique, sans précédent dans l'histoire du théâtre et qui, à ce point de vue, est digne d'être signalée: une artiste se faire presque concurrence à elle-même. Dans la même ville et dans la même soirée, Mlle Napierkowska paraissait au théatre et dans quinze à vignt cinémas.

> Car cette artiste incomparable, cette inimitable danseuse, ce mime cette comédienne extraordinaire appartient autant au cinématographe qu'au théâtre. Et cela dans un genre nettement différent. ("Mlle Napierkowska", *Le Cinéma*, 29 March 1912)

Another article from the same issue of *Le Cinéma* ("Silhouettes d'artistes") corroborates her synchronized appearance in the Parisian entertainment landscape as both a music-hall dancer and a film icon: "Hâtez-vous d'aller applaudir l'artiste à L'Olympia où elle vient de créer des danses japonaises et cambodgiennes d'une inoubliable beauté et au plus prochain cinéma dans *La Légende des Tulipes d'or*". It is significant that these authors point to the difference between Napierkowska's stage and screen style: unlike Bernhardt or

Mistinguett, Napierkowska's alternating medial incarnation demonstrated the plasticity of her performative range and image.

While these authors' promotional tone should be acknowledged, it is clear that by 1913 Napierkowska was a highly recognizable stage and screen star whose iconic resonance was found most centrally in her body's lithe display. In a satirical cartoon by "Gus" she is sketched as a human contortion standing upon one leg, arms overhead.[11] Puffs of smoke rise around her and underneath the caption reads: "Comment on rôtit le ballet à l'Odéon pour tacher d'allumer les vieux messieurs abonnés", suggesting that her nimbleness "heated up" an old entertainment form, in more ways than one.[12] However, it is interesting that Maurice Raynal, who became the first film critic for Apollinaire's journal *Les Soirées de Paris* in 1913, wrote in favour of popular, whimsical comedies such as *Polydore, savetier* while he criticized the lavishly costumed Films d'art in which Napierkowska was regularly starring and dancing:

> C'est dans ce sens que le cinéma pourrait, peut-être, créer quelque chose et non dans la reproduction de scènes historiques, telle que cette "Cléopâtre" écoeurante et vue ailleurs, que la vulgarité de Mlle Roch et les désarticulations de Mlle Napierkowska, la désossée, ne parvinrent pas à rendre intéressante. (Raynal 1913: 7)

Cléopatre was already three years old in 1913 (starring Madeline Roch as Cleopatra), but Raynal's distaste for an "out-moded" style anticipates what became a pervasive sentiment toward French film by the mid-teens among avant-garde artists.[13] By 1913, the "bonelessness" of Mlle Napierkowska was an insufficient and furthermore inelegant star-quality that had lost its appeal for this critic who may not have fallen prey to the "Cleopatra craze" of the 1910s that used the historical countenance to sell "everything from cigarettes to beauty soap and light bulbs" (Abel 1994: 258).[14]

A year earlier, however, Pathé Frères explicitly drew upon Napierkowska's appeal as an icon of modern terpsichore who hailed from the larger sphere of the Paris art and entertainment world and whose image embodied the company's haptical technology. Between 8 and 15 November 1912, a little more than a month before the Lorraine set sail, Napierkowska received top billing for the highly promoted release of *La Fièvre de l'Or*, a large production that claimed over sixty cast members; the film itself was released at the Omnia Pathé on 22 November.[15] Interestingly, the first, half-page advertisement for the film depends solely upon Napierkowska's name as a draw; a week later, another advertisement specifies that she will appear in the film's second act:

> Mlle Napierkowska, de l'Opéra, et le corps de ballet de l'Olympia dans Le Triomphe du Veau d'Or. La magnificence de sa mise en scène rehaussée par les merveilleuses couleurs naturelles dues à PATHECOLOR font de ce Film LE VERITABLE CHEF D'ŒUVRE DE L'ART CINEMATOGRAPHIQUE.

Here, the star's renown as a dancer is keenly associated with the vibrancy of Pathé's signature colour processing. The film's digital preservation in black and white at Pathé-Gaumont archives cannot speak to the full range of its original impact in colour. Yet its densely composed frames in which Napierkowska dances surrounded by an elaborately costumed dance corps suggest the extent to which this film was "consecrated *Painting in motion*" (Canudo 1911). As a symphony for the eyes in a dynamic swirl of complicated texture and colour associated with the star quality of Napierkowska's specific body and dance style, Pathé may have provided a kind of antecedent for Picabia's later tableaux which he described as "the idea of movement" (Picabia 1913: 9).

In light of Raynal's suggestion that popular physical comedies bore a more promising and modern aesthetic for the future of the film form, it is of special note that in the months (September 1912–January 1913) leading up to their early-January departure from Paris, Picabia could have seen Napierkowska in seven films starring and directed by the very popular comedian Max Linder. Picabia would have already been upon the Lorraine by the time *Mariage au téléphone* came out at the Omnia-Pathé on 10 January, but considering his love of all things burlesque it is likely that he would have seen Linder's *Peintre par amour* (released at the Omnia Pathé on 6 September 1912), *Max et la fuite de gaz* (Omnia Pathé on 9 September 1912) or *Amour tenace* (Omnia Pathé on 4 October 1912) – all of which starred Napierkowska.

Arguably the first French film star, Max Linder's popularity reached such great proportions by 1910 that, as Richard Abel (1994: 240) has remarked, Pathé renamed his film series simply as *Max*. By this time, Linder had developed his character's particular iconicity as the "young bourgeois [...] consistently inhabiting well-appointed apartments, fully equipped with servants [...] Max rarely worked; instead, he either courted young women (not always unmarried), frequented restaurants and nightclubs, or indulged in various sports" (Abel 1994: 240). While I will forego a full comparison to Picabia's own mythic identity as bourgeois sportsman and flirt, hence the potential points of Picabia's spectatorial identification with Linder, I will quote Abel's description of *Peintre par amour* at length for how it creates an interesting constellation of references considering that Napierkowska played the object of Linder's attention:

> Mlle Cabaneilles (Napierkowska), whom Max is courting on the sly, suggests that he make himself out to be a painter and do a portrait of her mother (Gabirelle Lange) so that she will assent to their engagement. Max's initial strategy, however, is to use his easel as a screen to keep the mother from seeing the couple kissing, but the mother exposes him as a fraud when she discovers the childish caricature he has drawn. His next strategy is to take on the guise of Léonard de Vincennes and portray the mother as a "Mona Lisa," which he produces by tearing off the canvas's top layer to reveal a copy of the famous painting stolen from the Louvre. The problem now is to reproduce the plumed hat the mother insists on wearing, and his witty solution is to clip off several feathers and stick them directly onto the copy, in a very up-to-date form of collage. (Abel 1994: 412–13)

Undoubtedly, the theme of the Mona Lisa in this and a spate of other films from this period has contemporary currency in the painting's 1911 theft from the Louvre (Napierkowska also appeared in *Le Tragique amour de Mona Lisa*, Albert Capellani, 1912, SCAGL-Pathé).[16] Yet Linder's whimsical collage aesthetic can also be thought of as part of the densely woven visual and cultural sources that nurtured Marcel Duchamp's *L.H.O.O.Q* (1919) as well as Picabia's subsequent "theft" of it for publication in *391* (no. 17, March 1920) (Baker 2001, 2007).

The similarly dense fabric of film and entertainment culture surrounding Napierkowska conditions a re-reading of Picabia's subsequent encounter with her on the Lorraine. I use the word "conditions" for several reasons. First, while it remains unknown if Picabia attended any of the many popular spectacles in which Napierkowska appeared – either live performance or cinematographic – it is certain that on some level he was a spectator, so to speak, of the star discourse about her in the press. This particular situation is by and large a more cinematographic than theatrical scenario insofar as it is an inherently voyeuristic equation that is positioned on the absence of the object. Christian Metz's classic formulation of the "imaginary signifier" is helpful in terms of the cinema's "scopic regime" that may be rethought here to include the extra-textual materials of a growing star system's promotional tools for the star body and identity: an experience of Napierkowska *in abstentia* – viewing an image of her rather than viewing the woman herself – activates perception in a way that is very distinct from the theatre in which case the object and subject produce a fictionalized scenario of voyeurism through simultaneous physical presence (Metz 1986). On the contrary, at the cinema this relationship is imaginary from the very beginning and produces in the subject "infinite desire" for what is endlessly inaccessible, an "effigy". Hence, in the instance of meeting or "seeing" Napierkowska in person Picabia is revealed as, effectively, star-struck – or gripped by a state of over-determined fascination with a particular body's signification as, indeed, *real*, present, and, even if by default, consensual to the scenario of voyeurism that the theatrical spectatorial relationship engenders.

Second, the "conditions" surrounding the Picabia-Napierkowska meeting have consequences for how we understand Picabia's arrival in New York (cinema culture), the subsequent production of *Mechanical Expression* as well as a host of other works that figure the "memory" of Napierkowska, the sensations of a foreign metropolis and that present real people as inhuman forms. In short, the preparatory, cinema-cultural context of his brush with celebrity on the Lorraine seems to be the condition out of which Picabia developed a style based on present absences and the omnipresence of his own perceptual experience: "Mais moi, je ne peins pas ce que voient mes yeux. Je peins ce que voit mon esprit, ce que voit mon âme... Mon esprit s'imprègne de chaque mouvement" (Picabia 2005: 51). Picabia's words to describe his painterly style seem to encapsulate what Metz (1986: 49) argues is actually perceived during cinematographic spectatorship: "[T]he spectator *identifies with himself*, with himself as a pure act of perception (as wakefulness, alertness): as the condition of possibility of the perceived and hence as a kind of transcendental subject, which comes before every *there is*".

New York, *la ville*

To date, there is little evidence of the extent of Picabia's cinema-going in Paris before 1913 where an exponential rise in the entertainment form's domination over the city occurred over the span of only a few short years. A reporter for the Catholic newspaper *Le Correspondant* wrote on 25 May 1913:

> [I]ts development has been prodigious; six years ago there were only two cinemas in Paris, and today there are 160. Day and night, the screenings follow fast on one another, and the cinemas are anything but empty. In every quarter of the big cities, we see a "cinema-theater," a "cinema-concert", or a "cinema-brasserie" – which at least are better than the "magic-cinemas" and "folies-cinemas". (Abel 1988: 78)

Incidentally, the Folies-Bergère began including short cinematographic projections as *entr'actes* as early as 1898; shortly thereafter film became a regular feature in most café-concert programs (Abel 1994: 16). Hence, Picabia's cinema-going in Paris may have occurred only by happenstance while attending a music-hall show. However, it is likely that his Parisian film-going habits were more developed, if not part of his social rituals, if we consider how Gabrielle Buffet-Picabia describes their time in New York. Once in America, Buffet-Picabia recalls that Picabia became an openly engaged *cinéphile*, a fact that would be confirmed years later in Paris upon publishing his article "Cinéma" in the true cinéphile's magazine, *Cinéa* (*Le Journal du Ciné-Club*), in May 1922. In 1913, however, her husband spent leisurely days going to the cinema where he was marked by a different cinematographic style and content that provided a sense of the American cinema's spontaneity and an adventurous *dépaysement*:

> Il passait ses jours au cinéma, émerveillé par les acteurs de l'époque, qui, je crois bien, n'ont jamais été dépassés: Charlot (déjà), William Hart, Lilian Guish [sic], l'héroïne de ce film extraordinaire: *The Birth of a Nation* qui durait quatre heures et qu'on suivait sans fatigue, peut-être parce que, pour la première fois, la partition musicale avait été écrite spécialement pour le film; mais ces westerns et films historiques, interprétés avec une telle ferveur et recherche de vérité, étaient particululièrement révélateurs de certains caractères essentiels du pays; on y ressentait vivement que la vie dure et avanetureuse des pionniers n'était pas encore très loin. (Buffet-Picabia 1977: 183) [17]

Buffet-Picabia also boldly asserted in her memoirs that the cinematographic vision more generally revealed "des décompositions de mouvements ignorés jusqu'alors" to avant-garde artists from which they drew "new conventions of vision and realisation" (Buffet-Picabia 1977: 224). This was the case for Picabia's particular experience across the Atlantic insofar as the style of American cinema exhibition differed distinctly from Parisian practices and provided him with a completely new context in which to consider the plasticity of cinematographic signification and the hapticality of cinema spectatorship. The charm and the sensorial explosiveness of American cinema-going were created first in the diverse sound-scape of American cinemas and, more precisely, nickelodeons – the cheap, store-front theatres that dominated American cinema exhibition practice until roughly 1915. In these theatres, a highly heterogeneous program of both live and mechanically reproduced spectacles footed the bill. Buffet-Picabia describes the aural components of la salle:

> [L]es spectateurs si proches des héros, l'intervention brutale du "faiseur de bruits" qui imite la mer ou le moteur d'aéroplane, surtout l'orchestre rudimentaire à base de tambour et le rythme continu du ragtime, dont la pression et la dépression stimulent l'effet visuel, forment une ambiance légèrement engourdissante, où l'esprit se degage plus facilement des impressions externes et s'adapte plus intégralement à l'écran lumineux, source de son plaisir. (Buffet-Picabia 1977: 391)

Considering her description of the "rudimentary" musical accompaniment of the piano-centric rag-time musical genre, this context is highly likely the nickelodeon whose sound-scape was more often than not created by a sole pianist whose work was also that of a sound-effects technician. Furthermore, the nickelodeon context also provided a wealth of specifically American visual forms whose sensorial radius included live singing and spectatorial participation: the Illustrated Song Slide was a standardized nickelodeon feature to roughly 1914 that, in most cases, featured an amateur singer who performed at the foot of the screen.[18] The singer would lead the audience in a chorus "sing-along" as slides "illustrating" the popular song's narrative were projected behind her. The colourful, elaborately designed slides commonly depicted images of surreal whimsy that often referred to the electric, urban and visual sphere of New York entertainment culture or, when necessitated by the song's narrative, the immigrant experience.

The Brevoort Hotel, the Picabias' address during their first New York adventure, was located at 5th avenue and 8th street, in proximity to a wealth of nickelodeons and more established high and low-brow theatres filled with mixed entertainment programs. Just six blocks north on east 14th street stood Keith's Union Square Theater, one of four important vaudeville and music-hall theatres that by 1908 had become one of the earliest and most reliable moving picture venues in the city. Coincidentally, on 17 February, just under a month after the Picabias had settled into the Brevoort, Thomas Edison débuted his

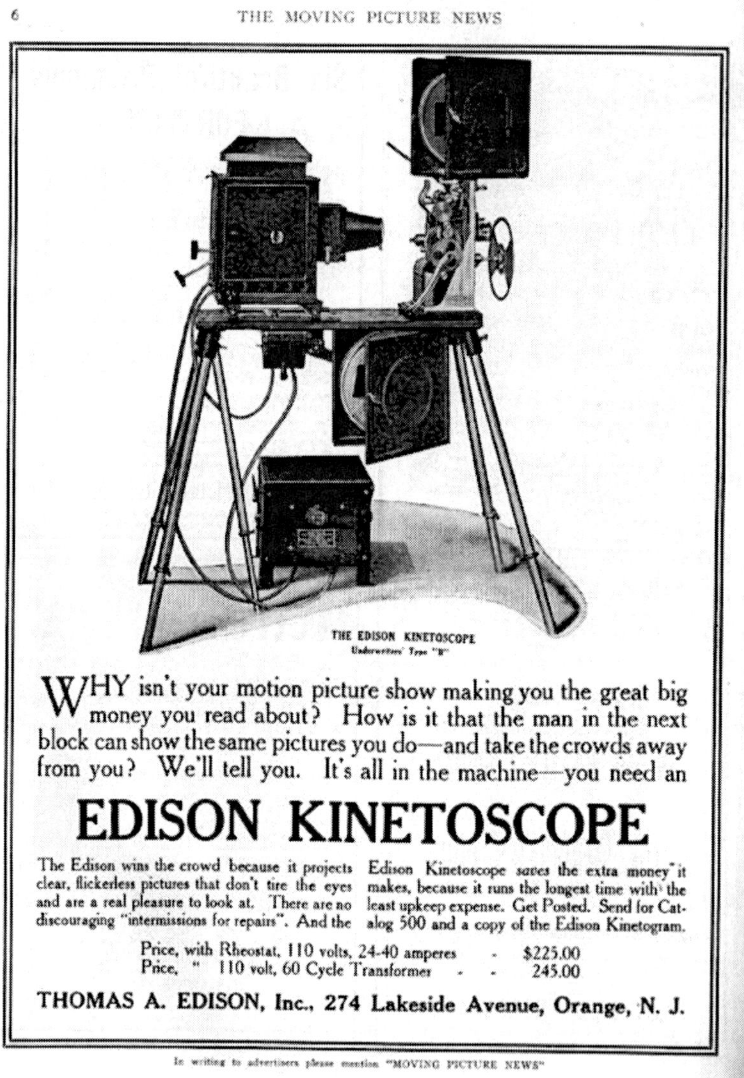

Figure 5. *The Moving Picture News* (March 29, 1913)

newest invention at all four Keith's theatres: the "Kinetophone" or his "talking pictures" that for the first time synchronized his sound and image recording/projecting devices. "Edison's latest" amazed and humored a large and attentive public:

> The first number of the exhibit was a descriptive lecture... Gesture and speech made the thing startingly real. He broke a plate, blew a whistle, dropped a weight. [...] Then he brought on a pianist, violinist, and soprano, and "The Last Rose of Summer" was never listened to with more fascinated attention. Finally, the scope of kinetophonic powers was further illustrated by a bugler's apologetic efforts, and the barking of some perfect collies. The second number was a minstrel show with orchestra, soloists, end men and interlocutor, large as life and quite as noisy. ("New York Applauds the Talking Picture" in *The New York Times*, 18 February 1913)

Indeed, in February of that year, Edison was the talk of the town in both popular and cinema-industry trade press publications that marveled at his latest invention or promoted his by now more standard fare of cinema devices: "It's all in the machine – you need an EDISON KINETOSCOPE. The Edison wins the crowd because it projects clear, flickerless pictures that don't tire the eyes and are a real pleasure to look at", declared a common advertisement from *The Moving Picture News* (29 March 1913) [figure 5].

For Picabia, the density of the "Edison context" surrounding the motion picture culture in New York that year must have heightened what was the original Edison legacy most thoroughly associated with the experience of New York City: electricity, or the city's "bright lights of Broadway", the "footlights" that shone upon a dancer, or the electrified amusement park at Coney Island, for example. In the context of Napierkowska, the moving pictures, and the sensory landscape of New York, the inventor's 1880 patent drawing for the light bulb [figure 6] acts as a direct bridge to *Mechanical Expression*. Evoking yet re-routing Bohn's interpretation of the 1913 work, I would like to suggest that *Mechanical Expression* depicts the sensorial objects that both illuminated and conditioned his meeting with Napierkowska and his passage into Edison-land, so to speak. *Mechanical Expression* thus reads like a travel itinerary and a map of Picabia's perceptual interiority: first, the viewer's eye engages the words "New York" that are written in the center of the "bulb". The viewer then adjusts her focus to the large dot above "New York", which may represent the Brevoort Hotel – or the stable destination that became the Picabias' home away from home in the foreign city.

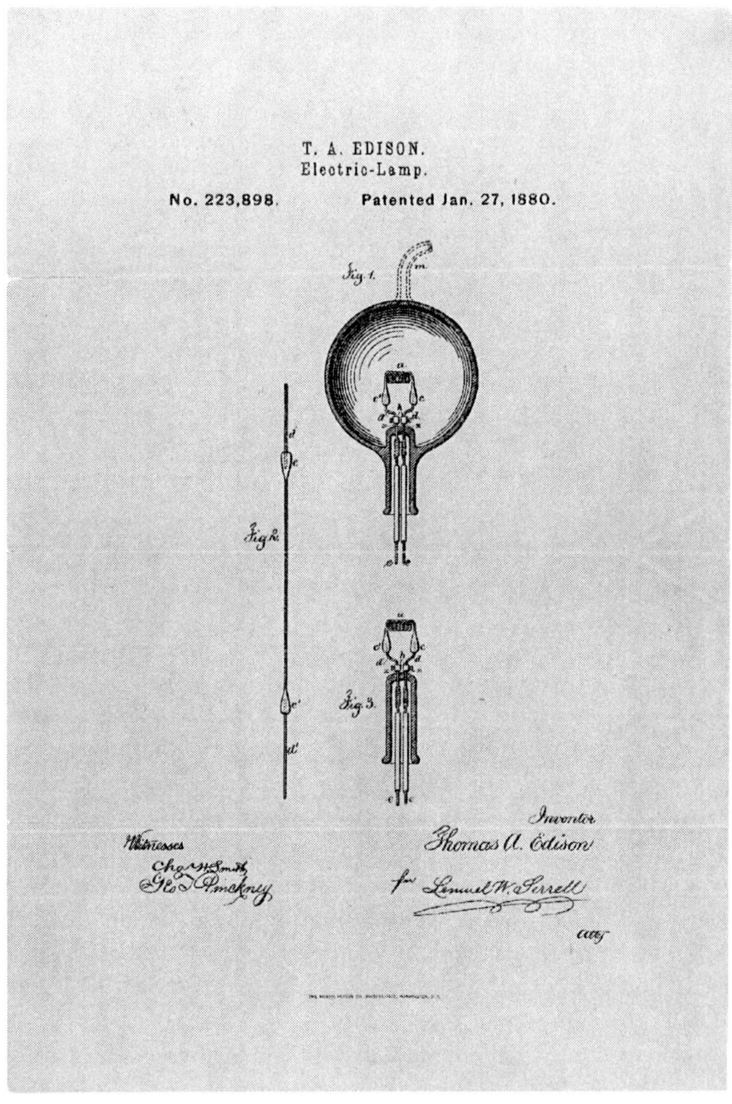

Figure 6. Thomas A. Edison, Electric Lamp patent drawing (1880)

Traveling down the circuit path that leads out of the "bulb" and toward the detached, stage-like form of its base, the viewer finally reads "Npierkowska" inscribed in a curved line. Yet, to arrive at this point, the viewer's gaze must pass through a diagonally shaded zone, which, for all intents and purposes, divides France from America, the flicker of Napierkowska's screened image from the bright glare of New York and the cinema culture therein. Finally, the shaded strips on either side of the drawing that contain elongated, rectangular bars become newly readable as the sprocket holes that align both sides of a strip of celluloid: this image depicts the very materials of cinematographic movement while evoking motion itself. Subsequently, the dividing line between New York and "Npierkowska" transforms into the line separating the cells of a strip of film, which is also echoed in the form located directly behind the bulb that Bohn (1984: 676) interpretes as a stack of commercial beehives. Finally, what seems to be "Npierkowska" 's miniature stage converts into a reel of film, while the distance between her name and the reel depicts the distance between her real body and its cinematographic projection.

Following Bohn's estimation that *Mechanical Expression* was created between 28 March and 9 April 1913, it is no coincidence that Napierkowska had one last appearance in New York – this time in a *New York Times* article (30 March 1913) [figure 7]. Entitled "Woes of the One Night Stand: An Actress on Tour Tells of the Strange Things Encountered in Small Town Opera Houses and Hotels", Napierkowska's image appears surrounded by a circular frame. Her image rushing back into his memory that was by now saturated by the electric landscape of New York (and that would also soon become a fleeting sensorial trace), Picabia created *Mechanical Expression* and thereby began what would be the first in a series of iconic forms within his Dada vernacular: the light bulb. *Américaine* (1917), would not only explicitly redefine the light bulb with mechanical precision, the words "Flirt" and "Divorce" that appear like projections on a white screen in the bulb's interior recall the sexually charged atmosphere of seduction on the Lorraine. In his "Poème banal" of 1918, the light bulb would take on a more graphic form but the words inscribed inside, just below the bulb's "filament" – "Les visions sont imprimées dans le téléphone" – become a refracted reference once again to Napierkowska. This time, the words recall her screen performance with Max Linder in *Mariage au téléphone*: Picabia surely would have been able to see a second, third or fourth run of this popular comedian's film in Paris throughout the mid-teens.

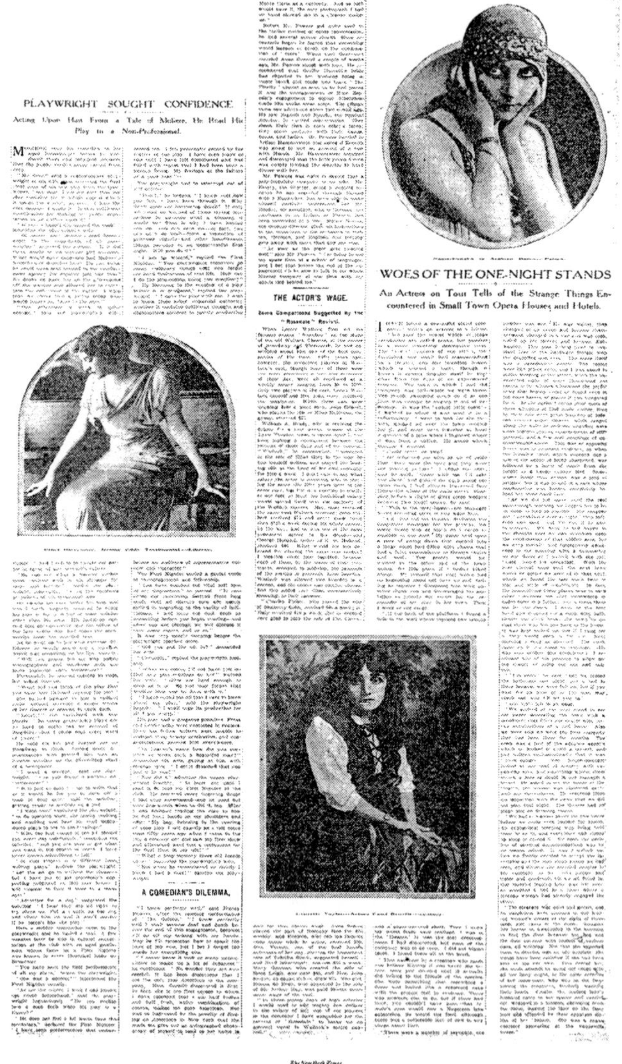

Figure 7. "Woes of the One Night Stands," *The New York Times* (March 30, 1913).

Finally, by 1924, we find the production of his ballet *Relâche* for which he commissioned his film, *Entr'Acte*, from René Clair. From its blinding, high-voltage décor, to Satie's modern score that Fernand Léger (1931) recalled as "lumineuse, éléctrique, cinématographique", to its cinematographic projection that opened ("déclenché") the ballet: "Rideau blanc, à plat. Projection cinématographique à déterminer, de trente secondes environ, accompagnée de musique", wrote Picabia (2005: 530). He ensured that any notion of theatrical unity was fractured. Its spectatorial experience was not "safe", but a full-body sensation capable of damaging if not assaulting the audience: "c'est une sensation de *nouveau*, de plaisir, la sensation d'oublier qu'il faut 'réfléchir' et 'savoir' pour aimer quelque chose" (Picabia 2005: 535). Not only did he hope that the cinematographic projection of *Entr'Acte* would incite whistles and screams from the audience – "Tant mieux! J'aime mieux les entendre crier qu'applaudir!" (Picabia 2005: 533) –, the posters for the event warned that the audience would indeed be visually assailed as if by a blinding light: "Apportez des lunettes noires..." Picabia structured cinematic elements throughout the ballet that were overt gestures of spectatorial assault in order to convey, to the fullest extent possible, "le mouvement perpétuel" of unmediated "life" and the thrill of un-intellectualized modern motion and its experience at the cinema (Picabia 2005: 533, 534).

Yet, amidst all of this commotion, there stands one figure who has yet to be identified, and who might be called the pivotal "centre" of *Entr'acte*: the ballet dancer, whose tutu forms a floral abstraction when first filmed in a low-angle shot from directly below through a transparent flooring – an angle that evokes passage between the levels of a transatlantic liner's decks. However, the following shot that travels up the dancer's pirouetting body does not eventually reveal the countenance of a beautiful performer or film star. Rather, the camera unveils the jarring image of a man's fully bearded face. At this point and in guise of a conclusion, it seems safe to ask: might this dancer be a mechanical expression of Picabia's memory of Napierkowska as seen through his own (Dadaistically charged) mechanical expression?

Notes

[1] "Copy London Halls at Palace Theater'" in *New York Times* (25 March 1913).

[2] Camfield's conversation with Gabrielle Buffet-Picabia in 1968 confirms the plastic influence of Napierkowska's dancing upon Picabia (Camfield 1979: 49). Carole Boulbès points to an unidentified article, "Les passagers du Lorraine" (Picabia 2005: 44).

[3] See also "Paris Dancer Dislikes Us" in *The New York Times* (17 April 1913), in which Napierkowska expresses her unpleasant experience performing for "uncivilized" and "narrow-minded" Americans, opinions that were surely informed by her brush with censorship.

[4] Bohn's work has spurred Linda Dalrymple Henderson's detailed interpretation of *Mechanical Expression's* light bulb form as rather Crookes cathode-ray tube which the author uses to position contemporary X-ray discourse as central to Picabia's and others' work (Dalrymple Henderson 1989: 114–23). See also Linda Dalrymple Henderson (1988).

[5] Camfield cites articles featuring Napierkowska in the entertainment weekly, *Comoedia* (15 February 1912 and 20 March 1912). Picabia begins publishing in *Comédia* by 1921.

[6] See the collection, "Stacia Napierkowska" (Paris: BNF, Richelieu, Arts des spectacles, 4 ICO PER 1937).

[7] Unidentified material, hand-dated (Paris: BNF).

[8] Unidentified material (Paris: BNF).

[9] *Catalogue Pathé des années 1896-1914* (Paris: Edition Henri Bousquet, 1995): 547–617. Information provided at www.imdb.com suggests that she made 47 films between 1908 through 1912. Various sources combined suggest she made a total of 88 films in her film career between 1908 and 1924. In 1917, she directed *L'Héritière de la mandade.*

[10] Bernhardt signed with Pathé's Films d'art in 1908, the same year Napierkowska made her first film with Pathé Frères: *L'Arlésienne* (Albert Capellani 1908) which depicts the tragic story of a troupe of *comédiens.*

[11] A photograph depicting Napierkowska in a similar position standing on one leg, arms raised to her sides, has often been reproduced. See Camfield (1979: illus.6, fig.66), Bohn (1985: 674) and Pierre (2001: 67).

[12] Unidentified material (Paris: BNF).

[13] Soupault (1924) describes how French cinema had become a wasteland of bourgeois melodramas filled with "tranches de vie".

[14] See also Lant (1992: 98), who states that "cinema's overlap with Egypt is bound to discourses on death, on preservation, on silence and on light projection".

[15] Ads from *Le Cinéma* (8 and 15 November 1912).

[16] Other films about the theft of the Mona Lisa are: *Gribouille a volé la Joconde* (Capellani 1911), *Nick Winter et le vol de la Joconde* (Paul Garbagni, Pathé 1911), *C'est Nick Winter qui a retrouvé la Joconde* (Pathé 1914).

¹⁷ It should be noted that *Birth of a Nation* did not appear until 1915; Buffet-Picabia therefore conflates both trips to New York since she could not have seen the film during her 1913 sojourn.

¹⁸ For an account of the Illustrated Song Slide and its demise in especially New York cinema culture see Altman (2004) and Wild (2005).

Bibliography

391 (191 –1924). 1975. (ed. M. Sanouillet). Paris: Belfond.

Abel, Richard. 1988. *French Film Theory and Criticism: A History/ Anthology I. 1907–1929*. Princeton: Princeton University Press.

Abel, Richard. 1994. *The Ciné Goes to Town: French Cinema 1896–1914*. Berkeley: University of California Press.

Altman, Rick. 2004. *Silent Film Sound*. New York: Columbia University Press.

Baker, George. 2001. "The Artwork Caught by the Tail" in *October* 97: 51–90.

——. 2007. *The Artwork Caught by the Tail: Francis Picabia and Dada in Paris*. Cambridge: MIT Press.

Bernardini, Aldo. 1994. "Le Film d'Arte Italiana" in Kernabon (1998).

Bohn, Willard. 1985. "Picabia's 'Mechanical Expression' and the Demise of the Object" in *The Art Bulletin* 67(4): 673–7.

Borras, Maris Lluïsa. 1985. *Picabia*. London: Thames and Hudson.

Buffet-Picabia, Gabrielle. 1956. "Picabia l'inventeur" in *L'Oeil* 18: 35.

——. 1977. *Rencontres avec Picabia, Apollinaire, Cravan, Duchamp, Arp, Calder*. Paris: Belfond.

Camfield, William. 1966. "The Machinist Style of Francis Picabia" in *The Art Bulletin* 48(3–4): 309–22.

——. 1979. *Francis Picabia: His Art, Life and Times*. Princeton: Princeton University Press.

Canudo, Ricciotto. 1911. "La Naissance d'un sixième art" in *Les Entretiens idéalistes* 61: 169–79.

Dalrymple Henderson, Linda. 1988. "X Rays and the Quest for Invisible Reality in the Art of Kupka, Duchamp, and the Cubists" in *Art Journal* 47(4): 323–40.

——. 1989. "Francis Picabia, Radiometers, and X-Rays in 1913" in *Art Bulletin* 71(1): 114–23.

Kermabon, Jacques (ed.). 1998. *Pathé: Premier Empire du cinéma*. Paris: Editions Centre Georges Pompidou.

Lant, Antonia. 1992. "The Curse of the Pharaoh, or How Cinema Contracted Egyptomania" in *October* 59: 86–112.

Léger, Fernand. 1931. "Vive *Relâche*" in *Les Ballets suédois dans l'art contemporain*. Paris: Le Trianon.

Metz, Christian. 1986. *The Imaginary Signifier: Psychoanalysis and the Cinema* (tr. C. Britton and A. Williams). Bloomington: Indiana University Press.

Picabia, Francis. 1913. "Picabia, Art Rebel, Here to Teach New Mouvement" in *The New York Times* (16 February): 9.

——. 1922. "Cinéma" in *Cinéa* 52: 9.

——. 2005. *Francis Picabia: Ecrits critiques.* (ed. C. Boulbès). Paris: Mémoire du Livre.

Pierre, Arnauld. 2001. "Picabia, danse, musique: une clé pour *Udnie*" in *Les Cahiers du Mnam* 75: 59–81.

Raynal, Maurice. 1913. "Chronique Cinématographique" in *Les Soirées de Paris* 19: 7.

Soupault, Philippe. 1924. « Le cinéma U.S.A" in *Films* 15.

——. 1979. *Écrits de cinéma 1918–1931* (eds A. and O. Virmaux). Paris: Plon.

Weiss, Jeffrey. 1994. *The Popular Culture of Modern Art: Picasso, Duchamp, and Avant-Gardism*. New Haven: Yale University Press.

Wild, Jennifer. 2005. "Sur le déclin d'un dispositif culturel, la chanson illustrée" *1895* 47: 9–37

Chapter 5

Patterns of Duality – Between/Beyond Dada and Surrealism: Man Ray's *Emak Bakia (1926)*

Kim Knowles

One of the most interesting aspects of the artist Man Ray is the overriding presence of duality in his life as well as in his work. Whether intentionally or unintentionally, he was constantly balancing one thing with another: an American of Russian heritage living in Paris; painter and photographer; Dada and Surrealist. In California during the 1940s, his decision to grow a beard was apparently met with mixed opinion, some liking and others disliking the way it looked. In direct response to this divide, he shaved one side of his face, leaving the beard intact on the other. "Un côté avec barbe pour ceux qui préféraient avec. Un côté sans, pour ceux qui préféraient sans", he stated (Bourgeade 2002: 32). Placing a mirror down the centre of his face, he allowed himself to be seen alternately in two different versions. This anecdote is important to our conception of Man Ray since it functions as a concrete manifestation of his divided self and his desire to be more than one thing at any time. It also gives us a sense of his idiosyncratic personality and his refusal to commit to any one camp, appearing to belong to both by carving out a unique position between them.

Nowhere is this more evident than in his participation in the movements of Dada and Surrealism and through the incorporation and interpretation within his work of the principles related to those movements. When Man Ray exhibited in the first Surrealist exhibition in 1925, he simply re-presented many of the objects, paintings and photographs that had already been shown in his Dada exhibition a few years earlier, demonstrating an important element of interchangeability between them. The present discussion explores this phenomenon from the perspective of Man Ray's film, *Emak Bakia* and attempts to understand its difficult positioning between the movements of Dada and Surrealism. It places particular attention on the way in which duality is actually woven into the fabric of the film, existing not simply in the simultaneous presence of Dada and Surrealism as influencing factors, but as a crucial element of Man Ray's exploration of the medium. In other words, it will argue that, although *Emak Bakia* is situated at the crossroads of Dada and Surrealist expression, Man Ray uses this interrelationship as a springboard for the exploration of his own obsessions related to cinematic vision and structure. Through this investigation, an awareness of the way *Emak Bakia* is simultaneously *between* and *beyond* Dada and Surrealism will emerge.

Although Man Ray's participation in the Dada and Surrealist movements is most frequently assessed through his two principle activities at the time – photography and collage (or object-creations), his work in film offers an equally valuable perspective on the nature of this participation. Despite his apparent decision to "ne jamais m'occuper du cinéma, sauf comme spectateur de temps en temps" (Bourgeade 2002: 49), Man Ray made four short films during the 1920s: *Le Retour à la raison* (1923), *Emak Bakia* (1926), *L'Etoile de mer* (1928) and *Les Mystères du Château du Dé* (1929). These now canonical avant-garde works provide an excellent context in which to study his relationship to Dada and Surrealism, since they are often understood as demonstrating a trajectory from one mode of expression to another, in a way that would seem to reflect the historical development of the movements. Yet, they are also extremely complex and evade straightforward categorisation. As Arturo Schwarz (1977: 286) has noted:

> It is hard to classify Man Ray's films; they are provocative in their originality and pioneering in their content [...] they are products of his deep-rooted individuality and independence. His films anticipated moods and modes. It may be said that they are the most Dada of the Surrealist films, the most Surrealist of the Dada films.

This comment provides a starting point for an investigation into the way Man Ray's cinema creates a dialogue between Dada and Surrealism, whilst expressing a unique and idiosyncratic approach to the medium. Rather than representing the films as simply moving from one set of principles to another, Schwarz draws attention to the way they slide back and forth between them. Whilst this view does, to a certain extent, relate to all four films, it is in *Emak Bakia* that this interrelationship is most clearly detected. It is also the work that most effectively demonstrates what Schwarz significantly refers to as the *anticipation* of moods and modes, specifically in terms of its approach to Surrealism.

In his autobiography, Man Ray (1998: 222) describes that, in making the film, he had "complied with all the principles of Surrealism: irrationality, automatism, psychological and dreamlike sequences without apparent logic, and complete disregard of conventional storytelling". Yet he also refers to the force of Dadaism, stating: "The Dada instinct was still very strong with me" (Man Ray 1998: 220). Indeed, the reference to psychology and dream aside, Man Ray's list of Surrealist principles reads almost like a recipe for Dada. What is interesting about this comment is the way Surrealism enters into the process by way of compliance – working to the rules and respecting boundaries –, whereas Dada is represented and understood as an instinct or a state of mind that simply *is*. *Emak Bakia* therefore seems to emerge from a dual sensibility and indeed many critical accounts of the film draw attention to the simultaneous presence of elements relating to both Dada and Surrealism. However, as Mimi White (1984: 43) has argued, these discussions "often end up as no more than catalogs of the respective Dada and Surrealist 'moments' in the film, and admit the impossibility of approaching it from any coherent critical position". Her own analysis is based on the view that *Emak Bakia* is concerned, not with the illustration of Dada and Surrealist principles, but rather with exploring issues of representability and vision in the cinema. The main problem with White's otherwise enlightening approach is that it discards the Dada and Surrealist context, dealing with the complex issue of interrelatedness by bypassing it altogether. Whilst it is important to examine the film's overall formal insistence, we must be careful not to ignore the way these formal patterns might be informed by a Dada-Surrealist dialectic, and the principle of duality to which it gives rise.

Emak Bakia was made in the summer of 1926, with money provided by American patron of the arts, Arthur Wheeler. The shooting was divided fairly equally between Biarritz, in the south of

France, where Man Ray was invited to spend a holiday with the Wheelers, and the artist's studio in Paris. This gives rise to an extremely diverse range of imagery (in contrast to Man Ray's first film, *Le Retour à la raison*, which was filmed entrirely in the studio) and signals the first, most general, instance of duality in the overall structure of the film. Duality is present from the very beginning of the film in the subtitle "cinépoème" that appears immediately after the title. Bringing together the two modes of expression, Man Ray presents his film as a lyrical mode of expression, that draws on the cinematic representation of reality as a subjective activity.

Despite claims about *Emak Bakia*'s lack of structure,[1] the film actually betrays an extremely intricate system of organisation. This can be seen first of all in the use of a framing device, with the first and last shots creating an element of circularity. Interestingly, this structural feature would become a recurring element in the rest of Man Ray's cinematic works – the opening and closing window at the beginning and end of *L'Etoile de mer* and the wooden hands in *Les Mystères du Château du Dé*. The first shot shows a mirror reflection of Man Ray in profile, operating his film camera. The image is manipulated in such a way as to show the lens that should appear on the right-hand side of the camera pointing directly towards the viewer, with an upside-down eye superimposed onto it. The visual composition of the shot is striking, radically rearranging the correct order of things and drawing attention to the themes of distorted vision and the mechanics of the cinema that create the impression of reality. The presence of Man Ray in what could be seen as a prologue to the film, as well as the reference to vision, has strong affinities with the eye-slicing scene of *Un Chien andalou* (Luis Buñuel and Salvador Dalí, 1929), in which Buñuel himself also appears. Although these two works differ greatly in their cinematic approach, this similarity offers an interesting example of Schwarz's notion of anticipation in Man Ray's films, prefiguring future developments in the realms of Surrealist expression.

In the final shot, a woman (Kiki de Montparnasse) with open eyes raises her head and, revealing the eyes to be painted onto her eyelids, opens her eyes for real. An upside-down version of the same image is superimposed onto the original, highlighting the confused sense of perception. Steven Kovács (1980: 132) has described this shot as a "Dada trick perpetrated on a Surrealistic motif", emphasising the dual significance of the image and the "inextricable fusion of Dada and Surrealist intentions". He fails to mention, however, the significance of the image within the structure of the film, notably in the way it reiterates the concentration on vision that is expressed at the beginning. The similarity between the two images is vital, since they place emphasis on the dual nature of cinematic vision as both reality and illusion. The upside-down superimposition that appears at the beginning and end of the film also expresses the contradictory nature of the way vision itself is processed, i.e. through a double inversion: once on the retina and then again in the brain. Whilst the presence of the filmmaker and his apparatus within the film has affinities with the Dadaist's strategies to undermine illusionism in order to make perceivable the construction of cultural artefacts, the reference to different levels or hierarchies of vision suggests the influence of Surrealism and its desire to uncover other ways of viewing the world. This is further highlighted through the techniques of inversion and superimposition in the opening and closing sequences which, whilst foregrounding cinematic technique, can also be understood in terms of André Breton's 1924 call, in the first *Manifesto of Surrealism*, for the uncovering of "what can be" and for the fusion of reality and imagination (Breton 1969: 4).

Following on from the prologue, the film moves into a sequence of Rayograph images taken from *Le Retour à la raison*.[2] A moving abstract mass of tiny circular forms fills the screen, followed by the frantic dance of nails and drawing pins. This recycled footage forms the most concrete link between the two works, building into *Emak Bakia* the same subversion of accepted forms of cinematic vision through the rejection of the film camera itself. As with the previous film, the illusion of reality, normally created through the cinema, is replaced by a confusing array of abstract and semi-abstract forms, which emphasise the flatness of the screen rather than the usual depth of the cinematic space. Man Ray's use of the introductory image becomes even more significant here, since it serves to establish a clear division between two types of imagery: camera-based and camera-less. The former is perfectly illustrated in the opening shot, as the camera is both the source *and* the content of the image – a double, even circular reference, since the camera films itself in the act of filming. The sudden appearance of images produced without the previously glimpsed apparatus establishes a very clear juxtaposition between the two forms of representation, further illustrated through the insertion of a camera shot of a field of daisies. Although this alternation between camera images and Rayograph images does not continue through the rest of the film, as is the case with *Le Retour à la raison*, it nonetheless provides the first reference to alternative modes of seeing. The Dadaist concern with materiality – highlighting the filmmaking apparatus – therefore comes into contact with a Surrealist interest in different layers of reality.

This relationship also reflects another duality that is established early on in the film, that is, the tension between abstraction and figuration. Already present in *Le Retour à la raison*, this aspect becomes even more crucial in *Emak Bakia* and represents one of its most central structural details. Even before the initial figurative image gives way to an abstract mass of forms, the eye that is superimposed onto the camera lens appears as abstracted from its context and floats in a space to which it does not belong. Yet, since the image itself is figural, that is, identifiable to us as an object, we could say that it floats metaphorically between abstraction and figuration. This dual conception is important in terms of Dada, as the statement by Berlin photomontage artist Raoul Hausmann suggests: "Anti-art withdraws from things and materials their utility but also their concrete and civil meaning; it reverses classical values and makes them half-abstract" (Elsaesser 1996: 23). Through the use of the Rayograph technique, Man Ray effectuates a reversal of classical values by isolating and emphasising form, presenting, in the words of Jean Sachet (1973: 26), "des nus d'objets". The object is thus stripped of its utlilitarian function and enters into the realm of the poetic.

The notion of the "half-abstract" is particularly useful in understanding the next section of images featuring moving lights against a black background. Since there is no identifiable object of reference, these two shots can only be understood in terms of abstraction, even if they have their basis in concrete reality. The amorphous forms provide a counterpoint to the sharply defined contours of the previous set of Rayograph images, yet their overriding similarity as simple white, circular and oblong phenomena transcends any difference that may exist on the level of signification. Thus, by shifting meaning onto the level of form through abstraction, Man Ray brings together disparate material, creating a new system of understanding. Continuing the theme of light and movement, the following shot presents a scrolling electric news bulletin filmed at night, bringing us back to the world of the figurative. The message reads: "Au milieu du bassin du Neptune au cours de deux grandes fêtes". The nonsensical nature of the bulletin seems to refer to the illogical progression of images, since they both evade conventional cinematic systems of signification. The insertion of text into these sequences of visual exploration seems to have a dual function. Whilst, as Mimi White (1984: 43) has commented, the message relates to preceding visual material through its significance as a simple "arrrangement of light", thus expressing the film's theme of the "similarity between all visually perceivable material", it also serves to demonstrate the fusion of image and text suggested in the subtitle "cinépoème". This reference brings us back to the idea of the film as an exercise in poetry and reiterates the importance of structure.

After a return to the abstract imagery produced using a range of distorting lenses, mirrors, crystals, reflecting prisms and a rotating turntable, the film then changes tone, switching to a concentration on figuration, through a number of short sequences that suggest narrative development. A great number of structural developments take place during this section of the film, many of which draw on the organising theme of duality. The transition is made through another image of an eye superimposed over a set of car headlights, which frame it on either side. In its similarity to the shot at the very beginning of the film, the reference to the eye again functions as a kind of prologue to the visual developments in this section. Like the juxtaposition of the eye with the camera in the opening shot, this image equates vision with technology – this time in the form of the automobile, signalling a concentration on speed and movement.

A car journey ensues, during which the rapidly passing countryside is presented from the perspective of the passenger or driver of the vehicle. The possibility of it representing the driver is stronger, however, due to the emphasis placed on the alternation between objective and subjective vision in this part of film. Since the driver has already been presented to the viewer from an objective point of view, the subsequent viewpoint is automatically related to this person, since no one else was visually present in the car as it began its journey. In one shot, Man Ray attempts to recreate the subjective visual impression of a collision by throwing the camera into the air. This is preceded by a static shot at ground-level where the car appears to literally drive over the spectator. These two experiments into the expression of subjective vision also play with different forms of cinematic movement, one involving the movement carrried out in front of the camera and the other created by the camera itself. The constrasting approaches are nonetheless brought together in the way they point to the filmmaking apparatus, once again emphasising the film's central focus: the relationship between human and cinematic vision. Again, the source of this relationship can in many ways be traced back to the simultaneous presence of Dada and Surrealist related ideas in Man Ray's approach – the attempt to give psychological significance to the film, whilst at the same time breaking with the cinema's ability to create a seamless illusion of reality that is dependent on the invisibility of technique.

As well as the interweaving of objective and subjective viewpoints, this part of the film makes extensive use of repetition and duplication. Whilst repetition is created through the editing together of separate shots showing the same action and thus disrupting normal temporal relations, the duplication of the image relies on techniques such as superimposition within the shot, giving rise to spatial distortion. The first, most interesting instance of duplication occurs immediately after the collision, in a shot showing a pair of legs dismounting a car (perhaps the one we have just seen). As they disappear out of the frame, the same action is repeated over and over again until the shot eventually contains a multitude of superimposed feet. An impression of reality is transformed into a reality of impressions. Using legs as a transition, the following sequence switches modes to that of repetition. A pair of legs dancing the Charleston is alternated with the arms of a banjo player in a total of nine shots, demonstrating the role of editing in bringing together potentially unrelated spaces. Parallels are also drawn between the aesthetic and emotive effects of superimposition and montage, with humour being central to the former, whilst an awareness of visual rhythm emerges from the latter.

These structural details continue into the following sequence that begins with Rose Wheeler entering her dressing room. Three different images show her brushing her hair, applying lipstick and putting on pearls. Although not exactly a repetition as such – there is an element of development in the sense that each shot is different – the similarity of these banal actions gives rise to a sense of repetition that is further heightened by the jump-cuts between them. As she gets up and looks out of the window, the focus shifts from an objective viewpoint to a subjective shot of the sea seen from above. A smooth transition is thus made into the next set of images in a tighter framing showing the repeated action of waves breaking onto the shore. The frame of vision narrows further still into what is understood as representing an underwater shot of fish swimming back and forth in front of the camera. As in the shot of superimposed feet, the fish gradually multiply as different layers of reality are created. The chain of associations ends with Man Ray's sculpture, *Fisherman's Idol*. As the object rotates at different speeds, it is gradually brought into play with shadows and superimpositions of itself, resulting in a complex composition in which reality and illusion are inextricablely linked.

Later sections of the film centre on the technique of animation, leading this discussion towards the final example of duality. During these sequences, Man Ray breathes life into inanimate phenomena, reversing the laws of reality as the earlier 360° camera rotation reverses the sky and sea, literally turning the world upside down. Various abstract shapes and forms magically appear and disappear, group together and disperse, and chase each other in and out of the frame. More light distortions and reflections are alternated with shots of women's faces, their eyes opening to look directly into the camera. The tension between objective and subjective vision once again becomes the central focus, commenting also on the cinematic conventions of looking. The gaze of the viewer is reflected in the returned gaze of the women, destabilising the traditional viewer-subject relationship and pointing to the camera as mediator in this exchange. Through the opening and closing eyes, the light distortions and reflections that both precede and follow these images come to develop a direct relationship with the sleeping or dreaming subject in a complex binding of abstraction and figuration with subjective and objective vision.

The final section consolidates many of the film's developments related to Dada and Surrealism. Beginning with the intertitle, "La raison pour cette extravagance", it procedes into another figurative section. A man (no other than the Dada dandy, Jacques Rigaud) arrives outside a building and enters. Once inside, he opens a briefcase and takes out shirtcollars, methodically tearing each one apart before letting the pieces fall to the ground. Finally, he rips off his own collar in what could be seen as the ultimate Dada gesture: the rejection of bourgeois respectability represented through the traditional dress-codes. The fall of the collars is reversed then slowed down, giving way to a final dance of forms and the return of the earlier rotations and distortions. The incongruous insertion of an intertitle suggesting a logical explanation for the diverse visual material that precedes it in many ways looks ahead to the use of text in *Un Chien andalou*. Man Ray obviously realised the potential for textual inserts to create the Surrealist effect of disorientation, as his later film, *L'Etoile de mer*, testifies. Furthermore, although the tearing of shirt collars can be explained in terms of Dada, as I have already mentioned, it also reveals yet another similarity with Buñuel and Dalí's film, in which the bourgeois uniform is seen as a symbol of constraint. In *Emak Bakia*, the defiant act of tearing apart the shirt collars is seen as giving way to creative freedom, as the film once and for all escapes its figurative connection to reality.

The concentration on visual relationships and the simultaneous demonstration of harmony and contrast in *Emak Bakia* provides an important perspective on Man Ray's cinematic approach. By making the expression of duality a central feature of the film, he succeeds in weaving together seemingly contradictory forces, balancing chaos with order, destruction with construction, and conscious with unconscious modes of exprssion. This study has drawn attention to the way Dada and Surrealist forces come together in the film, pointing out specific areas in which Man Ray appears to adapt his Dada sensibility to achieve a Surrealist effect. It has tried to emphasise, above all, that this approach results in the creation of a film that belongs to neither Dada nor Surrealism exclusively, but channels their correspondences and contradictions into a wider exploration of the cinematic medium.

Notes

[1]   See for example, Barbara Rose's commentary on the film, in which she states: "Because of the randomness of Man Ray's approach, one cannot really speak of the structure of *Emak Bakia*, which like *Un Chien andalou*, is basically a series of disconnected visual gags" (Rose 1971: 70).

[2]   The Rayograph, or photogram, technique involves the registering of images by placing objects directly onto or above the photo-sensitive paper, therefore

removing the mechanical intervention of the camera and placing emphasis on the physical materiality of the cinema.

Bibliography

Bourgeade, Pierre. 2002. *Bonsoir Man Ray*. Paris: Maeght.

Breton, André. 1969. *Manifestoes of Surrealism* (tr. R. Seaver and H. R. Lane). Ann Arbour: The University of Michigan Press.

Elsaesser, Thomas. 1996. "Dada/Cinema?" in R. Kuenzli (ed.). *Dada and Surrealist Film*. Cambridge, Mass.: MIT Press: 13– 27.

Kovács, Steven. 1980. *From Enchantment to Rage: The Story of Surrealist Cinema*. London: Associated University Presses.

Man Ray. 1998. *Self Portrait*. New York: Bullfinch Press.

Rose, Barbara. 1971. "Kinetic Solutions to Pictorial Questions: The Films of Man Ray and Moholy-Nagy" in *Artforum* 10(1): 68–73.

Sachet, Jean. 1973. "Rayographies" in *Man Ray* (ed. S. Alexandrian). Paris: Editions Fillipachi.

Schwarz, Arturo. 1977. *Man Ray: The Rigour of Imagination*. London: Thames and Hudson.

White, Mimi. 1984. "Two French Dada Films: *Entr'Acte* and *Emak Bakia*" in *Dada/Surrealism* 13: 37– 47.

Chapter 6

Spectres of Dada:
From Man Ray to Marker and Godard

Ramona Fotiade

A recurrent motif of early experimental films associated with the Dada movement in Paris consisted in the playful reference to the mechanism of the recording camera and the processes involved in creating the illusion of movement through the rapid succession of static images projected on the screen. Almost forty years later, the protagonist of Jean-Luc Godard's *Le Petit Soldat* (1960) was to announce, in typically provocative manner, that "cinema is truth 24 times per second". However, neither Godard nor the Dada filmmakers of the 1920s ignored the careful manipulation of both technical and psychological conditions of visual representation that went on behind the truthful reproduction of reality "24 times per second". For Dada artists as well as for some New Wave directors (such as Chris Marker and Godard) the debates over the faithful or the contrived nature of cinematic realism can be said to undercut any simple opposition between the documentary and the fictional traditions. In seeking to subvert the conventions that ensure the viewer's belief in the factual or fictitious sequence of events presented on the screen, Dada as much as New Wave practitioners of avant-garde cinema invite the audience to question the status of photographic and film images. It is no longer a matter of deciding whether moving or still images, documentary or fictional modes of representation have more chances of providing an accurate and reliable account of reality. The very possibility of capturing reality through photographic or cinematic means is called into question and denounced as illusion. As the cartoon bubble above Godard's photograph on the cover of the 1976 special issue of *L'Avant-Scène Cinéma* famously states: "Ce n'est pas une image juste, c'est juste une image" [This is not an exact/just image, this is just an image]. Dada cinema prefigured most strategies of disruption and distanciation that became incorporated into the New Wave onslaught on classical cinematic narrative and viewing conventions.

The legacy of early filmmakers such as Man Ray can perhaps be best appreciated in light of his experiments with cameraless photography (rayographs) and optical illusion that led to the elaboration of an "aesthetics of spectrality" – as I would choose to call it – with reference to static as well as moving images. Man Ray stumbled upon the rayograph technique when he accidentally mixed in an unexposed sheet of photosensitive paper with exposed sheets in the developing tray in 1921. Having waited in vain for an image to appear on the photosensitive paper, he placed a few objects on it (probably intended to serve as paper-weights), then turned the light on. The contour of the objects that began to emerge on the paper was an image produced not only without a camera, but also without the need to use photographic film: the shadow or the spectral trace of an object was directly impressed on the photosensitive paper support by means of light alone. In a similar manner, Man Ray made *Retour à la raison*, in 1923, partly without a camera, by applying his technique of the Rayograph to the film celluloid:

> On some strips I sprinkled salt and pepper, like a cook preparing a roast, on other strips I threw pins and thumbtacks at random: then I turned on the white light for a second or two, as I had done for my still Rayographs. (Man Ray 1963: 260)

The opening sequence of Man Ray's *Emak Bakia* (1926) includes the rayograph strip of film first used in *Retour à la raison*, with the addition of a figurative shot of a field of daisies spliced between two abstract rayograph images. It is also worth mentioning that Man Ray started to experiment with solarized photography in 1929–30 and possibly earlier. However, the final sequence in *Retour à la raison* can already be said to illustrate a strikingly similar technique in the medium of cinema. The image of a nude female torso, filmed from chin down with arms raised, is shown turning to face the light filtered through the curtains of a window. The moving torso serves as a screen on which shadows of the curtain pattern are projected. This stunning transformation of the human body into a quasi-spectral apparition, through the play of light and shadow, is then further enhanced by the sudden reversal of the contrast values in the negative version of the same set of shots, repeated twice at the end of the film. Technically, the partial reversal of contrast values in solarization is similar although not identical to the eerie aspect of negative images in motion. One of the early examples of a series of negative shots used to great effect in silent cinema was the accelerated arrival and departure of Count Orlok's phantomatic coachman in *Nosferatu the Vampire* (1922). It is not surprising that the caption, which exerted the most powerful fascination on the Surrealists, came from Murnau's legendary feature of 1922: "Passé le pont, les fantômes vinrent à sa rencontre". Desnos's articles on cinema, no less than Man Ray's avant-garde films, point to the diffuse yet consistent preoccupation with the possibility of defining the nature of the cinematic *merveilleux* in relation to notions of spectrality.

Although negative images come up only twice in Man Ray's films, both times in the closing sequences of *Le Retour à la raison* and *Les Mystères du château du Dé* (1929), it is obvious that he continued to experiment with means of subverting the realistic appearance of cinematographic representation. Virtually all the films he made during the 1920s display this aesthetics of spectrality. For example, he includes the double exposure shot of fish swimming in *Emak Bakia* (1926) or the mottled-glass effect consistently used in *L'Etoile de mer* (1928). An explicit thematic concern in *Les Mystères du château du Dé*, the spectral condition of photographic and film images is rendered through the peculiar use of silk stockings to conceal the identity of the actors. Apart from the striking resemblance with Magritte's painting, *The Lovers* (dating from 1928), this simple device reminds one of the much-celebrated screen heroines of Feuillade's serials, Musidora and Irma Vep. But what seems by far the most significant allusion to *Les Vampires* and *Fantômas* is Man Ray's accumulation of visual and verbal designators of phantoms, spectres and shadows. The effect of a dissolve transition between shots, that makes the masked characters disappear, resonates with the earlier image of shadows cast by steps near the swimming pool, then with the silhouettes of bathers projected on the wall, that are coupled with the enigmatic caption: "Passe, il faut que tu suives cette belle ombre que tu veux" [Pass by, you must follow this beautiful shadow that you want]. Most conspicuously, another caption in the film links the visual motif of ghosts or fleeting apparitions to the temporal condition of photographs and cinematic images, as impressions or traces of the past: "Existe-t-il des fantômes d'action?… Des fantômes de nos actions passées? Les minutes vécues ne laissent-elles pas de traces concrètes dans l'air et sur la terre?" [Are there phantoms of actions?… Phantoms of our past actions? Are there not concrete traces of lived instants in the air and on the ground?]

In his 1980 essay, *Camera Lucida*, Barthes (1993: 77) was to provide added theoretical support to Desnos and Man Ray's reflections on the cinema, through his analysis of the uncanny superimposition of reality and of the past that is the essence of photography. Although Barthes repeatedly denied cinema the spectral status that he attributed to the stillness of the photographic image, defined as "the living image of a dead thing" which induces the "perverse confusion between the Real and the Live" (Barthes 1993: 79), his conclusions accurately match the subversive strategy of avant-garde filmmakers such as Man Ray and Chris Marker. In exploring the subtle interference between still and moving images, or in denouncing the mechanical artifice and optical phenomena that create the illusion of cinematic movement, Man Ray and Chris Marker highlighted the contradictory status of both photographic and filmic representation. Fraught with memory, death and what Barthes (1993: 119) calls "intractable reality", cinema as well as photography present us with a closed world, a vestige of actual existence, to which movement can only surreptitiously, and ephemerally, attach the openness of life. If Desnos and Man Ray found more reasons to rejoice in the potential blurring of the boundaries between lived experience and the spectral manifestation of characters on the screen, it is nevertheless true that their conception of the cinema finds adequate expression in Barthes's description of photography as "the ectoplasm of 'what-had-been': neither image nor reality, a new being, really, a reality one can no longer touch" (Barthes 1993: 87).

Chris Marker's photo-roman, *La Jetée*, persuasively queries and unsettles the assumed "intractable reality" of photography through the hypothesis of time travel, and the possible interaction between different temporal dimensions: present, past and future. Still images in *La Jetée* are not only the conveyors of a retrospective account of events, unfolding in the characteristic snapshot mode of disjointed or loosely connected memories, but also the means by which the scientists of the post-apocalyptic world depicted in the story seek to access the past. The voice-over commentary that accompanies the montage of frozen pictures informs the viewer from the outset that "this is the story of a man marked by an image of his childhood", a violent scene that he witnessed on the main pier at Orly, "sometime before the outbreak of World War III". Having set the narrative about to begin in the near, yet indistinct, future of a post-nuclear war struggle for survival, the rest of the commentary proceeds in the past tense, not so much to project the viewer's standpoint further ahead along the temporal axis, as to draw attention to the implacable reality of the photographs, "a reality one can no longer touch". The aorist, as Barthes (1993: 91) pointed out, is the tense of the Photograph, and the diegesis in *La Jetée* subtly appropriates this signifier of documentary evidence in order to turn a sequence of utopian images of holocaust into the implacable still-shot reminiscence of what has come to pass:

> And soon afterwards Paris was blown up. Many died. Some fancied themselves to be victors. Others were made prisoners. The survivors settled beneath Chaillot in a network of galleries. Above ground in Paris, as around the world, everything was rotten with radioactivity. The victors stood guard over a kingdom of rats.

The narrative then focuses on the experiments carried out by a team of unidentified scientists led by Herr Doktor Frankenstein. Through an advanced form of psychoanalysis that seems to have accomplished the Surrealist aspiration of capturing and visualizing unconscious phenomena, the scientists aim to send "emissaries into time", and thus "call past and future to the rescue of the present". After various failed attempts resulting in madness or death, a man with "very strong mental images" is selected on account of an obsessive dream relating to a childhood memory. His initial forays into the past generate compelling tableaux of life in the pre-war world, and the voice-over commentary insists on the heightened reality of these images as compared to the nightmarish underworld of the man's waking consciousness: "a peacetime morning, a peacetime bedroom, a real bedroom, real children, real birds, real cats, real graves". Not surprisingly, the enumeration of photographic remnants of real life builds up to a designator of death, the very eidos of photography as manifestation of "a defeat of time", according to Barthes (1993: 96). At first, the protagonist in *La Jetée* remains confined to the position of a voyeur, whose time travel possibilities do not extend beyond the passive contemplation of closed and inaccessible images of the past. However, soon he starts looking for the face of the woman that he remembers seeing as a child on the main pier at Orly. The status of this image is uncertain, as the prologue of *La Jetée* informs us: "he often wandered if he had ever seen it or if he had dreamt a lovely moment to catch up with the crazy moment that followed it", the death of a man shot down on the pier. It is only when he eventually manages to conjure up the image of the woman during one of the sessions of induced sleep that his travel into time really starts. For he does not simply go back to the event he witnessed as a child at Orly, but he somehow becomes capable of accessing the "intractable reality" of frozen moments in the past, as his present, adult self, and meet with the woman in several different surroundings.

Barthes's remark on the "temporal hallucination" of photography (Barthes 1993: 115) is taken one step further when the man and the woman in *La Jetée* freely converse about their incompatible spatio-temporal frameworks. She calls him her ghost, and he tells her "the truth" about his journeys through time by referring to "an unreachable country, a long way to go". The most disturbing reflection on the superimposition of past, present and future that the protagonist experiences during the sleep experiments comes up in a scene which is a direct quotation from Hitchcock's *Vertigo* (1958): like the haunted Madeleine (Kim Novak) and Scotty (played by James Stewart) in Hitchcock's feature, the man and the woman in *La Jetée* look at the rings in the cross section of a sequoia tree. Unlike Madeleine, who pinpoints the moments when she was born and when she died in a previous existence, the man in *La Jetée* shows his companion a point beyond the tree and, "as in a dream", hears himself say: "This is where I come from". The sudden disclosure of an incongruous temporal reference breaks down the reality of a shared moment in the past, and the man, exhausted, regains consciousness in the present-time underground lab. But the meaning of the latest sequence of frozen frame images has radically altered the status of photographic representation. Far from merely prompting the "vertigo of time defeated", as Barthes (1993: 97) claimed, still images exceptionally acquire the protensity of film shots in *La Jetée*. The crucial difference between photography and cinema, according to Barthes, resides in the melancholy and spectral nature of the former, which "is without future". If cameras can be understood as "clocks for seeing", the only relationship to the future of a photographic image corresponds, in Barthes's account, to a "prophecy in reverse: like Cassandra, but eyes fixed on the past" (Barthes 1993: 15, 87). To a certain extent, this description matches the function of the obsessive childhood memory in *La Jetée*. However, the man's gesture pointing beyond the cross section of the sequoia tree to a moment in the future explodes the closed temporal frame of the image. The viewer is intrigued by the very possibility of the protagonist's coming back as an adult to moments in time when the woman is no older than she was in his childhood memory. The still frame narrative of such meetings cannot logically belong in the past, for its protensive meaning exceeds even Madeleine's assumed anamnesis of a previous existence in Hitchcock's *Vertigo*. These are no memories, properly speaking, since no one can recall events that have not yet, or rather, have never actually come to pass. The exploration of the past through photographic snapshots of reality in *La Jetée* brings recollection, and its visual documentary evidence, displayed as fragments of arrested time, much closer to the proleptic mode of certain dreams or of premonitory visions, to delirium and the psychoanalytical projection of desire. Contrary to Barthes's assertion, the suggestion or the actual use of cinematic movement in this case does not exclude or "tame" the spectral potential of photographic images. The man's apparent recollection of his meetings with the woman in *La Jetée*, just like the only instance of animated vision in Marker's photo-roman (when the woman opens her eyes and blinks looking straight into the camera), or – again – Madeleine's anamnesis in *Vertigo*, properly pertain to the notions of ecmnesis and hallucination, that Barthes opposes to the essentially oneiric illusion of film. Cinema, no less than photography, can be spectral and ecmnetic, can explore phenomena of paramnesis and temporal hallucination, especially when it deliberately highlights the illusion of cinematic movement, or when it employs both still and moving images to subvert the realism of photographic representation.

Man Ray's exploration of the rayograph technique, along with his use of arrested motion and the decomposition of cinematic movement, prompted Breton's compelling remarks on the spectral quality of both photographic and film images which reveal the paradoxically immaterial presence of perceived reality:

> Almost at the same time as Max Ernst, but in a different and, at first sight, almost opposite spirit, Man Ray also derived his initial impetus from photographic precepts. But far from entrusting himself to photography's avowed aims and making use, after the event, of the common ground of representation that it proposed, Man Ray has applied himself rigorously to the task of stripping it of its positive nature, of forcing it to abandon its arrogant air

> and pretentious claims. [...] The same considerations apply, indeed, to the
> taking of cinematographic images, which tend to compromise these figures not
> only in an inanimate state but also in motion. (Breton 1972: 32)

Most interestingly, in a short text on Max Ernst, dating back to 1921, the heyday of Dada manifestations in Paris, Breton (1978: 7) provocatively identified photography and automatic writing, whose revolutionary impact on poetic language he described as the advent of "a genuine photography of thought". In the same article, Breton turns his attention to the possibility of transgressing the mimetic and utilitarian aspect of photographic images in the manner in which Duchamp's readymades attributed a poetic functionality to everyday objects:

> It would be equally sterile for us to reconsider the ready-made images of objects
> (as in catalogue figures) and the meaning of words, as though it were our
> mission to rejuvenate them. We must accept these conventions, and then we can
> distribute and group them according to whatever plan we please. (Breton 1978:
> 7)

Although the passage itself gives no clear indication of the kind of images Breton was referring to – whether mental images or actual photographic prints – another text he wrote about the same time, entitled "Caractère de l'évolution moderne et ce qui en participe" (1922–23), unambiguously establishes the analogy between Man Ray's rayographs and Duchamp's readymades, such as the bird cage filled with marble sugar lumps, entitled *Why not Sneeze?*.[1] The sensorial effect of estrangement achieved by means apparently intended to reproduce or display everyday objects brings to light, according to Breton, the undeniable affinity between such "properly speaking poetic experiments". Similarly, in Breton's 1921 article on Max Ernst, the notion of "*dépaysement*" or estrangement relates the opening remarks on photography and automatic writing to a landmark statement about the new spatio-temporal conditions of Dada visual representation:

> It is the marvelous faculty of attaining two widely separate realities without
> departing from the realm of our experience; of bringing them together and
> drawing up a spark from their contact [...] and of disorienting us in our memory
> by depriving us of a frame of reference – it is this faculty which for the present
> [holds the attention]. (Breton 1978: 8)

In inviting the viewer to query the assumed documentary evidence and conventional spatio-temporal framework of photographic and cinematic means of expression, Man Ray's as well as Chris Marker's experimental films deliberately highlight the estrangement potential of images that can "nous dépayser en notre propre souvenir" [disorient us in our memory]. Far from merely reproducing the flow of mental images prompted by the reminiscence of past events or by the direct perception of reality, photographs and moving pictures, in this case, bring into view the full range of unconscious processes that constantly re-arrange and interpret what we see. The snapshots illustrating the man's recollection of his meetings with the woman in *La Jetée* have little in common with actual memories. They remain outside time, as the voice-over commentary points out ("no memories, no plans"), so that one can reasonably surmise that the spatio-temporal paradoxes outlined by the narrative properly pertain to an unconscious exploration of the past, more akin, for instance, to Brassaï's engravings on exposed photographic plates, that he entitled "latent images", and that went on to inspire his interpretation of the Proustian "remembrance of time past" as a recurrent preoccupation with the latent, or as Annick Lionel-Marie (2000: 159) described it: "what could have been and what has not been, what is buried, and yet close at hand, beneath reality". The virtual rather than factual meaning of unconscious images thus forms the object of *La Jetée*'s journey across the disconcerting spatio-temporal conundrum of events that take the viewer deep into the protagonist's mind, and make him share the experience of what Brassaï (1997: 20) aptly called, with reference to Proust, "the photographer of mental images with his own being as the sensitized plate". Several verbal and visual allusions to Brassaï's photographs of Parisian graffiti (among which arrow shot hearts and skulls figure prominently) punctuate the narrator's comments on the freeze frame perception of suspended moments in the present: "They have no memories, no past. Time builds itself painlessly around them. As landmarks they have the taste of this very moment they live, and the scribbles on the walls". Significantly, time flows "around" rather than within such vividly evoked images of Paris, filled with the premonition of both love and imminent death.

Two suggestive sequences that can qualify as "ecmnetic" encounters with the past, in Barthes's terms, explicitly deal with sleep and death. The first occurs just after the sequoia tree scene, when the man goes back once more to the pre-war world and finds the woman sleeping in the sun. "He knows", the voice-over commentary informs us, "that in this world where he has just landed again for a while, in order to be sent back to her, she is dead". The mise-en-scène and montage of still images take up the verbal hint at the photographic temporal hallucination and subtly render it through the initial positioning of the characters on a deep focus visual axis (that foregrounds the woman's profile); then through a middle shot of the man and the woman aligned, as it were, horizontally across the screen. The sudden change of direction, amounting to a jump cut in filmic terms, brings the two characters together in a homogeneous spatio-temporal frame, after having allowed the viewer to contemplate the woman's death-like stillness in her sleep and the temporal distance, rather than merely spatial depth of field, that separates her from the man. The second sequence uses continuity editing across a swift succession of still images linked through dissolves, that build up to the only instance of animated vision in *La Jetée*. The background sound of birds chirping gradually swells along with the increasingly rapid pace of fluid transitions between shots and leads to the moment when the life-like cinematic movement is miraculously restored. When the woman opens her eyes, looks into the camera and blinks, the viewer witnesses the ecmnetic coincidence of the present and the past, as the cinema fleetingly brings back to life the spectrality of still photographic images.

The symbolic "awakening" of a freeze-frame portrait to life-like movement in *La Jetée* displays a strong formal similarity with the final sequence of Man Ray's *Emak Bakia*, which features a high-angle shot of a woman who opens her eyes and smiles to the camera. However, the second pair of eyes painted on Kiki's closed eyelids in *Emak Bakia* accomplishes an astounding mise-en-abîme of photographic and cinematic vision, by confronting the viewer not just with the denounced illusion of presence-as-absence, wakefulness-as-sleep, but also – ultimately – with the staring, deadly gaze of the cinema. For what is staring back at the viewer, in this obvious recall of the opening sequence which shows Man Ray filming himself in a mirror while the image of his eye appears superimposed upside down in the camera lens, is the blank, unyielding eye of the camera. As Godard later remarked in *Histoire(s) du cinéma* (1998), by paraphrasing Blanchot's own considerations on the image in *L'Amitié*:

> Cinema [...] was not sheltered from time, but was a shelter for time. Yes, the
> image is joy, but alongside it nothingness lingers, and the entire power of the

image can be expressed only by appealing to that nothingness. One ought perhaps also to add: that the image, which has the capacity to negate nothingness, is also the gaze of nothingness upon us. The image is light, and nothingness immesurably heavy; the image glimmers, while nothingness is the diffuse impenetrability in which nothing shows up. (Blanchot 1971: 48, 50-1; tr. Temple, William and Witt 2004: 411)

At the limits of visual representation, cinema, no less than the stillness of photographic prints, ceases to be the faithful "mirror with a memory" and returns the viewer's gaze, along with his or her reminiscent re-enactment of the past, as the unconscious premonition of death: nothingness that lingers and shows up on the edges of our intermittent presence in the camera-eye. Unlike Barthes, Godard has explicitly and repeatedly expressed, since the early 1960s, his belief in the hallucinatory, death-laden potential of film:

The cinema is the only art which, as Cocteau says (in *Orphée*, I believe) "films death at work". Whoever one films is growing older and will die. So one is filming a moment of death at work. Painting is static: the cinema is interesting because it seizes life and the mortal side of life. (Milne 1986: 181)

Among the best examples of radical Dada nihilism in Godard's work, *Week-end* (1967) provides not so much a direct meditation on human mortality as a wider-encompassing exploration of the outer frontiers and death of cinema itself. The caption that precedes the title shot describes *Week-end* as "a film found on a scrap heap" [à la ferraille], and the grotesque, yet visually arresting, accumulation of car and plane crashes, traffic jams, burning or calcified carcasses, clearly signals an aesthetics of debris, of waste and disintegration. Although *Week-end* and *La Chinoise* (also made in 1967) have primarily attracted critical attention on account of their analysis of a social and political state of affairs that foreshadowed the violent upheaval of May 1968 in France, there is certainly a lot more that goes on under the ominous ideological discourse of these two films. *Week-end*, in particular, evinces a powerful affinity with the subversive illogicality of Dada pronouncements. The collapse of the established social order, and of the mode of thinking associated with it, is not only anticipated but also actually effected through the systematic dismantling of the entire edifice of bourgeois axiology. Nothing is spared, from aesthetics to religion, from ethical values to political convictions, and the ferocious sarcasm of destruction in *Week-end* gradually and self-consciously acquires apocalyptic undertones that hark back (well beyond Chris Marker's bleak utopian vision) to Picabia's *Manifeste cannibale Dada* of 1920:

> You are all indicted; stand up! Stand up as you would for the *Marseillaise* or *God Save the King*....
> Dada alone does not smell: it is nothing, nothing, nothing.
> It is like your hopes: nothing.
> like your paradise: nothing.
> like your idols: nothing.
> like your politicians: nothing.
> like your heroes: nothing.
> like your artists: nothing.
> like your religions: nothing. (Picabia 1975: 213)

Considerably more Dada than committed left-wing party manifesto, *Week-end* is a sweeping indictment of humanity, of modern "civilization" and technological progress. From the moment the two protagonists leave their bourgeois apartment and set off on a cross-country pursuit of frustrated consumerist desires to the cannibalistic epilogue of their adventures, *Week-end* traces the accelerated decline of so-called "civilized" human society, and its regression to an uncontrolled state of anarchy and bestiality. Halfway through the film, a striking reference to Buñuel's *Exterminating Angel* (1962) makes the viewer aware of the similarities between Godard's anthropological study of social behaviour and his predecessor's absurd parable of bourgeois values rapidly backsliding into murderous savagery, when the guests to a dinner party find they are trapped in the drawing room. The manner in which Godard consistently uses intertitles to provoke the viewer's spatio-temporal disorientation and highlight the disruption of film narrative and editing conventions is also highly indicative of his affinities with both Man Ray and Buñuel's experimental practice. Intriguing temporal markers such as "The Week of 4 Thursdays" or "One Tuesday in the 100 Years War" that punctuate Godard's increasingly fragmented narrative in *Week-end* unavoidably seem to recall the groundbreaking impact of Buñuel's intertitles in *Un Chien andalou* (1929): "Once upon a time", "Towards three in the morning", "In the spring". However, Godard is more often treading in Man Ray's Dada footsteps when he uses verbal puns and graphic effects of word division on the screen in order to enhance or even accelerate the dismantling of linguistic codes and cinematic grammar. Man Ray and Duchamp's rotating disks with spirally printed verbal puns that featured first in the *Rotary Glass Plates*

(Precision Optics) installations then in the short film *Anémic cinéma* (1926), effectively managed to denounce the illusion of cinematic movement and make the verbal constructs compete with the hallucinatory effect of images. The samples of *Rrose Sélavy*-like word games and automatic writing that Man Ray later added to Desnos's scenario for *L'Etoile de mer* (1928) further emphasised the intended discrepancy between intertitles and the visual narrative of the film. Godard similarly explored the effects of asynchrony in *Week-end* by allowing incongruous written messages to compete with the visual information for the viewer's attention, and frustrate any attempts at assembling the vestiges of narrative continuity in line with established rules of cinematic syntax. The enigmatic hitchhiker that Roland and Corinne encounter during their journey, and that a repeated intertitle identifies as the "exterminating angel", confirms Godard's intentions, when he declares, in unadulterated Dada fashion: "I am here to proclaim to these modern times the end of the grammatical era and the beginning of an age of flamboyance in every field, especially the movies".

There is no doubt that the apocalypse prefigured in the opening sequence, which portrays a dysfunctional couple in a social environment ridden with greed, violence and resentment, will sooner or later spill over into the worn-out mechanism of cinematic representation, and lead us from the first intertitle announcing "a film adrift in the cosmos" and "a film found on the scrap heap" to the inevitable conclusion written on the screen: "end of story", quickly followed by "end of cinema". Several times during Roland and Corinne's journey from Paris to Oinville we are reminded, in typical Dada fashion, of our own voyeuristic position as spectators, and of the artificial nature of narrative conventions based on the viewer's suspension of disbelief. When Roland fails to get directions from Emily Brontë and Tom Thumb (two of Godard's ghostly mouthpiece contraptions that provide vocal and visual support to an intricate web of literary, philosophical, or filmic quotations in *Week-end*), he vents his frustration like any run-of-the-mill, naïve member of the audience: "Ça fait chier ce film, on tombe que sur des malades!" [What a rotten film, all we meet are crazy people]. To add to the confusion, Corinne tries to put an end to Emily's nonsensical discourse by pointing out: "That's enough. This isn't a novel, it's a film. A film is life". Having exhausted all their arguments, Roland and Corinne set Emily's dress on fire and watch her die, while musing on the possibility of her – and implicitly – their real existence:

> Corinne: It's rotten of us, isn't it? We've no right to burn even a philosopher.
> Roland: Can't you see they're only imaginary characters?
> Corinne: Why is she crying, then?
> Roland: No idea. Let's go.
> Corinne: We're little more than that ourselves.

Later on, when they try to hitch a ride after days of walking through a desolate landscape strewn with the remains of car crashes, that they mercilessly scavenge, they are confronted with a riddle every time a driver stops. The first time, a woman asks Roland: "Are you in a film or in reality?" As Roland promptly replies: "In a film", the woman snaps back: "In a film? You lie too much", then drives away without a look back at Corinne and Roland who are helplessly shouting: "Salauds! Salauds!" The joke not only destabilizes the characters' already precarious status within a self-referential narrative, but also forces the viewer to reconsider his or her presuppositions at each stage.

It is not by chance that the only vehicle which eventually offers Corinne and Roland a ride is a garbage truck, and that the longest political speeches in the film are delivered, in turn, by the two drivers, one of whom is black, and the other of North African Arab origin. For the aesthetics of debris, of junk yard accumulation and social decay in *Week-end* meets the postmodern ideology of collage, citation, pastiche and parody in a truly flamboyant remake of the Dada anarchistic warfare on bourgeois civilization. When the Arab driver praises the effectiveness of guerilla tactics, of "bloody acts of sabotage", and then goes on to provide a crash course in Morgan and Engels' account of the evolution of mankind from "primitive barbarism" to the "confederation of tribes", a flash-forward brings into view the members of the so-called Seine and Oise Liberation Front, whose cannibalistic rituals will bring Corinne and Roland's initiatory journey to its gruesome conclusion. If the two protagonists' murderous intentions are clearly stated throughout their cross-country drive to collect Corinne's inheritance by speeding her parents' death, the final answer to their reflections on reality and fiction, on the origin and aims of civilization, comes as an equally explicit debunking of the viewer's expectations and of narrative conventions. The savage mores of the Seine and Oise Liberation Front represent not only a sarcastic fulfilment of the proletariat's utopian aspiration towards an egalitarian, classless society, but also an illustration of the violent demise of old visual codes of representation, within a process of cinematic cannibalism. *Week-end* literally feeds on several established genres and traditional editing and narratorial strategies that it slowly and deliberately pushes to the point of self-destruction. All political and ideological concerns are explored as part of a parodic and self-referential engagement with visual narrative form that subverts rather than upholds any expected propagandistic clichés. One salient example is the comical rendition of the fatal crash between a farmer's tractor and a Triumph sports car that constitutes the first overtly political sequence of the film. Labelled by an intertitle which reads, in turn "SS", then "SS STRUGGLE" and, eventually, "THE CLASS STRUGGLE", this episode displays an extravagant use of the interaction between words and images, as well as a form of extreme asynchrony between sound and image. The violent argument between the middle-class girl who survived the accident and the tractor driver who killed her boyfriend in the accident starts offscreen, while the camera lingers on Corinne and Roland who have stopped their car nearby, and are discussing what to do in case Corinne's father has dictated an updated will on his "little Japanese tape recorder". When the emphasis on the soundtrack shifts to the rather incongruous exchange of insults off-screen: "You bourgeois turd!", "You disgusting fat rat of a peasant", the intertitle appears, shortly followed by still images of the dead driver in the red sports car. Then, instead of an establishing shot that would bring the two interlocutors together, the girl alone is shown in close up against an advertising billboard, looking pensively into the camera, while the tractor driver continues angrily off-screen: "Why drive so fast? This isn't St Tropez!" The increasingly comical illogicality of the situation is underscored by another image of a group of three working-class men posing for the camera in front of the same billboard. Cutting back and forth between the car crash and several images of unknown and motionless characters looking straight into the camera, the editing fragments the ongoing argument, and makes the viewer aware of the cartoon-like succession of photographic portraits gazing back at the audience, as it were, with the mirror-reflection of their apathetic or amused participation in the events. Every time a recall shot of the dead driver in his sports car threatens to disrupt the parodic mood of the scene, the voice-over dialogue and the smiling or laughing expression of the anonymous bystanders take the edge off any potentially dramatic statements, such as: "He had the right of way", when the argument quickly degenerates into more colourful interjections: "You big lump of shit!", "You wretched little tart!", "Your cut-price tractor", and so on. Failing to get Roland and Corinne to intervene as witnesses to the crash, the girl and the farmer end up uniting against the hateful couple who drive off amongst incongruous protestations and insults: "You can't leave just like that! Aren't we all brothers like Marx said? Bastards! Bastards!", to which the girl adds: "Jews! Dirty Jews!" [Juifs, fascistes, pourris, dégueulasses!]. The conclusion to this double-edged lampoon that puts Communists on a par with anti-Semites (indeed, Fascists), comes up in the form of a quizzical intertitle: FAUX/TOGR/APHIE, which introduces the last picture-like shot of the sequence, showing the girl, the tractor driver and all the dislocated bystanders in one group happily posing for the camera, while the instrumental, yet badly out of tune, version of *L'Internationale* (the anthem of International Communism) is played on the soundtrack. The ironic insertion of *L'Internationale* at the beginning of the sequence (when the farmer is heard whistling it joyfully off-screen just seconds before the car crash) and at the end of this parodic interlude on the "class struggle" matches the constant visual play on the illusory realism of both photographic and cinematic images, apparently meant to convey a straight political message.

Revolutionary in its subversion of film narrative and representational practices rather than in its false attempt at flogging the dead horse of Russian agitprop, *Week-end* successfully tackles the discrepancy between the assumed realism and the spectrality of film images by literally making cinema "the only art that films death at work", that can film not only the death of its own mimetic conventions, but also the inevitable decline and demise of the worldview which engendered the naïve belief in the "mirror with a memory". Far from simply recording and preserving reality, the camera prefigures, through a palimpsest of filmic and literary quotations, the end of a "chapter in the history of humanity", as Godard argues in Pierre Desfons' documentary, *Vie et mort de l'image* (1995), based on a scenario by Régis Debray. A "montreur d'ombres", a conjurer of shadows, according to Godard, the cinéaste-filmmaker knows that the memory of the camera does not capture Proust's madeleine but the image that each viewer has formed in his or her mind of the madeleine. So that if one were to throw, as Godard literally (and symbolically) does in *Vie et mort de l'image*, Proust's *Remembrance of Time Past* to the unfathomable waves of generation upon generation of viewers, what will eventually come back to the shore of postmodernity is not the mirror reflection of a resurrected moment in history but James Joyce's *Ulysses* – or the ever-changing puzzle of what our unconscious cinematic memory makes of man's passage through time.

Notes

[1] "Through a personal technique, Man Ray arrives at a similar result on a sheet of paper. Without any doubt this opens up the perspective of an art that has more surprises in store than painting, for example. I think of Marcel Duchamp who went to fetch his friends to show them a cage that seemed birdless and half-filled with sugar lumps. When he asked them to lift the cage, they were astonished to find it was so heavy, because what they took for sugar lumps were in fact little pieces of marble. [...] This anecdote paraphrases quite well the novelty of Man Ray's experiments. And it is from this point of view that it becomes difficult to distinguish them from properly speaking poetic experiments" (Breton 1988: 300).

Bibliography

Barthes, Roland. 1993. *Camera Lucida. Reflections on Photography* (tr. R Howard). London: Vintage

Blanchot, Maurice. 1959. *Le Livre à venir*. Paris: Gallimard.

——. 1971. *L'Amitié*. Paris: Gallimard.

Brassaï. 1997. *Marcel Proust sous l'emprise de la photographie*. Paris: Gilberte Brassaï and Gallimard.

Breton, André. 1972. *Surrealism and Painting* (tr. S. Watson Taylor). London: MacDonald and Company (Publishers) Ltd..

——. 1978. *What is Surrealism? Selected Writings* (ed. F. Rosemont). London: Pluto Press.

——. 1988. *Œuvres complètes I*. Paris: Gallimard (Collection La Pléiade).

Milne, Tom (ed.). 1986. *Godard on Godard* (tr. T. Milne). Cambridge: Da Capo Press.

Man Ray. 1963. *Self-Portrait*. Boston: Little, Brown.

Picabia, Francis. 1975. *Ecrits* I (1913-1920). Paris: Editions Belfond.

Temple, Michael, J. S. William and M. Witt (eds). 2004. *For Ever Godard*. London: Black Dog Publishing.

Sayag, Alain and Annick Lionel-Marie (eds). 2000. *Brassaï. "No Ordinary Eye"*. London: Hayward Gallery.

DADA CULTURES

Chapter 7

The Location of Dada Culture:
Revising the Cultural Coordinates

Dafydd Jones

We might recognize today collisions and theoretical self-destruction as consistent principles in the most productive of western cultural formations, visible from the enlightenment's critically enlightened self-interrogation, to the "radical evil" of emancipatory politics, to postmodernism's evolution into a cultural dominant, and beyond. Strategies validated under the cultural logic of late capitalism, we have seen, have effected their own undoing – pastiche, for instance, is dissolved by using the instruments of pastiche itself; alternatively, some genuine historical sense is reconquered by using the instruments of what have been called substitutes for history. As thought systems collapse in on themselves, they instigate their own dissolution through anti-logic, or invert and thereby reproduce the flawed logic that was ostensibly the object of their critique at the outset. Even to talk about a postmodern text, Fredric Jameson (1986b: 72) observes (and as is surely the case when we talk about Dada), is "to reify it, to turn it into the work of art that it no longer is, to endow it with a permanence and monumentality that is its vocation to dispel". Through "alert sinuousness", in turn, and "discontinuous scintillation", even anarchic thought systems and formations become subject to theoretical inversion, as procedures are argued to founder under their own presuppositions; among such recent philosophical critiques, for instance, has been the charge brought by Alain Badiou against his older (and absent) contemporary Gilles Deleuze, that in the latter's thought equivocity is "reinstalled at the heart of being itself and [...] the virtual finally [gains] the status of a 'final cause' that explains everything only to the extent that it explains nothing at all" (Burchill 2000: xv). Badiou's ordered conception of chaos wades in to indict Deleuze's chaotic conception of order, giving us Deleuze "as the joyous thinker of the world's confusion" (Badiou 2000: 10). The eventual dispute between the two may indeed have proved a one-sided affair in Deleuze's absence, but the difference was already documented between the anarcho-desirer contra the Maoist during the so-called "red years", the invective charge of "Bolshevik" against the counter-charge of "fascist" at Vincennes leading to "the reflective determination of intellectual incompatibilities" (Badiou 2000: 2–3) – and the eventual establishment, in Badiou's words, of the two thinkers' "mobile divergence in its exact confused clarity (or obscure distinctness)" (Badiou 2000: 5).

The difference here cited is a difference argued to result from equivalence – a complicated proposition indeed, and one that relies in the above instance on Badiou's application of the terms and methods of set theory, where the disparity between equality (=) and equivalence ($\leftrightarrow$) demonstrates how two sets named "Deleuze" and "Badiou" do not have to be equal in order to be equivalent. But as such, the emerging difference from equivalence is affirmative of a current and critically necessary rethinking of oppositionality – most notably oppositionality as invoked in the context of a cultural avant-garde, and in practical terms as it enters into states of suspension through cooption and containment, and achieves a final, depressing redundancy. Attempting to reconfigure the familiar or not-so-familiar components of historical Dada (a category that already and formally exceeds itself with its pre-, proto- and neo- principles), and locating our encounter with Dada in both conceptual and practical terms, becomes an immediate concern if Dada is now to rupture historical containment and demonstrate a continued critical charge in renunciation (or so one argument goes – Baudrillard's) of "its own aesthetic rules of the game [defaulting] into the transaesthetic era of the banality of the image" (Baudrillard 1993: 11). Recognizing the rupture demands recourse to Dada's own demarcation of limits, and philosophical redress in the opportunity provided by those limits to test and to exceed them through unconditional adjustment – to argue then for theoretical stability understood not as fixity but always as variation within limits. It is for this reason at the outset that I pose Deleuze and Badiou on their high plateau as an instance where the conventional terms of binary opposition collapse, and radically revised and rethought relations between components become urgent.

Revision is an ongoing practical and theoretical exercise, as controlling structures reconfigure – literally change shape – in response to any critical or hostile emergency, so forcing responses in turn that move to free themselves from, or evade, the imposition of the "new" structure. Freedom is, of course, problematic: as an idea that is privileged within (and actually symptomatic of) bourgeois-anarchist individualism, historically it became untenable in marxist thought against what Lenin spoke of in 1905 as the real freedom to be actualized when revolutionary thought breaks out of bourgeois slavery and merges with "the movement of the really advanced and thoroughly revolutionary class" (Lenin 1992: 140). Lenin's hostility to the idea of freedom in its uncritical state was in continuation of Joseph Dietzgen's hostility in the nineteenth century to the materialist theory of knowledge espoused by self-styling "free thinkers" who constituted a reactionary mass in relation to social democracy. Against these "free thinkers" Lenin posed the "integral people" he favoured, in whose practice theory is embedded and their systems inscribed – even, potentially, when such systems are opiate religious ones. Our delusion of freedom in liberal democracy is simultaneously our failure to see ideological envelopment and structural containment, and the painful truth that there can be "no real and effective 'freedom' in a society based on the power of money" (Lenin 1992: 139). Lenin's recognition is productive, as his comparison of a living movement with a mechanism at least makes the structure visible, at which point we can begin to think, rethink and revise our relation to the structure. To think, and to think about thinking, is to participate in a common activity; thinking takes the specific instance to construct a generalization, but Dietzgen (1906: 357) cautions that the general proves of little consequence unless it is "conceived in its relation to its special [specific] forms". Through contradiction, necessarily struggling between generalization and specialization, the activity of thought is not however bound to move towards synthesis and resolution (although Dietzgen clearly identifies the dialectic – ahead of Marx and Engels – suggesting that it is in the nature of the mind to seek to "harmonize" the contradictions of the world, to relativize and equate them). Rather, the opposite gains the initiative, as contradiction and conflict are actively cultivated in revised strategic cultural and political engagement.

Rehearsing the problem of Dada

This paper then proposes preliminary delineation of the ground from which Dada, culturally and politically at the start of the twentieth century, developed integral and deliberately critical modes of engagement that, in continued practice, will reconstitute the movement as significantly more than the charge against it at the end of the twentieth century as constituting little more than "trivial irreverence" (Jameson 1986a: 38). Jameson's resignation on this point as, in his own words, "the impulses of negation and revolt, not to speak of those of social transformation, are increasingly perceived as vain and trivial" (Jameson 1984: 57), is symptomatic perhaps of poststructuralist pessimism in relation to the postmodern taken as an indicator of critical and creative crisis in the west. To accommodate the viability today – as in 1916 – of the same avant-garde practice that we were famously told by Peter Bürger had ceased as "historical" demands revisiting, as well as revising readings of, the historical instances and to think beyond the immediate:

> At any point in time, there is a tendency when one "thinks" about world society to "think" that things are fixed, cannot change. This non-changeability is imaginary, invented by "thought" to simplify the process of "thinking". But thinking is nowadays complex [...] Our minds are changing [...] to a courageous seeing of things in movement, life as revolution. (Cage 1979: 166)

The words of John Cage, here resonant of Richard Huelsenbeck's resistance to sedimentation and fixity – "to be a Dadaist", Huelsenbeck said in 1920, "means to let oneself be thrown by things, to oppose all sedimentation" (Motherwell 1981: 246) – and of Raoul Vaneigem's 1967 treatise on the revolution of everyday life, recognize "thinking" itself as counting among the controlling state apparatuses: for "free thinkers" now read free "thinkers". Lenin obligingly identifies those first in line for his dismissal as "muddled idealists", professors of philosophy whose very vocation comes under scrutiny for the committed proletarian militant of early marxism. Lenin, moreover, provides the apposite contradiction in this context that "in order to follow a true path it is necessary to study philosophy, which is *the falsest of all paths* [...] [and this means] that there can be no true path without a study and eventually a *theory of philosophy as a false path*" (Althusser 1971: 31). To this extent, Lenin isolated himself and was tarred as "philosophically intolerable", but his concession to his own vague and unpolished formulations in the face of the sophisticated ruminations of others underscored the critical distinction he wanted to make: "not only do I not 'philosophize' like them at all […] I treat philosophy differently, I practise it", he writes in a letter to Gorky (7 February 1908) (Althusser 1971: 31). It is Althusser who argues our indebtedness to the Bolshevik leader for contributing to the conditions under early marxism that made the anticipation of a non-philosophical theory of philosophy possible; in actualizing a procedural truth by direct engagement of that which is false (masquerading as truth), even in consciousness that problematically yet necessarily remains captive to its own falsity, I would now argue an indebtedness to Dada in anticipation of a non-artistic theory of art. Lenin is a seductive proposition when it comes to Dada: the collision of revolutionary politics, philosophy and art on Zurich's winding Spiegelgasse in 1916 is tantalizing, just eighteen months before the momentous events of October 1917. In Lenin's room at Spiegelgasse 14, future change was studiously being planned while the Cabaret Voltaire blasted off at Spiegelgasse 1, the waking and the dreamt revolution just a few doors apart. Resident in the seedy Niederdorf quarter, however, Lenin was hardly at one with his environs, the "smoky breeding places of endless tirades, in which day and night the revolutionary 'declamators' prostituted themselves" (Solzhenitsyn 1971: 113). As far as he was concerned, the cafés of the quarter attracted "unfathomable foreigners", variously "adventurers, wheeler-dealers, racketeers, students, deserters, and intellectual babblers, who rebelled with philosophical manifestos and artistic protest-actions against what-not" (Solzhenitsyn 1971: 113). Ironically, though, activities at the Cabaret Voltaire raised the suspicion of the Swiss authorities long before Zurich's Bolshevik émigrés (Lenin, Radek and Zinoviev) even registered. In more restrained mode, the brooding Russian revolutionaries pursued their own goals: of the two camps, Richter (1966: 16) later recalled, it was of course the Dadaists who were most "capable of perpetrating some new enormity at any moment". From the "strange protectedness" of Zurich's cafés, the Dada revolution unravelled through deliberate and strategic incoherence in the process of transforming the individual, and thereafter the revolutionized self was unlikely again to be politically, socially, economically or artistically unified. This, at least, was one distinction between Zurich's two revolutionary groups – the Dadaists and the Bolsheviks – as the Russians emphasized unity, specifically political unity, in the face of the divisive threat posed by philosophical disputes among "free thinkers". Within disciplined unity, however, Althusser (1971: 26) importantly observes "a 'practice' of philosophy, and the consciousness of the ruthless, primary fact that philosophy divides", finally to conclude that "philosophy divides, and it can only unite by dividing". This principle of unity through division, we note, was to become imperative for the Dadaists.

Practice is to be understood in this context as practice in the process of knowledge (Althusser 1971: 52). Its particular form, described by Althusser among Zurich's Bolsheviks and as I submit here among the historical Dadaists, is divisive and in the first instance debilitating. Arguably the one consistent casualty when it comes to radical cultural and avant-garde practice is communication. Its breakdown was, however, cultivated by the Dadaists – famously in the optophonetics of Berlin Dada, for instance – in opposition to communication that seemed tantamount to collusion with the bourgeois order, and the engineered breakdown of communication was prerequisite for the Dadaists' cultural arrest (and remains today the most potent means of immediate cultural arrest). But it does not follow from failure to recognize the transmitted impulse that the action in question is ineffective (or that it has no impulse), specifically so if we attend to the impulse itself. We are told how Lenin's loud and riotous neighbours on Spiegelgasse "were known to laymen and experts alike, more by our roars of laughter than by the things we were really doing [...] we laughed and laughed" (Richter 1966: 64), and indeed by the Dadaists' assumption of a deliberately transgressive stance we are perhaps now placed to recognize what Nietzsche (1987: 62) once described as "play as artists and children engage in it [...] coming-to-be and passing away, structuring and destroying". What Nietzsche the thinker poses are impulses and relations as the effects of chance – and ultimately the existence of the individual as the effect of chance – chance therefore as radically innocent because of its necessity, and entirely just because of its release from any purpose. Necessity transforms the game of chance into one where the stakes are high, as chance is positively identified "with multiplicity, with fragments, with parts, with chaos: the chaos of the dice that are shaken and then thrown" (Deleuze 1983: 25–7). In affirmation of innocence, necessity and multiplicity, Deleuze is emphatic:

> To abolish chance by holding it in the grip of causality and finality, to count on the repetition of throws rather than affirming chance, to anticipate a result instead of affirming necessity – these are all the operations of a bad player.[1]

Certain among the participants at the Cabaret Voltaire quite clearly took the stage as what Deleuze would presumably have termed "supreme players", as unimpeded by causal motives as they were by the idea of a goal. But the deferral of unity and completion as the idea of a goal becomes redundant is not the prompt to any open hostility towards unifying principles that we might expect from such a thinker as Deleuze. Yes, there is resistance to permitting the reduction of thought to unifying principles, but unifying principles are never ruled out as conceptual options – no more, for example, than Deleuze rules out the strategic use of conceptual binaries. The application here to Dada is that Deleuze's admission of any conceptual strategy in the process of thinking permits (philosophical) thought that freely operates as "the capture of a life that is both total and divergent" (Badiou 1994: 55), by virtue of a "positive ambivalence" that emanates from his total repudiation of negation and refusal to conform or be forced into any one position.

Reading the Zurich manifestos

The idea of revolution as a practical proposition demands revision now as late twentieth-century revolutionary philosophical thought realigns western cultural and political coordinates. Aping radicalism is certainly not revolutionary when the resulting "revolution" condemns a system and then asks that same system for acceptance; more than once during the twentieth century, it was forcefully and sometimes violently demonstrated that people involved in revolutions do not become part of systems, but that they destroy systems. How we should invoke the idea of revolution in view of this, and how we apply that idea retrospectively to the early twentieth century avant-garde, requires a deliberate revision of readings that have hitherto dominated art historically, prescriptive (and predictable) readings of Dada that characterize it as anarchic, a nihilist gesture, an act of cultural destruction offering nothing to replace what it set about destroying. If, however, we read revolution as committed to breaking down systems in all their forms, the revolutionary agent increasingly assumes the recognizably destructive, anarchic and nihilist traits already ascribed to the Dada type, crucially abandoning binary schemata and engaging cultural logic itself – revolution, therefore, that is not defined by preemptive conclusions. Such becomes revolution without a goal, but revolution with effect; not revolution as Lenin envisaged it emanating to Russia and beyond from its filterbed in neutral Switzerland, but revolution revised practically and theoretically throughout the twentieth century in reflection upon the sobering aftermath and ultimate failure of October 1917. Problematically, critical or oppositional posturing will prove unproductive unless the engagement demonstrated moves to embrace the institutionalizing of political change: failure to move to the latter implies a conservatism underlying the "radical" stance being described (so the "radical" form is "conservative"), and it is what makes possible the almost effortless cooption of radical cultural forms within a very short space of time, even when those forms are generated from a broadly, and consequently vaguely, defined anarcho-nihilist position. Such a position distinguishes itself as resistant to the conceptual inversions of revolution as conventionally exercised, but by that same resistance any effective and lasting (therefore institutionalized) change is put in serious question. Arguably nothing beyond surfaces change when one order is replaced by its opposite and the cultural, political, social or economic logic is simply inverted. Critically resisting binary logic, however, forgoes institutionalized change, and it is at this point that Dada might appear to collapse as an effective critical force, yielding to its characterization as the great radical yet wholly negative cultural gesture of the early twentieth century, at the impasse of subjugation that denies the adequate theorizing of a possible critique of hegemonic power or authority.

Oppositionality falters when it stakes itself against its object, precisely as the idea of the avant-garde breaks down when it takes on directly state morality and economy; and here lies the task in hand, to revise how "oppositionality" is thought, and along with it how "revolution" is thought. Reading Tristan Tzara and Walter Serner's manifesto soundings of 1916–20 provides instances that patently refuse to yield to direct oppositionality, and so resist reduction to revolutionary claims. Nowhere, for example, do they allow the reader or listener to find the stability of meaning that is anticipated by "system", ideologically or politically defined, and the enclosure of subjects by systems:

> If there is a system in the lack of system [...] I never apply it.
>
> In other words, I lie. I lie when I apply it, I lie when I don't apply it, I lie when I write that I lie because I do not lie [...] for myself has never been myself. (Tzara 1992: 27)

Tzara, here as elsewhere, destabilizes every expectation that might fall upon him to refute the authority of a containing ideology, and takes issue even with his own cynical reason in the process. The complexity of this introspection is apparent in the blunt admission that "myself has never been myself", signalling the subject's loss of control as his lexicon takes shape outside of his thought but at the same time shapes it. The singular refusal to admit any stable meaning critically engages ideology's assumption of stable meaning and significance – however contingent or contestable – in "the symbolic" in order to break it down: this Tzara does, consistently I would argue, in order to open up a space that will relate to the ideological as it similarly relates to "the symbolic". Indeed, that this is a space permitted by the ideological means that it is at once immanent to the ideological, and its immanence makes redundant any invocation of the conventional space of oppositionality (coming from the outside) usually anticipated for dissenting voices. Whether such voices are on the inside or outside ceases to have any bearing in the struggle to orient ourselves to their various positions, as they renege equally on the reader as on themselves: "One should begin at long last to speak out against oneself! One should begin!! One!!" Serner's uncompromising stance is undiminished as he places himself in the line of his own critical fire, his self-loathing and subjective destitution exposed, as "for a long time now I have, in quiet hours, been spitting on my own head" (Serner 2006: 61). If it has been suggested that Tzara's notorious *Manifeste Dada 1918* carries Serner's heavy yet anonymous imprint, Serner retains full credit for "Der Schluck um die Achse" [The Swig about the Axis], a text as destructive and disorienting in intent as Tzara's offering of 1918. "Der Schluck um die Achse" appeared as a late submission to Zurich Dada, published in the single issue of *Der Zeltweg* in 1919 (by which time Serner had already left Zurich), and in practical terms it constituted a summation of the Tzara-Serner brand of anarcho-nihilism of the preceding years (subsequently to be integrated into the extended version of Serner's *Letzte Lockerung Manifest* of 1920). It is, nonetheless, a distillation of the nihilist tone and its incipient critical mode as already encountered in the *Manifeste Dada 1918* that Tzara took with him from Zurich to Paris at the close of 1919.

Both Tzara and Serner's positions immanent to the ideological are positions from which the manifesto writers necessarily bear witness to the meanings and assumptions current in the ideological formation itself, and the deployment of reason to contest any discourse within ideology then becomes active within a critique of ideology. The breakdown of the usually stable image of "social reality" is one critical consequence, as the space immanent to the ideological makes unstable the ideological projection of its "social reality". The challenge is then mounted in the form of Dada antagonistic resistance to ideological projections, resistance that marks critical distance and opens up critical, in-between space. Active politically in the cultural sphere, the Dadaists were anything but self-deluding in their "oppositionality" and revolutionary stance, as Tzara (1992: 1) reminded his audience at the first Dada demonstration in July 1916: "we are wise enough to know that our brains are going to become flabby cushions, that our antidogmatism is as exclusive as a civil servant, and that we cry liberty but are not free; a severe necessity with neither discipline nor morals and that we spit on humanity". The concessions made at the outset placed Dada on a trajectory that was never intended to destroy art: "anti-art" is not concerned with the obliteration of the category, after all, and the eventual recuperation or cooption of Dada by and for the reigning order is, as a result, inadmissible as evidence of any stated "failure" on Dada's part. Huelsenbeck (1981b: 399), indeed, with remote retrospection, observed how Dada "was positive and pursued positive aims from the very beginning of its existence", and in its critical engagement with cultural and social constraints the movement's resistance to outright rejection and destruction is recognizable. The practical and theoretical necessity of constraints and limits are reaffirmed by Deleuze's observation that:

> you have to keep small supplies of signifiance and subjectification, if only to turn them against their own systems when the circumstances demand it ... and you have to keep small rations of subjectivity in sufficient quantity to enable you to respond to the dominant reality. (Deleuze 1987: 160)

The sustained Dada assault on the dominant reality, at every manifest level, retained always that reality's privileging function of art and the reception of art, as well as what was (and remains) perpetually categorized under current cultural forces, in unashamed mercenary fashion, whenever such categorization proved useful for Dada engagement. Hence the artistic and political legitimacy of using forms that the Dadaists were at least theoretically opposed to – "I write a manifesto [...] and in principle I am against manifestos", said Tzara (2006: 36) in 1918 – and the acute increase in the destructive potential of such forms when they are put into operation from the performative sites that Dada itself created, those very places that "put, or kept Dada squarely 'inside' culture, or better yet, inside 'culturing' " (Foster 1994). The necessary impermanence of the coordinates of Dada engagement, continuously revised and reconfigured as a matter of course, allows culture's ongoing process, which in turn provides the legitimate context within which effective (I mean really effective) oppositionality becomes viable. Direct, hostile engagement with a concept has limited use: far better, Deleuze (1991: 94) suggests, "to build the new functions and discover the new fields that make it [the concept] useless or inadequate". I submit that the Zurich manifesto writings of Tzara and of Serner patently enter into such new fields, and though in more recent parlance they may indeed struggle in environments of simulation and simulacra, as they do so they demonstrate efficient critical use of "the arms and weapons specific to that world which are themselves very precisely simulacra" (Jameson 1986a: 42–3).

Orienting ourselves, then, to the location of Dada culture means to think our relation to the encounter – where and how – of Dada, even as it turns against itself. If Dada is an event, its occurrence is located in the critical space that opens up, immanent to the ideological, the in-between or the "meanwhile" – or, more precisely, *un entre-temps* in Deleuze and Guattari's own usage, where "it is the event that is a meanwhile [un entre-temps] [...] it belongs to becoming" (Deleuze and Guattari 1994: 158). Here, more than locating the event in the space, the distinction between the event and the space is suspended and our apprehension of Dada both in and as the mean, still time (or "dead time") of the event remains vital: "nothing happens there [in the event], but everything becomes, so that the event has the privilege of beginning again when time is past.

Nothing happens, and yet everything changes" (Deleuze and Guattari 1994: 158) – what we are reading is revolution without a goal, but with effect. Dada tests and exceeds its own limits, unconditionally reconfiguring itself and submitting to our theoretical reflection a practical stability understood not as fixity but as continuous revision and variation within limits – declaring, in Huelsenbeck's words, an emphatic yes "to a life that strives upward by negation" (Huelsenbeck 1981a: 246). In void spaces and the interstices of culture, in its ruptures, collisions and fissures, political urgency makes itself known and Dada begins again.

---

[1] Deleuze (1983: 27). This very abolition of chance and anticipation of result is a flaw that Badiou reflects back onto Deleuze himself (who first made the observation), making of Deleuze a "bad player" whose thought progresses towards its own "destination" (result), which, for Badiou, is "the One".

Bibliography

Ades, Dawn (ed.). 2006. *The Dada Reader: A Critical Anthology*. London: Tate Publishing.

Althusser, Louis. 1971. *Lenin and Philosophy and Other Essays*. New York: Monthly Review Press.

Badiou, Alain. 1994. "Gilles Deleuze, *The Fold: Leibniz and the Baroque*" in C. V. Boundas and D. Olkowski (eds) *Gilles Deleuze and the Theater of Philosophy*. New York and London: Routledge.

Badiou, Alain. 2000. *Deleuze: The Clamor of Being*. Minneapolis: University of Minnesota Press.

Baudrillard, Jean. 1993. *The Transparency of Evil*. London: Verso.

Burchill, Louise. 2000. "Introduction" to Badiou (2000).

Bürger, Peter. 1984. *Theory of the Avant-Garde*. Minneapolis: University of Minnesota Press.

Cage, John. 1979. *A Year from Monday*. Middletown, Conn.: Wesleyan University Press.

Deleuze, Gilles. 1983. *Nietzsche and Philosophy*. New York: Columbia University Press.

Deleuze, Gilles and Félix Guattari. 1987. *A Thousand Plateaus: Capitalism and Schizophrenia*. Minneapolis: University of Minnesota Press.

Deleuze, Gilles. 1991. "A Philosophical Concept …" in E. Cadava, P. Connor and J.-L. Nancy (eds). *Who Comes After the Subject?* New York and London: Routledge.

Deleuze, Gilles and Félix Guattari. 1994. *What is Philosophy?* London: Verso.

Dietzgen, Joseph. 1906. *The Popular Outcome of Philosophy*. Chicago: Kerr.

Foster, Stephen C. 1994. "Zurich Dada: The Arts, Critique, and the Theatre of Radicalism". Unpublished keynote address to the Zurich Dada Conference, Manchester Metropolitan University.

Huelsenbeck, Richard. 1981a. "Collective Dada Manifesto" in Motherwell (1981): 242–6.

Huelsenbeck, Richard. 1981b. "Dada Manifesto 1949" in Motherwell (1981): 398–402.

Jameson, Fredric. 1984. "Postmodernism, or, the Cultural Logic of Late Capitalism" in *New Left Review* 146: 52–92.

Jameson, Fredric. 1986a. "Hans Haacke and the Cultural Logic of Postmodernism" in B. Wallis (ed.). *Hans Haacke: Unfinished Business*. New York: New Museum of Contemporary Art; Cambridge, Mass.: MIT Press: 38–51.

Jameson, Fredric. 1986b. "An Interview with Fredric Jameson by Anders Stephanson on Postmodernism" in *Flash Art* 131: 69–73.

Lenin, Vladimir Ilyich. 1992. "Party Organization and Party Literature" in C. Harrison and P. Wood (eds). *Art in Theory 1900–1990: An Anthology of Changing Ideas*. Oxford: Blackwell: 136–40.

Motherwell, Robert (ed.). 1981. *The Dada Painters and Poets: An Anthology*, Boston: G. K. Hall.

Nietzsche, Friedrich. 1987. *Philosophy in the Tragic Age of the Greeks*. Washington DC: Regnery Gateway.

Richter, Hans. 1966. *Dada, Art and Anti-Art*, London: Thames and Hudson.

Serner, Walter. 2006. "The Swig about the Axis" in Ades (2006): 58–61.

Solzhenitsyn, Alexander. 1976. *Lenin in Zurich*. New York: Farrar, Strauss & Giroux.

Tzara, Tristan. 1992. *Seven Dada Manifestos and Lampisteries*. London: Calder.

Tzara, Tristan. 2006. "Dada Manifesto 1918" in Ades (2006): 36–42.

Vaneigem, Raoul. 1967. *Traité de savoir-vivre à l'usage des jeunes générations*. Paris: Gallimard; *The Revolution of Everyday Life* (tr. J. Fullerton and P. Sieveking). London: Rising Free Collective, 1979.

Chapter 8

Le Cabaret Voltaire en perspective

Nadia Ghanem

Le Cabaret Voltaire véhicule une image mythique. Il est perçu comme un îlot de survie où se côtoient les réfugiés de tous bords, oscillant entre désespoir et volonté de s'ouvrir à de nouvelles expériences artistiques et poétiques.

Dès 1918, lors de sa première allocution Dada en Allemagne, Richard Huelsenbeck (2005: 258) entoure le Cabaret Voltaire d'une aura mystique: "Cela a donné un tel sabbat de sorcières que vous pouvez à peine vous l'imaginer: du tapage du matin au soir, une sorte de grand vertige avec trombones et tambours africains, une sorte d'extase avec claquettes et danses cubistes". La dimension extatique et apocalyptique du Cabaret est également évoquée par Tristan Tzara dans sa *Chronique zurichoise 1915-1919* (Huelsenbeck 2005: 10–13). Le poète y décrit une succession effrénée d'événements dans une ambiance "bordélique". D'autres membres fondateurs du Cabaret perpétueront ce mythe dans les décennies suivantes, à la faveur de récits qui laisseront le lecteur rêveur. Dans son essai judicieusement intitulé "Dadaland" (formule reprise à Georges Ribemont-Dessaignes), Hans Arp (2005: 308) se remémore la peinture, réalisée par Marcel Janco en 1916, qui figure une scène du *Cabaret Voltaire*. Arp convoque des images de rituels d'un autre âge et de contrées exotiques afin de rendre compte de l'agitation qui secouait le Cabaret. Janco, quant à lui, se souvient de la ville de Zurich comme d'une "île au milieu du feu, du fer et du sang", un "port de refuge", une "oasis de l'homme pensant" (Janco 2005: 20). Hans Richter, qui s'est fait l'historien du mouvement Dada, enrichit le mythe malgré sa non-participation au Cabaret (il arrive à Zurich à la fin du mois d'août

1916). Il fait sien les événements de l'époque et déclare: "Rien ne pouvait mieux exprimer notre optimisme, ce sentiment d'une liberté spirituelle nouvellement acquise sur notre île de la Vie, au milieu d'une mer de la Mort, que cette répétition vigoureuse de *da-da*" (Richter 1965: 27).

On serait tenté, à partir de ces quelques références, de lier le Cabaret à tout un imaginaire insulaire et utopique. La thématique de l'île est récurrente dans les récits utopiques fictionnels. Elle est dans un premier temps investie d'une utopie nostalgique, celle d'un retour à un Âge d'or, telles les "Iles Fortunées" ou "bien-heureuses" d'Horace. Elle devient le lieu d'une utopie humaniste, avec la parution, en 1516, de l'*Utopie* de Thomas More. Plus tard, elle apparaît comme le lieu de l'utopie libertaire – de l'anti-utopie ou contre-utopie – que cristallise le récit satirique de Jonathan Swift, *Gulliver's Travels* (1726). L'île d'utopie est tour à tour lieu de félicité et de cauchemar.

L'utopie désigne avant tout le projet imaginaire d'une société "autre", insulaire ou non. Mais du projet à la réalisation, il n'y a qu'un pas. Le Nouveau Monde verra se concrétiser nombre d'utopies, parmi lesquelles les utopies pirates sous la forme de "micro-sociétés hors la loi" (Bey 1997: 10). Ces micro-sociétés ne sont toutefois pas l'apanage des utopies pirates et peuvent surgir à n'importe quelle époque et dans n'importe quel lieu. Pour les désigner, Hakim Bey, gourou de la contre-culture des années 1990 qui se réclame entre autres de Dada, utilise le terme "TAZ", que l'on traduit en français par "zone autonome temporaire". Bey (1997: 14) définit la TAZ comme "une insurrection sans engagement direct contre l'État, une opération de guérilla qui libère une zone (de terrain, de temps, d'imagination)". L'insurrection porte atteinte aux "structures de contrôle" (Bey 1997: 15) de l'État, aux idées sur lesquelles repose la société. Les zones autonomes temporaires se situent en marge des institutions avec lesquelles elles cohabitent, aussi se caractérisent-elles par leur invisibilité. Elles participent d'une "tactique de la disparition" face à un pouvoir dominant (Bey 1997: 62).

La TAZ se donne comme un modèle d'alternance. Selon Henri Desroche, "l'alternance" est la première des trois altérités recherchées par l'utopie.[1] Desroche (1978: 25) situe l'alternance dans le rêve mais aussi dans "l'établissement de temps, de lieux ou même de micro-sociétés occasionnelles ou permanentes" qui sont autres "au sein même d'une société dominante, laquelle, en ces temps, en ces lieux ou dans ces micro-sociétés devient une société *vacante*". Dans cette configuration, le discours institutionnel s'avère caduc. Les sociétés d'alternance, soumises à leurs propres lois, sont les initiatrices de contre-cultures. C'est pourquoi Desroche (1978: 26) y voit des "temps et espaces de décompression, de débridement, d'inversion du jeu et des règles du jeu". Ce sont les sabbats, la fête des fous, le carnaval, etc.

La dimension festive de l'insurrection est primordiale pour Hakim Bey. Elle instaure une relation directe entre des individus qui s'unissent dans la convivialité et au gré des affinités. Tout système hiérarchique est aboli pour permettre à l'individu de s'épanouir au sein du groupe. La TAZ rompt aussi bien avec le modèle de société dominant qu'avec les utopies collectivistes.

Il reste alors à s'interroger sur le mode d'apparition du Cabaret Voltaire à la lumière de ces zones autonomes temporaires, ou sociétés d'alternance.

Le Cabaret Voltaire doit avant tout son caractère utopique à son fondateur, Hugo Ball, poète allemand, exilé en Suisse depuis 1915. Lorsqu'on parle de ce dernier, on évoque volontiers la réflexion, engagée avec Wassily Kandinsky au début des années 1910, sur la synthèse des arts. Cette synthèse réside dans l'association d'effets visuels et auditifs susceptibles de procurer au spectateur une expérience multi-sensorielle. L'artiste, quant à lui, devient à la fois peintre, poète, danseur, auteur, interprète et metteur en scène. Mais l'idée d'œuvre d'art totale réside surtout dans l'établissement d'une communauté de spectateurs. Pour ce faire, Ball choisit de s'adresser à l'inconscient. Le théâtre est pour lui un espace de "liberté" et les artistes sont "les prophètes d'une renaissance" (Ball 1993: 27, 31). Il ira même jusqu'à qualifier Kandinsky et Picasso de "créateurs de mondes nouveaux" et de "paradis nouveaux" (Ball 1993: 31). On peut alors penser que le poète a souhaité – malgré son exil et les impératifs financiers – poursuivre sa réflexion et créer un espace théâtral qui réponde à son désir de reconstruction de la société. Hypothèse d'autant plus recevable que Ball aurait lancé son projet de Cabaret entre le 25 et le 31 décembre 1915, période qui symboliserait le "temps de palingénésie", c'est-à-dire celui d'une renaissance de l'univers (Lista 2005: 42).

Cependant, l'annonce que le poète publie dans la presse zurichoise, le 2 février 1916, ne laisse rien paraître de ses motivations.

Le Cabaret y est présenté comme un "centre de divertissement artistique" ouvert à toutes les "tendances" et à toutes les "suggestions et propositions" (Ball 1993: 111). Dans un premier temps, le Cabaret Voltaire s'inscrit dans la tradition des cabarets littéraires d'avant-garde dont les principales sources d'influences sont l'expressionnisme et le futurisme.

Son premier signe distinctif – et non des moindres en ces temps de guerre – réside dans le fait que les soirées ont lieu en plusieurs langues, notamment en français et en allemand. Les artistes prennent également le parti de créer une revue bilingue, intitulée *Cabaret Voltaire*, où figurent, juxtaposés, poèmes français et allemands et œuvres d'artistes d'origines diverses. Ce plurilinguisme témoigne d'un désir de dépasser le clivage des nationalismes. La nécessité de décloisonner les catégories artistiques se conjugue avec celle de détruire les frontières entre les nations. Les artistes et les poètes s'interrogent sur l'État et l'Europe moderne jugés responsables de la guerre, et s'attaquent à la pensée rationnelle. Dans une même volonté de réduire à néant les fondements de la civilisation occidentale et de dépasser l'esthétique expressionniste et futuriste, un nouvel état d'esprit se dessine au Cabaret Voltaire. Celui-ci prend pour cibles le langage et l'image.

Hugo Ball compose une poésie sonore qui témoigne de son refus du discours logique. Le langage, "dépouillé de son pouvoir de signifier", tire désormais toute sa "puissance" du "rythme", de "l'intonation" ou du "cri", explique Henri Béhar (1967: 18). La poésie phonétique prend tout son sens lorsqu'elle est récitée. Vêtu d'un costume carcan, Ball déclame *Karawane*, le 23 juin 1916, et se métamorphose en chaman pour accomplir une sorte de rituel. Le poète-chaman perd peu à peu le contrôle de son corps, il entre en transe. Dans les rituels primitifs, la transe est provoquée par le chant, la musique ou la danse. Le chaman part ainsi à la recherche de l'âme égarée. La mise en scène de Ball se situe à mi-chemin du rite païen et de la cérémonie liturgique.

On pourrait rapprocher la poésie sonore des glossolalies, que Marina Yaguello (1984: 131) définit comme "une émanation directe de l'individu, non médiatisée par le social", mais qui "transcende l'individu". Dès lors, toute communication "discursive" est abolie au profit d'une communication "immédiate et ineffable". La glossolalie, à l'instar de la poésie sonore de Ball, n'est pas du domaine de l'expérience mais de la nature. Les sons ne répondent à aucun processus linguistique et s'apparentent au cri animal. Jean-Jacques Courtine (1988: 10) y voit un "infra-langage" qui surgit à une période critique de l'histoire, pour annoncer l'avènement d'un monde nouveau. Et c'est précisément au tournant du 19e et du 20e siècle que les glossolalies réapparaissent, réaction, selon Marina Yaguello, au développement de la pensée positiviste et matérialiste. Elles appartiennent à une tradition de l'Église primitive et témoignent d'une croyance en l'irrationnel et le fantastique. Chez Ball, la poésie sonore revêt une dimension mystique conforme à ses croyances religieuses. Mysticisme qui n'est pas partagé par les autres membres fondateurs du Cabaret, qui se rassemblent en revanche autour d'un même refus de la modernité. Les collages abstraits de Hans Arp mêlent indifféremment les formes géométriques et les formes organiques en un agencement aléatoire, "selon la loi du hasard" pour reprendre le concept cher à l'artiste. Les compositions abstraites de Arp se distinguent de celles des artistes russes et hollandais qui obéissent à des règles strictes de structure et d'équilibre. Arp (2005: 307) voit en celles-ci un "hommage à la vie moderne, une profession de foi à la machine et à la technique". Il leur oppose une œuvre proche de l'élément naturel qui surgit accidentellement sous l'impulsion d'une force propre. C'est pourquoi Leah Dickerman (2005: 998) définit l'art abstrait Dada comme une "forme moderne qui s'attaque à la modernité".

Le hasard, que Arp associe à une méthode, n'est toutefois pas absolu. Le jeu, né de cette alliance, relève d'un processus de régression vers un stade infantile. Le plaisir de la régression va de pair avec une lutte contre la réalité et donne naissance à une œuvre double où cohabitent le sens et le "sans sens" (Arp 2005: 312). Hugo Ball note, pour sa part, le 8 avril 1916:

> [D]ès que cesse la croyance en une chose ou en une cause, cette chose et cette cause retournent au chaos, redeviennent des territoires libres. Mais peut-être est-il nécessaire de produire très énergiquement ce chaos [...] avant de pouvoir envisager une reconstruction solide. (Ball 1993: 125–6)

Grâce au jeu, l'artiste devient démiurge: il détruit dans le but d'édifier son univers propre.

Pour créer les conditions du jeu, les artistes et les poètes prennent également pour modèle l'art "primitif". Depuis la fin du 19e siècle, la vie des peuples d'Afrique et d'Océanie, préservée du processus historique lié au progrès, est associée à un Âge d'or. Cette forme d'authenticité se retrouve dans l'art des tribus; c'est du moins ce que pensent nombre d'artistes. Marcel Janco et Sophie Taeuber confectionnent des masques et des costumes inspirés de ces traditions ancestrales. Sous l'emprise du masque et du costume, l'artiste accède à un autre niveau de conscience, que Dickerman (2005: 1005) qualifie de "conscience primitive", source d'épanouissement et de création. Les bois gravés et les sculptures en reliefs de Janco sont également inspirés de pratiques tribales.

Tristan Tzara et Richard Huelsenbeck se livrent, quant à eux, à de véritables récitals "nègres". Leurs œuvres ont la spécificité de créer une cacophonie par l'appropriation des principes du simultanéisme et du bruitisme. Le duo soigne particulièrement l'accompagnement sonore. La grosse caisse, instrument favori de Huelsenbeck, joue un rôle symbolique primordial dans l'imaginaire des artistes. Le bruit de la grosse caisse couvre le bruit des canons. La grosse caisse, et par extension les activités du Cabaret, deviennent un instrument de déraison face à la guerre moderne et mécanique qui résulte du prétendu pouvoir de la Raison. N'hésitant pas à s'en prendre physiquement et verbalement au public, Huelsenbeck et Tzara préfèrent l'affrontement à l'expérience collective, proche d'une communion mystique, préconisée par Ball. Les artistes et les poètes du Cabaret affirment la présence de l'œuvre et de l'artiste dans une immédiateté de l'expérience.

Ce qui pourrait ressembler à une utopie primitive, combinée à la nostalgie d'un Âge d'or, est rapidement travestie en une bouffonnerie mortuaire. Cette bipolarité parcourt l'ensemble du mouvement émergeant et est contenue dans le mot "Dada". Le petit cheval de bois auquel fait référence ce terme symbolisait déjà pour les expressionnistes allemands "un état primordial de l'enfance non corrompue par la civilisation" (Lista 2005: 41). État primordial que Ball tente désespérément de protéger au Cabaret comme pourrait l'indiquer la parution, dans la revue *Cabaret Voltaire,* d'un chapitre extrait de *Tenderenda le fantasque*, et intitulé "Johann, le cheval de manège". En voici quelques lignes révélatrices: "Nous sommes des fantasques. Nous ne croyons plus à l'intelligence. Et nous nous sommes mis en route pour protéger de la populace cet animal, objet de toute notre vénération" (Ball 2005: 21). L'intelligence dont souhaitent s'émanciper les artistes est intimement liée à l'intellectualisme jugé responsable des maux dont souffre la société. Les artistes choisissent donc paradoxalement d'être idiots suivant une démarche réfléchie. L'idiot est celui à qui la raison fait défaut, le fou. C'est aussi celui qui, par souci d'individualisme, se situe en marge de la société. L'idiotie Dada relève d'un projet intellectuel et permet aux artistes et aux poètes de prendre leur distance à l'égard de la figure prophétique – voire héroïque – de l'artiste moderne. Ils deviennent des anti-héros.

Au Cabaret Voltaire, toute structure autoritaire est dissoute dans la convivialité. Cet esprit se perpétuera dans les différentes tendances de Dada, et amènera Huelsenbeck (2005: 166) à déclarer: "Dada n'est ni une politique ni un mouvement artistique, il ne vote ni pour les idées humanitaires ni pour la barbarie – il 'tient la guerre et la paix dans sa toge mais il se décide pour le Cherry Brandy Flip' ". Huelsenbeck emploie une métaphore qui évoque les dîners mondains et qui n'est pas sans rappeler le projet de fonder une *Société Voltaire.* Le regroupement d'individus en "Société" participe d'une attitude proche du dandysme.

Cette structure festive anti-autoritaire se rapproche également d'une conception anarchiste. Influencé par les idées de Bakounine dont il est le traducteur, Ball (1993: 344) établit en 1920 un parallèle entre Dada et l'anarchisme: "Politiquement je suis allé jusqu'à l'anarchie, et artistiquement jusqu'au Dadaïsme, qui fut, à vrai dire, ma création ou pour être précis, mon grand éclat de rire". Cependant, l'anarchisme suppose la révolution qui s'inscrit dans la durée, tandis que le Cabaret Voltaire s'apparente à un soulèvement en raison de son caractère éphémère et de son impact somme toute limité sur la société. Dans un siècle sans *terra incognita,* où les frontières sont omniprésentes, les artistes font émerger un espace libre, dans une sorte d'interstice. En ce sens, Huelsenbeck (2005: 165) qualifiera ultérieurement Dada de "phénomène parallèle".

On pourrait inscrire dans l'héritage Dada l'œuvre de Maurizio Cattelan qui se caractérise par son "idiotie". Cattelan et le commissaire d'exposition Jens Hoffmann organisent, en novembre 1999, la *6ᵉ Biennale des Caraïbes,* intitulée "Blown Away". Dix artistes, parmi les plus en vogue du moment, sont invités à participer à cette biennale qui consiste à prendre une semaine de vacances (du 10 au 17 novembre 1999) sur l'île St. Kitts aux Caraïbes.[2] Cattelan et Hoffmann préparent un projet curatorial, avec à l'appui communiqués de presse et encarts publicitaires qu'ils publient dans *Artforum, Frieze* et *Flash Art*: encarts publicitaires qui ne sont d'ailleurs pas sans rappeler ceux dont usent les agences de voyage. Comme pour n'importe quelle biennale, les critiques d'art affiliés à ces magazines sont conviés sur l'île. En somme, la *6ᵉ Biennale des Caraïbes* est présentée comme "un événement international majeur de l'art contemporain ouvert au public" (Cattelan 2001: n.p.).

La procédure suivie par Cattelan et Hoffmann ne manque pas d'évoquer celle suivie par Hugo Ball pour lancer le Cabaret Voltaire. Cette mise en perspective nous permet de mieux saisir les intentions de Ball. On peut penser que ce dernier, à l'instar de Cattelan, a emprunté les modes d'apparitions médiatiques de l'époque afin de les détourner. L'annonce de Ball, qui présentait le Cabaret comme "un centre de divertissement artistique", pourrait alors acquérir une dimension subversive insoupçonnée au premier abord.

Maurizio Cattelan entend parodier les biennales d'art contemporain et par extension offrir une critique du monde institutionnel de l'art, auquel il participe par ailleurs. Sa stratégie d'utiliser les mêmes outils de communication que les institutions incriminées lui donne la possibilité de subvertir de l'intérieur la société médiatique occidentale, vue par l'artiste comme une dictature qui impose un seul et unique modèle social, idéologique et artistique. L'effacement des frontières – tant désiré par les artistes Dada – a finalement pris une dimension tragique à travers la globalisation. Dans cette conjoncture, l'île apparaît une fois de plus comme le lieu d'un refuge et d'un espace de liberté créatrice. Cette liberté créatrice prend forme dans la posture idiote adoptée par les artistes. Ils disparaissent dans une sorte de rituel pour devenir des vacanciers parmi tant d'autres. L'île devient alors un miroir déformant de la société consommatrice de biens culturels sous toutes ses formes, qu'il s'agisse d'art ou de tourisme.

De la même manière qu'au Cabaret Voltaire, la tactique de la disparition cohabite avec celle de la célébration. Celle-ci réside dans le choix des artistes de renom, ainsi que dans la publication d'un catalogue d'exposition en 2001. Cattelan reprend l'idée du catalogue, objet fétiche de célébration du monde institutionnel de l'art, qu'il transforme en un album-photo de vacances. Des images des artistes à la plage, sous les palmiers, et d'autochtones sont entrecoupées de textes liés à leur réflexion sur la société. Cattelan a voulu son utopie insulaire conviviale, à l'instar des dîners mondains du 18ᵉ siècle auxquels il compare leurs soirées.

La biennale semble par ailleurs s'inscrire dans une tradition de la piraterie. Avec la découverte des Amériques, la piraterie, à l'œuvre depuis le début du 15e siècle, investit les Petites Antilles. Celles-ci deviennent au 17e et au 18e siècle le terrain d'enjeux économiques où s'affrontent deux sortes de pirateries: d'une part la piraterie dite "sauvage", composée de marins, de fugitifs et d'anciens esclaves et qui n'obéit à aucune autorité d'État, et, d'autre part, la piraterie soutenue par les Etats, aussi appelée la flibusterie. La flibusterie, également composée de marginaux, s'insère dans un processus légal.

La piraterie et davantage encore la flibusterie obéissent à une logique de conquêtes de territoires et de pillages. Philippe Jacquin (1992: 119) y voit la naissance d'une "économie-monde" dont le lieu symbolique n'est autre que l'île St. Kitts, dite aussi île St. Christophe. Elle est la première île des Petites Antilles à être officiellement colonisée en 1626. Et c'est précisément cette île que Maurizio Cattelan choisit comme terrain d'expérimentation d'une piraterie doublée d'une flibusterie. Cattelan, Hoffmann et les dix artistes invités se positionnent simultanément à l'intérieur et à l'extérieur d'une économie monde qui sévit à l'aube du 21e siècle et que Cattelan nomme la "nouvelle économie" (Cattelan 2001: n.p.). Cette nouvelle économie repose, selon l'artiste, sur une guerre médiatique entre les pays occidentaux qui semble remplacer le conflit armé.

Le Cabaret Voltaire et la *6e Biennale des Caraïbes* s'imposent comme des contre-cultures – des alternances – susceptibles d'échapper à leur époque. Deux époques plongées dans une guerre qui vide de leur sens tout discours langagier et artistique. Les artistes du Cabaret, à l'instar de Cattelan, se défendent de toute tentative "mélioriste" liée au projet moderniste. Leur individualisme se révèle par ailleurs non conforme avec l'utopie moderne qui repose sur un idéal de construction collective. Dans cette verve, Huelsenbeck parodie le *Manifeste du parti communiste* lors d'une allocution prononcée au Cabaret Voltaire au printemps 1916:

> Nobles et respectés citoyens de Zurich, étudiants, artisans, ouvriers, vagabonds, errants sans but de tous les pays, unissez-vous ! [...] Nous voulons changer le monde avec rien, nous voulons changer la poésie et la peinture avec rien. Nous sommes ici sans intention, nous n'avons pas le moins du monde l'intention de vous divertir ou de vous amuser. (Richard 1998: 74)

Contrairement à la 6e biennale qui repose sur un souci de démonstration, les événements du Cabaret sont de l'ordre de l'improvisation, animés par une urgence de guerre. Mais qu'elle soit improvisée ou mûrement réfléchie, la création d'un espace interstitiel répond à une nécessité. Ce processus se voit réactivé chaque fois que le besoin s'en fait sentir. Comme le prédit Huelsenbeck (2005: 170) en 1920 (dans une formule partiellement reprise à Nietzsche): "Dada ne meurt pas de Dada. Son rire a de l'avenir".

Notes

[1] La deuxième altérité de l'utopie est "l'altercation" ou contestation; "l'alternative", qui en est la troisième forme, réside dans la prise du pouvoir (Desroche 1978: 25–6).

[2] Vanessa Beecroft, Olafur Eliasson, Douglas Gordon, Mariko Mori, Chris Ofili, Gabriel Orozco, Elizabeth Peyton, Pipilotti Rist, Tobias Rehberger, Rirkrit Tiravanija.

Bibliographie

Arp, Jean. 2005. *Jours effeuillés: poèmes, essais, souvenirs, 1920–1965*. Paris: Gallimard.

Ball, Hugo. 1993. *La Fuite hors du temps: journal 1913–1921* [1927] (tr. S. Wolf). Monaco: Editions du Rocher.

Ball, Hugo. 2005. *Tenderenda le fantasque* [1967] (tr. P. Gallissaires). Paris: Vagabonde.

Béhar, Henri. 1967. *Étude sur le théâtre Dada et surréaliste*. Paris: Gallimard (Collection Les Essais).

Bey, Hakim. 1997. *TAZ. Zone autonome temporaire* (tr. C. Tréguier). Paris: L'Eclat.

Cattelan, Maurizio. 2001. *6th Caribbean Biennial. A Project by Maurizio Cattelan*. Dijon: Les presses du réel (n.p.).

Courtine, Jean-Jacques. 1988. "Les Silences de la voix: histoire et structure des glossolalies" in *Langages* 91: 7–25.

Desroche, Henri. 1978. "Les cavalcades de l'utopie" in *Magazine littéraire* 139: 20-7.

Dickerman, Leah. 2005. "Zurich" in L. Le Bon (ed.). *Dada*. Paris: Editions du Centre Pompidou: 986–1014.

Huelsenbeck. Richard. 2005. *Almanach Dada* (tr. S. Wolf). Dijon: Les presses du réel.

Jacquin, Philippe. 1992. "L'Age d'or de la grande piraterie" in G. A. Jaeger (ed.). *Vues sur la piraterie*. Paris: Tallandier (Collection Approches).

Janco, Marcel. 2005. "Dada créateur" [1957] in M. Dachy (ed.). *Archives Dada – chronique*. Paris: Hazan.

Lista, Giovanni. 2005. *Dada libertin et libertaire*. Paris: L'Insolite.

Richard, Lionel. 1998. *D'une apocalypse à l'autre*. Paris: Somogy.

Richter, Hans. 1965. *Dada, Art et anti-art*. Bruxelles: Editions de la Connaissance.

Yaguello, Marina. 1984. *Les Fous du langage: des langues imaginaires et de leurs inventeurs*. Paris: Seuil.

Chapter 9

Dada et la fonction écologique de l'art (à partir de *Fountain* de Duchamp)

Patrick Suter

Une œuvre prophétique

Les pages qui suivent partiront d'un lieu commun, c'est-à-dire de l'œuvre Dada sans doute la plus célèbre,[1] pour rejoindre notre lieu commun à tous: l'espace où nous vivons avec les plantes et les animaux, que "l'homme […] sale [...] tue", comme l'écrivait Tzara dans la "Note 2 sur l'art" (1917) consacrée à Arp (*Dada Zurich Paris* 1981: 118).

Tout le monde a en tête l'urinoir de Duchamp, l'emblème même de l'œuvre scandaleuse du 20e siècle. Les raisons qui président à ce sentiment de scandale sont évidentes. Il s'agit là d'une "non œuvre", et ceci non parce qu'elle n'a en fait été vue de personne au Salon des Indépendants où elle eût dû être exposée, mais parce qu'elle n'émane apparemment du *travail* d'aucun artiste. De même, elle semble ne relever que d'une pure décision de son "auteur" de considérer arbitrairement un objet comme de "l'art" – d'où l'impression que l'art est fait avec n'importe quoi, et qu'une telle œuvre, c'est le comble du "n'importe quoi", du "je-m'en-foutisme", de la "merde". Et ce dernier jugement est d'autant plus probable que cette pissotière constitue un objet évidemment recevable pour dégoûtant, associé aux lieux sales et malodorants.

On sait d'ailleurs que cet horizon d'attente ne fut pas démenti, puisque cette œuvre, signée R. Mutt, fut refusée par les artistes prétendument les plus libres, c'est-à-dire par le comité de la Société des Indépendants de New York. Comme le rappelait Louise Norton (1917: 5) en prenant la défense de l'urinoir (se muant alors selon toute vraisemblance en porte-parole sinon en prête-nom de Duchamp), c'est bien pour des raisons de cet ordre qu'il fut écarté: "Some contended it was immoral, vulgar [...] Others, it was plagiarism, a plain piece of plumbing".

De cette œuvre, souvent commentée, retenons les éléments suivants. Elle interroge évidemment l'essence de l'art, Norton (1917: 6) posant d'ailleurs explicitement la question: "What is ART?" Elle est provocante, dans la mesure où elle affirme que le seul critère permettant de définir comme telle une œuvre d'art correspond au "choix" de l'artiste: "He CHOSE", écrit encore Norton. Et elle tend à abolir les frontières entre objets esthétiques et non esthétiques, n'importe quel élément du monde pouvant se transformer en œuvre d'art (roue de bicyclette, porte-bouteille, pelle à neige, tout comme tel ou tel représentant des lieux d'aisance, soit les lieux peut-être les plus éloignés symboliquement des "salons", fussent-ils "artistiques" ou "indépendants"). Apparemment, donc, cette œuvre avait tout pour choquer, sa réception éventuelle comme œuvre d'art étant d'emblée compromise par son aspect dégoûtant et repoussant.

Et pourtant, l'on peut se demander si ce dégoût du public n'est pas lui-même dégoûtant. L'œuvre s'intitule *Fountain* [Fontaine]. Mais son titre se situe à l'opposé exact de son usage habituel, puisqu'une pissotière ne produit que des eaux usées et, plus précisément, scandaleusement usées. En effet, l'eau des WC n'est généralement pas retraitée; et si ce n'était pas le cas en 1917, actuellement encore, d'après Arno Rosemarin, les eaux d'une ville comme Milan ne sont pas assainies, pas plus que les deux tiers de celles de Londres.[2] De plus, l'épuration des eaux usées est fort dispendieuse en énergie, alors que, contrairement à une croyance largement répandue, elle ne produit pas d'eau potable (d'où l'insistance des environnementalistes – dans le cadre des programmes actuels des organisations internationales visant à généraliser partout sur la planète l'installation de toilettes – à réclamer que soient installées des toilettes sèches à compost, qui ont pour avantage d'être neutres sur le plan environnemental).

Or n'y a-t-il pas quelque beauté, par opposition, à imaginer un urinoir qui serait vraiment fontaine? Qui permettrait vraiment de produire une eau propre à la consommation et aux ablutions? Qui sauverait les matières rejetées en permettant qu'elles retournent à l'humus, ce dernier laissant à son tour la place aux sources d'eau pure? Et qui prendrait le contre-pied d'une civilisation acceptant, sous prétexte de préserver localement une hygiène, de compromettre la possibilité même d'habiter la terre en en salissant l'eau, c'est-à-dire le bien commun le plus précieux ?

Ainsi est-il possible de lire dans ce titre, *Fountain*, quelque chose comme la nostalgie d'un monde nouveau,[3] ou plus précisément (car la nostalgie n'est guère Dada, même si elle concerne le futur), comme la sommation exaspérée que s'accomplisse un retournement, qui contredirait l'impression de dégoût qui ressort de l'urinoir. Et peut-être est-ce d'ailleurs en ceci que cette œuvre est le plus précisément Dada, en ce sens qu'au-delà de sa provocation, elle ouvre la voie à la reconstruction de la civilisation sur des bases inédites, en permettant aux matériaux humbles de trouver de nouvelles fonctions.[4] Effectivement, en présentant une eau nouvelle,[5] la "fontaine" contribue à défaire une civilisation caractérisée par ce que Schwitters nommait la "misère érotique", dont la pissotière est un parfait emblème (dans la mesure où elle accueille la solitude masculine, tout en donnant à voir selon Norton (1917: 6) les "legs of the ladies by Cezanne" – son "exhibition", aux sens à la fois anglais et français du terme, constituant par conséquent le tabou suprême).

L'œuvre Dada et son environnement

Au-delà de son titre presque prophétique (selon l'interprétation que je viens de proposer), la "Fontaine-urinoir" touche encore à quatre niveaux au moins à la problématique de l'environnement.

Elle met tout d'abord en évidence la continuité susceptible de relier l'œuvre d'art et son milieu, dans la mesure où il suffit de quelques transformations minimes (le titre et la signature) pour qu'un objet du monde quotidien se transforme dans le monde du musée en œuvre d'art.

A l'inverse, elle donne à saisir que la réception d'un objet peut varier radicalement selon son environnement. Car si, comme le rappelle Norton, la perception du même urinoir dans la vitrine d'un plombier ne pose aucun problème,[6] sa présence dans le musée, qui le transforme en objet esthétique, constitue un scandale.

Dans cette perspective, elle rend manifeste le fossé existant entre l'idée de l'art en 1917, et l'art réel américain, qui, selon Norton encore, a apporté des créations fondamentales surtout en matière de ponts et de plomberie: "The only works of art America has given are her plumbing and her bridges". L' "art" des musées apparaît coupé du monde dans lequel il s'inscrit, "l'écologie de l'art" ne partageant rien avec "l'environnement réel".

Mais, en même temps, cette séparation est ici justement remise en cause. En effet, si des marques spécifiques d'une œuvre d'art sont inscrites dans cette œuvre (titre et signature, encore une fois), elles peuvent sembler gratuites, l'artiste ne signant pas apparemment une "création" personnelle, et le titre paraissant ironique. Et plutôt que d'établir clairement une frontière entre le monde de l'art et l'univers des latrines d'où provient l'urinoir, ces marques tendent à rendre une telle frontière ambiguë.

Or, en élargissant la perspective, on s'apercevra que cette continuité entre l'environnement et l'œuvre d'art, qu'interroge exemplairement *Fountain* de Duchamp, n'est nullement isolée dans le mouvement Dada, dont c'est sans doute l'une des caractéristiques les plus importantes. Parmi de nombreux exemples possibles, je me contenterai ici d'une brève remarque sur le type d'exposition organisée par les Dadas, et de quelques notes sur Schwitters – dont l'œuvre constitue peut-être, au sein de Dada, celle dans laquelle la relation entre art et environnement est la plus importante, et dont la pratique résume assez bien celle de l'ensemble du mouvement en la matière.

Foires et urinoirs

A l'exposition "Dada Vorfrühling", organisée en mai 1920 à la brasserie Winter à Cologne, les spectateurs devaient passer par les pissotières pour accéder à l'exposition – la visite commençant donc par celle des urinoirs, qui constituaient là aussi des objets présentés, et les premiers. Or cette exposition, où les œuvres, "très rapprochées les unes des autres […] donnent une impression de chaos, en écho à la réalité urbaine contemporaine", a influé sur "l'agencement révolutionnaire de la Foire" internationale Dada de Berlin de l'été 1920. A la Dada Messe de Berlin, justement, plusieurs installations étaient composées d'éléments empruntés au monde quotidien, telle l'œuvre anonyme intitulée *Das grosse Plasto-Dio, Dada-Drama,* constituée entre autres de journaux et d'assiettes, ainsi que d'appareils divers (Le Bon 2005: 322). Les expositions Dada ne présentaient donc pas de frontière nette entre les œuvres et le monde d'où provenaient leurs éléments. Mais surtout, les lieux de la "brasserie" ou de la "foire" étaient choisis par opposition au musée, que les œuvres devaient quitter pour entrer dans un autre environnement, ce dernier contribuant à déterminer de nouveaux regards esthétiques. L'exposition Dada tendait ainsi à modifier l'environnement de l'art, pour présenter des objets empruntés à la vie, et pour rejoindre en fin de compte la cité qui les a produits. C'est dans cette perspective qu'il s'agit de comprendre toute l'importance des slogans donnés à lire dans telle ou telle œuvre ("Dada ist politisch"). L'art Dada s'affiche comme ayant un rôle politique, et l'on verra que, plus précisément, il s'agit là d'un rôle écologique. Pour autant, c'est sans nullement trahir le langage de l'art que s'exercera ce rôle, l'art n'étant ici asservi à aucune cause qui lui serait extérieure. L'exemple de Schwitters en témoignera.

Merz

Dès le tournant des années 1918–19, Schwitters s'est mis à confectionner des collages à partir de rebuts trouvés dans la rue, recueillis, puis assemblés, collés, parfois peints, et disposés de manières diverses. Souvent, les collages ont été réalisés selon des échos assez aisément perceptibles, les couleurs et les formes se répondant comme des rimes plastiques, ainsi qu'il en va dans *Plume – Merz 410 Irgendsowas,* où les différents rouges, bruns et noirs sont disposés selon une organisation à la fois symétrique et circulaire. Il arrivait en effet fréquemment que Schwitters rajoutât de la couleur aux éléments collés pour faciliter des échos entre les différents fragments assemblés. Aussi, bien que recueillis dans l'environnement, ces derniers s'en retrouvaient désormais "ab-straits" – comme l'art "merz" échappait en général au "Kommerz" (Schmalenbach 1984: 95–6) – et étaient réorganisés selon les moyens de la peinture abstraite, c'est-à-dire comme des compositions (Dachy 1989: 47). Et sans doute reconnaît-on assez aisément dans ces collages une première fonction écologique de l'œuvre d'art Dada – fût-elle "merz" – , une telle œuvre constituant le lieu de retraitement d'objets de rebut, qui retrouvent une nouvelle fonction dans l'œuvre abstraite, les détritus étant recyclés de la meilleure façon et revalorisés par le jeu de leurs échos réciproques. Dans ce travail consistant à former des images à partir de détritus – "Man kann auch mit Müllabfällen schreien" [On peut aussi crier avec des ordures], écrivait Schwitters en 1930 (Schmalenbach 1984: 99) – s'effectue la "rédemption de ce monde obscur, de cette nature empestée" que Schwitters "implorait avec ferveur", comme le dira plus tard Arp (Bailly 1993: 34). Chez Schwitters, qui n'a cessé durant toute sa vie de recueillir des objets de rebut, puis de les réorganiser sur le tableau, l'artiste se fait recycleur, tout déchet pouvant retrouver une place en des sortes de "prodigieuses icônes".

Cependant, il n'est pas sûr que le geste de Schwitters soit toujours aussi aisé à interpréter. Certaines de ses œuvres constituent de simples présentations d'éléments qui pourraient presque se retrouver tels quels dans la nature, comme cette œuvre sans titre de 1923, qu'il serait aisé de prendre pour une épave. Et il en va de même de ce "fil sur fond rose", reproduit ici en noir-blanc; ou encore – et plus exemplairement – de cette œuvre portant le titre *For Ernst, 16. 1. 43, Dada-Dady*, qui pourrait être empruntée à bien des blocs issus par exemple de chantiers de construction. En effet, on a presque affaire ici à des ready-made d'environnement, sans aucun ajout ni aucune transformation – comme plus tard les tableaux de Daniel Spoerri, par exemple, "prendront au piège" des fins de repas et les transformeront en œuvres d'art, ne modifiant la scène ainsi capturée qu'en en fixant les différents éléments au moyen de colle. On peut donc former l'hypothèse qu'ici, comme chez Duchamp, n'importe quel élément du monde peut devenir œuvre d'art.

Enfin, on découvre également chez Schwitters un mouvement qui consiste à étendre l'art au-delà des limites qui lui sont assignées dans l'univers contemporain du musée. Si, pour Tzara (1975: 367), DADA est "LA VIE", il s'agit chez Schwitters d'étendre merz à l'ensemble de l'environnement. D'où la décision trois fois recommencée, malgré les déménagements successifs forcés, d'élaborer le *Merzbau*, l'habitat humain se trouvant transformé, et recueillant lui-même les rêves et les matières refoulées du monde, et les éléments de la "misère érotique", qu'illustre sa fameuse colonne. Dans cette perspective, Schwitters partage avec des artistes comme Sophie Taeuber-Arp le souci de transformer les objets quotidiens, de ne pas établir de frontières entre les Beaux Arts et l'art décoratif, l'ensemble des objets familiers pouvant être transformés en objets Dada, l'art merz s'étendant par exemple jusqu'à la confection de boîtes en marquetterie (Le Bon 2005: 892).

Autonomie de l'œuvre

Ainsi l'art a-t-il tendance pour Dada à s'étendre à l'ensemble de l'environnement. Et c'est bien là ce que retient par exemple Ben de l'aventure Dada: "Tout est art, et tout le monde peut le faire", affirme Ben, et il ajoute que "[l]'art total est de prendre conscience que tout ce qui se passe, s'est passé ou se passera dans le temps et dans l'espace est art total" (Béhar et Dufour 2005: 618).

Pour autant, cette contiguïté entre l'art et l'environnement n'a rien d'évident dans le cas de Dada. C'est qu'il était aisé de percevoir l'œuvre Dada comme horrible, son influence sur l'environnement pouvant de ce fait passer pour dangereuse. Mais c'est surtout qu'elle semble échapper complètement au monde dont elle provient.

Tzara, on s'en souvient, réclamait des "œuvres fortes, droites, précises et à jamais incomprises" (Tzara 1975: 365). Mais comment y parvenir ? Sans doute le plus simple consistait-il à prendre comme œuvres des "non-œuvres" soit des éléments non élaborés par l'artiste, en en variant l'ordre le cas échéant, et éventuellement en en augmentant le désordre. Ainsi en va-t-il dans la célèbre recette "Pour faire un poème Dada" (où un "poème" est "composé" à partir des mots d'un article de journal tirés au hasard), ou lorsque les composantes de l'œuvre sont empruntés directement à l'environnement, qu'elles soient choisies comme matériaux de rebut – papiers collés assemblés selon un apparent désordre, par exemple dans "P" de Raoul Hausmann (Le Bon 2005: 139) – ou comme appareils choquants (la pissotière de Duchamp), ou encore comme objets désespérément ordinaire (la pelle à neige du même Duchamp, entre autres). Par là même, les Dadas s'assuraient de l'incompréhension de leurs œuvres; et, en se présentant comme pur morceau d'environnement (fût-il réaménagé), et comme environnement repoussant, l'œuvre échappait à tout discours consensuel à son égard.

Or cette pratique avait alors une conséquence majeure et inattendue. Depuis des siècles, en Europe occidentale, l'œuvre d'art s'était développée en revendiquant de plus en plus son autonomie. La Renaissance italienne avait marqué à cet égard une étape importante, et, plus tard, dans le domaine littéraire, le romantisme théorique d'Iéna avait correspondu à ce moment où étaient remises en cause les anciennes organisations rhétoriques et artistiques relevant de l'âge des Belles Lettres, pour laisser la place à l'invention d'un genre en perpétuel devenir, la littérature ayant à se découvrir elle-même, c'est-à-dire indépendamment de tout ordre qui lui eût été extérieur (Lacoue-Labarthe et Nancy 1978: 277–80). Or voici qu'avec une œuvre comme *Fountain*, l'œuvre d'art atteint le comble de son autonomie, puisqu'elle s'affirme "faite, étant",[7] indépendamment de toute allégeance à quelque code que ce soit, fût-il d'ordre esthétique ou moral. Elle se voit donc parfaitement abstraite de son environnement premier, une solution de continuité apparaissant entre ce qu'elle est devenue et son existence antérieure.

Autonomie et environnement

Cet apparent paradoxe peut cependant être dépassé. Reprenons cet acte fondamental de Dada qui consiste à présenter comme art des éléments prélevés directement dans l'environnement, fussent-ils retravaillés par la suite. Ces éléments étant empruntés, leur organisation relève de leur environnement premier, et non de leur environnement second. "L'organisation" de la pelle à neige, par exemple, ne découle pas d'un travail artistique, et encore moins de techniques de compositions artistiques, ni d'aucune disposition propre à un genre littéraire ou artistique qui en constituerait une "structure à priori".[8]

Tout à la fois, en décrétant que tel élément du monde est œuvre d'art, et éventuellement, comme dans le cas de *Fountain*, en lui ajoutant des éléments propres à l'œuvre d'art depuis la Renaissance (titre, signature, etc.), Dada permet de contempler cet élément emprunté à l'environnement *comme on contemple une œuvre d'art.*

Mais de quel regard s'agit-il alors ? Selon Mallarmé, ce qui fait le livre, c'est le "pli", qui permet d'établir des relations entre les différents éléments qu'il contient, et d'y repérer ce qu'il nomme "constellation" ou "scintillations" (Mallarmé 1988: 387, 37–8). Or on peut en dire autant de l'œuvre d'art, dont la compréhension nécessite que soient tissées des relations entre ses différentes parties. Et alors, ce que permet l'installation Dada, l'œuvre-morceau d'environnement, à travers un retour sur l'œuvre, c'est précisément un retour sur ce morceau d'environnement. Dans le travail de l' "activité de l'esprit" (qui désignera à partir de 1930 l'authentique travail de la poésie selon Tzara (1975: 643), mais qui correspond également à l'attitude nécessaire à saisir le "petit Bouddha" que constitue selon Louise Norton l'urinoir de Duchamp, lequel n'est déchiffrable qu'à la manière des koans japonais), tout objet qui passe pour trivial se mue en objet complexe et hautement signifiant. Alors les pissotières, transformées en fontaines, apparaissent proprement renversantes – et sans doute n'est-ce pas pour rien que l'urinoir de Duchamp, dans la photo d'Alfred Stieglitz de 1917, est précisément disposé à l'envers.

Et voici comment, de la manière la plus forte, l'œuvre d'art Dada se retrouve dotée d'une fonction écologique. En décrétant tel objet de l'environnement "œuvre d'art", ou en abstrayant tels éléments de l'environnement pour les reconfigurer autrement dans un dispositif soumis à contemplation esthétique, le geste Dada permet d'isoler ces éléments du monde comme environnements autonomes, ou dans un nouvel environnement. Comme dans toute œuvre d'art, "l'activité de l'esprit" permet alors d'en relier les différents éléments, de relier les différentes parties du "système" de l'œuvre. Mais comme les marques d'origines de ces œuvres d'art ou de leurs constituants ne sont nullement effacées (les tickets et autres fragments de tissus des collages de Schwitters sont reconnaissables pour tels, et un urinoir existe évidemment ailleurs que dans un musée), l'œuvre, repliée sur elle-même en tant qu'œuvre, permet de prendre de la distance par rapport à l'organisation qui est la sienne dans son milieu d'origine — et qu'elle continue parfois de porter, mais dotée de nouvelles marques (titre, signature). Plus précisément, l'œuvre d'art Dada, en tant que nouveau milieu, permet de mettre en parallèle l'organisation de ce milieu ab-strait avec celle du milieu de provenance de l'œuvre. Ouverte à la contemplation, elle constitue un petit monde à déchiffrer, dont la compréhension permet d'envisager de manière nouvelle l'environnement dont elle provient – soit le "grand monde" où nous habitons. En particulier, dans le cas de la fontaine de Duchamp, la rédemption des eaux sales dans la fontaine permet de prendre conscience de la rupture des cycles écologiques qui caractérisent la civilisation moderne. Autonome par rapport au monde dont elle provient, mais tout en utilisant les éléments mêmes de ce monde d'origine, l'œuvre comme système abstrait permet de prendre conscience du (mé-)fonctionnement des écosystèmes du monde moderne. Et il n'est guère étonnant que, plus tard, dans la lignée de Dada, de très nombreux artistes se soient mis à créer ce qu'ils nommeront des "environnements" – qui poursuivront à leur manière cette interrogation de l'écologie du monde. Dans le sillage de Dada, l'œuvre se présentera désormais comme un petit environnement, qui permettra de questionner l'environnement dans son ensemble; et la visite d'un musée d'art contemporain devient nettement moins ardue dès lors que le spectateur prend conscience de cette fonction écologique de l'œuvre d'art.

L'œuvre laide

L'œuvre d'art comme microcosme ? Mais qu'y a-t-il là de nouveau? N'est-ce pas une idée ancienne, que l'on retrouve aussi bien à la Renaissance que dans le romantisme? Sans doute. Cependant, un passage d'un article de John Heartfield et Georges Grosz, intitulé "La Canaille artistique" (1919), permettra de saisir ce que la relation entre l'œuvre d'art et le grand monde a ici d'absolument singulier:

> En dépit de toute cette honte, ils ont peint le monde sous un jour apaisant. La beauté de la nature, la forêt avec les gazouillis des oiseaux et le soleil couchant: montre-t-on que la forêt est dans les mains poisseuses du profiteur qui la déclare propriété privée sur des kilomètres et des kilomètres, qui en dispose à sa guise, qui la déboise pour couvrir des dépenses somptueuses mais qui l'enclôt de barbelés pour empêcher ceux qui meurent de froid de venir ramasser des brindilles? (Béhar et Dufour 2005: 223)

Or, on le voit, par rapport à celle de la "canaille artistique", la stratégie Dada est toute différente. Dénonçant la main mise de l'homme sur la nature, l'œuvre d'art Dada montrera l'environnement en tant qu'il est laid, ou maltraité – pour faire apparaître cette laideur, mais aussi pour que, dans le lieu abstrait où la voici convoquée, soient réinventées les relations des éléments qui la constituent. Utilisant les déchets du "Kommerz", "merz" les fait entrer dans une nouvelle économie, que l'on pourrait appeler de rédemption, préfiguratrice d'un temps dans lequel économie et écologie ne pourront plus être "pensés contradictoirement". C'est en convoquant l'environnement défiguré dans l'œuvre d'art, et de la manière la plus brute possible, que Dada fait apparaître une dichotomie scandaleuse entre l'écologie des signes (le monde des musées, de l'art, des salons, de l'échange des bons mots, etc.), et l'écologie réelle, de plus en plus malmenée.

Notes

[1] Particulièrement en ces temps où l'une de ses "copies" vient d'être attaquée à coups de marteau par l'artiste français Pierre Pinoncelli à l'exposition Dada de

    Beaubourg (2005–6), l'affaire ayant fait grand bruit jusque dans les émissions télévisées destinées au grand public.

2   "Des toilettes sèches pour économiser l'eau et fabriquer du compost" (*La Revue durable* 2006: 26). "169 des 526 villes européennes de plus de 150 000 habitants n'ont pas de système d'assainissement satisfaisant et 25 n'ont même pas de système de traitement", lit-on encore sous la plume des rédacteurs de la revue (14).

3   Cette nostalgie a d'ailleurs trouvé des réponses ici ou là. Par exemple, toutes les eaux de la maison écologique de François et Olivier Guisan à La Tour-de-Peilz, récupérées du toit, puis utilisées dans la maison, sont ensuite recyclées dans trois filtres successifs (bacs de décantation, filtre de sable, étang naturel), pour être ramenées au haut du jardin à l'aide d'une pompe à énergie solaire, et retomber en fontaines successives qui les réoxygènent. Les urines ne sont pas récupérées, et les eaux ainsi retraitées ne sont pas bues – mais elles le pourraient (des analyses ont été effectuées). Voir Guisan (2006).

4   Arp (1966: 309) insistera sur l'humilité que cherchait Dada: "Les objets Dada sont formés d'éléments trouvés ou fabriqués, simples ou hétéroclites. Les Chinois, il y a plusieurs milliers d'années, Duchamp, Picabia aux Etats-Unis, Schwitters et moi-même pendant la guerre de 1919, étaient les premiers à inventer et répandre ces jeux de sagesse et de clairvoyance qui devaient guérir les êtres humains de la folie furieuse du génie et les ramener plus modestement à leur place équitable dans la nature".

5   Certes, cette "eau" est absente de *Fountain*; mais elle est évidemment suggérée dans le titre, qui constitue ici le véritable élément prophétique.

6   "Mr. Mutt's fountain is not immoral, that is absurd, no more than a bath tub is immoral. It is a fixture that you see every day in plumbers' show windows" (Norton 1917: 5).

7   Selon l'expression de Mallarmé (2003: 217), qu'il emploie au masculin à propos du livre dans "L'action restreinte".

8   C'est par cette expression que Christine Montalbetti (1997: 61) définit le "genre", littéraire en l'occurrence (mais cette définition conviendrait aussi au genre pictural).

Bibliographie

Arp, Jean. 1966. *Jours effeuillés. Poèmes, essais, souvenirs*. Paris: Gallimard.

Bailly, Jean-Christophe. 1993. *Kurt Schwitters*. Paris: Hazan.

Béhar, Henri and Catherine Dufour (eds). 2005. *Dada circuit total*. Lausanne: L'Age d'Homme (Dossiers H).

Dachy, Marc. 1989. *Journal du mouvement Dada*. Geneva: Skira.

Dada Zurich Paris 1916–1922. 1981. Paris: Jean-Michel Place.

Guisan, Françoise et Olivier. 2006. *Notre maison écologique: rêver, réaliser, partager*. Lausanne: Publi-Libris.

Lacoue-Labarthe, Philippe et Jean-Luc Nancy. 1978. *L'Absolu littéraire. Théorie de la littérature dans le romantisme allemand*. Paris: Seuil (Collection Poétique).

Le Bon, Laurent (ed.). 2005. *Dada*. Paris: Éditions du Centre Pompidou.

Mallarmé, Stéphane. 1998 et 2003. *Œuvres complètes I* et *II*. (ed. B. Marchal). Paris: Gallimard (Collection la Pléiade).

Montalbetti, Christine. 1997. *Le Voyage, le monde et la bibliothèque*. Paris: PUF (Collection Ecriture).

Norton, Louise. 1917. "The Richard Mutt Case" in *The Blind Man* 2: 5–6.

La Revue durable. 2006. 19, février-mars. Fribourg, CERIN Sàrl. Numéro comprenant un dossier intitulé "Des technologies appropriées pour la construction, l'eau et la santé": 13–55.

Schmalenbach, Werner. 1984. *Kurt Schwitters*. München: Prestel-Verlag.

Tzara, Tristan. 1975. *Œuvres complètes I* (ed. H. Béhar). Paris: Flammarion.

DADA LEGACIES

Chapter 10

Dans le sillage de Dada: Dubuffet, Michaux, Alechinsky et autres "périphériques"

Nathalie Roelens

> Max Loreau oppose avec une grande pertinence subversion et révolution. Révolution, c'est retourner le sablier. Subversion est tout autre chose; c'est le briser, l'éliminer. (Dubuffet 1968: 58)

Les propos qui suivent se situent à la fois dans la périphérie de Dada et dans son après-coup, son *beyond*. L'hypothèse qui les sous-tend se résume au fait que les héritiers de Dada s'attaqueraient surtout au visage comme emblème de la peinture figurative canonique, à ce que Gilles Deleuze qualifie de "machine de visagéité", machine despotique qui impose subjectivité et signification à l'organisme au sommet duquel elle trône. Le visage chez les post-Dadaïstes devient la tête d'un *corps sans organes*, le lieu non plus d'une oralité parlante mais d'une buccalité presque animale, tandis que le corps sans organes devient à son tour triomphe d'une esthétique de l'informe qui s'insurge contre l'anthropomorphisme et contre l'idée thomiste sous-jacente de "conformité" entre l'homme et son Dieu créateur (Didi-Huberman 1995: 40).

L'année clé de l'essor de ces irrévérences ou de ces dissidences semble être 1948, l'immédiat après-guerre, année de la fondation de la Compagnie de l'Art Brut par Dubuffet, du passage à la peinture chez Michaux, de la période vache de Magritte, de la création de CoBrA.

Jean Dubuffet

> A plus d'un qui aura goûté de ces ouvrages si indemnes de tout trivial souci
> d'applaudissement ou de gains, élaborés dans une solitude dramatique et pour le
> seul enchantement de leur auteur, les ouvrages des professionnels réputés de
> l'art culturel apparaîtront ensuite pompeuses – et oiseuses – grimaces. (Dubuffet
> 1967: 515)

La légitimité que donne le mouvement Dada à d'autres mouvements provocateurs se traduit chez Jean Dubuffet par sa découverte de l'ouvrage très largement illustré de Hans Prinzhorn, *Bildnerei der Geisteskranken* de 1922. Ce médecin et historien de l'art avait constitué une importante collection de travaux d'aliénés à des fins de recherche pour le compte de la clinique psychiatrique de l'université de Heidelberg. Une des figures obsédantes des patients semble être les "Kopffüsser", des céphalopodes ou bonshommes sans tronc. Sous le Troisième Reich, dans l'exposition "Entartete Kunst" [Art dégénéré] de 1937, cette collection fut cependant détournée de sa vocation originaire dans le but de calomnier et de montrer le caractère pathologique d'artistes d'avant-garde comme Kandinsky, Nolde, Klee, Kircher, Kokoschka ou Chagall qui, quelques années auparavant, en avaient découvert la valeur artistique (Martin 2005: 11).

Dès les années 1940 Dubuffet était fasciné par tout ce qui relevait d'une créativité à l'état brut, donc à la fois par les dessins d'enfants, qui représentent d'ailleurs souvent des macrocéphales, "un têtard géant, un clown, un gros boudin ou une énorme betterave", comme dira plus tard Henri Michaux (2004: 1331),[1] et par les œuvres d'autodidactes, de malades mentaux, d'adeptes du spiritisme, de détenus ou encore de solitaires et de marginaux, bref par tout ce qui relève de l'exclusion ou de la clandestinité. Il découvre grâce à eux une approche intuitive, non informée, des anatomies protéiformes et surtout la brutalité et l'archaïsme des procédés employés à l'écart de l'art savant, par exemple le plaisir de manipuler diverses substances insolites ou la fascination pour les univers organiques.[2] Pour désigner cette diversité de formes, Dubuffet inventera la notion d'Art Brut: un art "cru", inventif et non éduqué.

Un voyage de prospection en Suisse en 1945, qui le conduit dans plusieurs cliniques psychiatriques, lui vaut d'heureuses trouvailles, ainsi les *Barbus Müller*, des statues sculptées dans des pierres volcaniques, utilisées probablement à l'époque comme bornes délimitant les chemins. Elles tiennent leur nom du célèbre collectionneur suisse, Josef Müller, qui les a acquises au début des années 1940 dans un magasin d'antiquités. Il découvre encore Aloïse Corbaz (1886–1946, Lausanne), amoureuse de l'empereur de Prusse, Pascal-Désir Maisonneuve (1863–1934, Bordeaux) anarchiste qui compose des effigies de souverains et d'hommes politiques, Heinrich Anton Müller (1865–1930, Versailles et Suisse), interné à l'asile psychiatrique de Münsingen près de Berne, Adolf Wölfli (1864–1930, Berne), ce patient psychotique dont les travaux sont conservés grâce au Dr Morgenthaler, qui les avait étudiés dans une monographie publiée en 1921, *Ein Geisteskranker als Künstler.*

En 1946, dans *Prospectus aux amateurs de tout genre*, Dubuffet émet l'hypothèse d'un art praticable spontanément par n'importe qui, un art qui ne nécessiterait ni don ni instruction, qui procéderait de la jubilation et non de l'initiation. Même si Dubuffet a voulu se démarquer des dessins d'enfants "pour prévenir une assimilation de la sauvagerie telle qu'il l'entendait à l'angélisation niaise dont il est question à l'époque" (Thévoz 2005: 64), même si vers 1945, c'est la folie qui se substitue à l'enfance en tant que source vive de l'invention, entre les cures de folie et l'enfance l'alternative n'est pas exclusive. L'enfance n'a rien à voir pour lui avec le mythe de l'innocence perdue, mais avec l'émergence de fonctions plus archaïques, chaotiques, asociales, maniaques, ce que Lyotard (1988) qualifierait d' "inhumain". A en croire Michel Thévoz (2005: 65), "Dubuffet rejoint la conception psychanalytique d'un recouvrement entre la disposition psychique polymorphe de l'enfance, la folie adulte, et la création artistique".

La galerie Drouin, place Vendôme, expose en octobre 1947 les *PORTRAITS/ à ressemblance extraite,/ à ressemblance cuite et confite dans la mémoire,/ à ressemblance éclatée dans la mémoire de Mr JEAN DUBUFFET,/ Peintre.* Dans ces portraits comme incisés en pleine matière, dans une gamme de tons brunâtres et avec le dessin expressif jusqu'à la caricature inspiré de ses découvertes, Dubuffet exalte la ressemblance en la contrariant et en violentant la face humaine. L'inventaire des titres est déjà éloquent de la façon dont il dit en pleine face aux écrivains tutélaires de l'époque que leurs tête (aux drôles de nez, aux dents plantées de travers, aux oreilles dissymétriques) est plus suggestive que leur littérature. Premier délit de faciès lancé au visage de l'écriture: *Léautaud sorcier peau-rouge, Bertelé chat sauvage, Edith Boissonnas démon tibétain, Ponge plâtre meringué, Limbour façon fiente de poulet, Tapié grand-duc, Dhôtel velu aux dents jaunes, Fautrier araignée au front, Fautrier vielle femme, Michaux façon momie, Michaux acteur japonais, Michaux botaniques, Michaux façon momie, Tapié petit théâtre de rides.* Que Dubuffet s'intéresse à la même époque à un dialecte algérien d'El Goléa qu'il transpose phonétiquement pour ensuite écrire des poèmes d'illettré, "Ler dla campane" (1948), "Anvouaiaje par in ninbesil avec de zimaje" (1950), accroît encore la gamme de ses élans rebelles.

En novembre 1947 Dubuffet ouvre, dans le sous-sol de la galerie Drouin, le Foyer de l'Art Brut, fréquenté par quelques initiés. On peut s'étonner de ce paradoxe de l'Art Brut: son lieu de naissance se situe certes dans une cave mais à deux pas de l'hôtel Ritz, place Vendôme, l'un des endroits les plus huppés de Paris. Pour torpiller la culture, on ne peut rêver lieu plus élégant! Le terme Art Brut lui-même porte la contradiction entre un expression visuelle, comme la définit justement Prinzhorn qui privilégie le neutre *Bildnerei*, et le système de l'art avec ses codes, sa valorisation et son histoire.

En 1948, Dubuffet fonde à Paris la Compagnie de l'Art Brut, entouré de quelques amis écrivains comme André Breton, Jean Paulhan et Henri-Pierre Roché. Au fil du temps, l'association s'essouffle pourtant. Elle se dissout en 1951. En 1955 Dubuffet s'installe à Vence où il essaie de se rapprocher du monde naturel (collages, ailes de papillon) et où il entame sa série de *Barbes*, d'*Eléments botaniques* et de *Matériologies*.

Le cycle de *L'Hourloupe,* amorcé en 1962, introduit une nouvelle mutation, cette fois dans le sens de la dématérialisation, utilisant des substances comme le vinyle ou le polystyrène expansé. "Je l'associais, par assonance, à 'hurler', 'hululer', 'loup, 'Riquet à la Houppe', et le titre 'Le Horla' du livre de Maupassant inspiré d'égarement mental".[3] Il passe à un registre tricolore bleu, blanc, rouge cerné de noir qui dessine un entrelacs sans fin.

L'expatriation de sa collection en 1971 vers une francophonie périphérique nous semble le couronnement de son œuvre de "déterritorialisation" contre "l'asphyxiante culture". Depuis son premier voyage helvétique, il considère que ce pays entretient une relation privilégiée avec l'Art Brut. En 1971, la Ville de Lausanne prend en charge la Collection sous la direction de Michel Thévoz. Aujourd'hui, sous l'égide de Lucienne Peiry, la collection est étoffée par des acquisitions d'œuvres du monde entier (Martin 2005: 10).

Henri Michaux

La dette envers Dada est sans doute moins évidente à première vue dans le cas du poète namurois Henri Michaux. Son autoportrait fictif, intitulé *Quelques renseignements sur cinquante-neuf années d'existence*, porte pourtant toute la rancune d'un citoyen indocile, d'un périphérique qui se muera en déserteur:

> 1929
> Mort de son père. Dix jours plus tard, mort de sa mère.
> Voyage en Turquie, Italie, Afrique du Nord...
> Il voyage *contre.*
> Pour expulser de lui sa patrie, ses attaches de toutes sortes et ce qui s'est en lui
> et malgré lui attaché de culture grecque ou romaine ou germanique ou
> d'habitudes belges. (Michaux 1998: cxxxiii)

Raymond Bellour établit lui-même le lien entre cette "expatriation" et la déterritorialisation de Deleuze-Guattari (Michaux 1998: lxv). La proximité entre Michaux et Deleuze est en effet indéniable et on peut même avancer que l'expatriation volontaire a commencé bien avant les voyages imaginaires ou réels. Dès sa prime enfance, Henri Michaux entame un travail de sape existentielle proche de l' "anorexie" deleuzienne: ce sont les mots "inappétence", "résistance", "gréviste", "secret", "retranché", "honteux", "mépris", "dégoût" qui ponctuent ce même autoportrait. Deleuze reconnaîtra dans le refus anorexique un geste politique, une façon de trahir la famille, d'échapper aux normes de la consommation, signe que la provocation n'est pas nécessairement dans l'outrance ou dans l'excentricité mais au contraire ici dans la réserve, dans la dissidence introspective: "L'anorexique est un passionné [...]. Il trahit la faim, parce que la faim le trahit, en l'asservissant à l'organisme; il trahit la famille parce que la famille le trahit en l'asservissant au repas familial et à toute une politique de la famille et de la consommation" (Deleuze et Parnet 1996: 132–3). Or, chacun sait que la culture belge, si elle existe, est une culture de la bonne chère, de la ripaille, de la peau du ventre bien tendue, du *Banquet* (1568) ou du *Pays de Cocagne* (1567) de Bruegel, de "Et ça sent la morue / Jusque dans le cœur des frites / Que leurs grosses mains invitent / A revenir en plus cuit / Puis se lèvent en riant / Dans un bruit de tempête / Referment leur braguette / Et sortent en rotant", que Jacques Brel chante dans *Amsterdam*, ou encore, des tartes à la crème que l'illustre entarteur Noël Godin balance allègrement à la figure des célébrités.

Dans sa *Lettre de Belgique* de 1924 Michaux (1998: 51) s'en prenait déjà à cette goinfrerie proverbiale: "Les étrangers se représentent communément le Belge à table cependant qu'il boit, qu'il mange. [...] Truculent – ripaille – goinfrerie – ventru – mangeaille". Dans un pamphlet encore plus virulent de 1930, intitulé *En Belgique*, digne de *Pauvre Belgique* de Baudelaire, Michaux (1998: 268) renchérira: "N'importe où l'on plonge la main on en tire une betterave, ou des pommes de terre, ou un navet ou un rutabaga; de la bourre d'estomac; pour le bétail et pour toute cette race mangeuse de farineux, autant qu'il se peut et de lourdeurs". Il est clair que son célèbre *Monsieur Plume* ne fera pas le poids. Léger comme une plume, il est ballotté d'une mésaventure à l'autre, transparent, "les uns lui passent dessus sans crier gare, les autres s'essuient tranquillement les mains à son veston" (Michaux 1998: 625). Ceci dit, la minceur ontologique du personnage le rend en quelque sorte invulnérable.

A la trahison du repas familial s'ajoute, vers quinze ans, le rejet des parents, qui se traduit d'abord par l'évasion dans des lectures effrénées, "pour découvrir les siens, épars dans le monde, ses vrais parents" (Michaux 1998: cxxxi), ensuite par une véritable répudiation du père chapelier et puis rentier. Celui-ci ne sera en effet pas épargné par l'œuvre de Michaux. Tantôt extrêmement fuyant – "Il s'effaçait parfois comme une tache" (Michaux 1998: 608) – tantôt roué de coups par son propre fils dans "La séance de sac" (Michaux 1972: 9). La première tête à claques dans l'imaginaire de Michaux est donc la figure du père, celui qu'il appela encore le "macrocéphale", détenteur de valeurs paternalistes, autoritaires, réactionnaires. Et si Plume est plutôt une tête à claques lui aussi, un clown qui se fait marcher dessus, celui-ci peut soudain, dans certains chapitres, se muer en bourreau, en arracheur de têtes et donc en mangeur de chefs (si l'on renoue avec l'étymologie "caput"). Doit-on y voir un meurtre symbolique du père? L'ironie du sort veut cependant que le père meure vraiment en 1930 (la mère mourra 3 semaines plus tard). Ce qui n'empêche pas Michaux de renchérir avec sa "mitrailleuse à gifles", une machine qui sévit surtout au sein de la "vie de famille, comme il fallait s'y attendre":

> Ma colère tout à coup se projeta hors de ma main, comme un gant de vent qui en serait sorti, comme deux, trois, quatre, dix gants, des gants d'effluves qui, spasmodiquement, et terriblement vite se précipitèrent de mes extrémités manuelles, filant vers le but, vers la tête odieuse qu'elles atteignirent sans tarder.

> Ce dégorgement répété de la main était étonnant. Ce n'était vraiment plus une gifle, ni deux. Je suis d'un naturel réservé et ne m'abandonne que pour le précipice de la rage.
> Véritable éjaculation de gifles, éjaculation en cascade et à soubresauts, ma main restant rigoureusement immobile. (Michaux 1972: 18)

En malmenant le visage, Michaux dénonce la "machine abstraite de visagéité", selon le concept de Deleuze et Guattari (1980: 207), qui "surcode" la tête avec un visage, qui visagéifie le corps physique et social, une machine qui épingle, identifie, produit des visages conformes et écarte les déviances. Deleuze et Guattari ont eu le mérite d'étudier le visage comme une production sociale remontant à celui du Christ et traversant toute notre culture occidentale, ce "large visage aux joues blanches, avec le trou noir des yeux". Aussi incitent-ils précisément à échapper au visage, à le défaire, à le libérer du joug des significations et des subjectivations imposées. Echapper au visage – à en croire Deleuze – suppose en effet soustraire les "traits de visagéité" à l'organisation du visage, mais aussi lui ôter tout signe identitaire, le rendre méconnaissable. Notre hypothèse du lien indissoluble entre culture et visage comme cible des post-Dadaïstes se voit donc à nouveau vérifiée ici.

Michaux reproche en effet à ses ancêtres de lui avoir donné une forme, un visage. C'est ce qu'il dénonce dans cette longue invocation intitulée "Visages de jeunes filles" et où il déplore que la beauté se voie si vite altérée par un "nez d'ancêtre alcoolique et goinfre ou malade [qui] se met à grossir bientôt, bientôt, trop tôt, à grandir insidieusement" ou que la malléabilité de ces jeunes visages se voie durcie par la volonté d'être quelqu'un "femme, citoyenne, scout, soldate?" (Michaux 1963: 41–2). Ces visages, à la lisière de l'informe et du formé, annoncent déjà leur enfermement futur, "tel ce visage d'un enfant de riche où l'on discerne déjà la vocation militaire, la nuque saint-cyrienne" (Deleuze et Guattari 1980: 217). Il n'est pas étonnant dans ces conditions que Michaux ait peint surtout des visages informes non marqués, si je puis dire, et se soit intéressé aux dessins d'enfants, et qui désarçonnent "les visages tendus et résolus" (Michaux 2004: 1335) des adultes.

Autre chef d'accusation: le royalisme, la bêtise du pouvoir, autre père putatif: le roi. Aussi le visage du Roi sera-t-il la cible par excellence de la soif d'irrévérence de Michaux.[4] Le peintre surréaliste belge René Magritte a également attenté à la vie du roi dans une toile intitulée *Le Mat*: "Un fou déguisé en évêque assassine le roi châtré dont le sexe, divisé en trois parties, meuble l'avant-scène" (de Heusch 1992: 38). Or le roi s'avère un père plus tenace que le père biologique, il n'est pas du genre à perdre la face:

> Dans ma nuit, j'assiège mon Roi, je me lève progressivement et lui tords le cou.
> Il reprend des forces, je reviens sur lui, et lui tords le cou une fois de plus.
> Je le secoue, et le secoue comme un vieux prunier, et sa couronne tremble sur sa tête.

N'étant pas parvenu à le vaincre par force en l'étranglant, il tente de le rabaisser, de l'humilier, de le détruire par la honte:

> Dans le secret de ma petite chambre, je pète à la figure de mon Roi. Ensuite j'éclate de rire. Il essaie de montrer un front serein, et lavé de toute injure. Mais je lui pète sans discontinuer à la figure, sauf pour me retourner vers lui, et éclater de rire à sa noble face, qui essaie de garder de la majesté.
> [...] Et maintenant je le renverse par terre, et m'assieds sur sa figure. Son auguste figure disparaît; pantalon rude aux taches d'huile, et mon derrière − puisque enfin c'est son nom − se tiennent sans embarras sur cette face faite pour régner.
> [...] Et si je me retourne, sa face imperturbable règne, toujours.
> Je le gifle, je le gifle, je le mouche ensuite par dérision comme un enfant.
> Cependant il est bien évident que c'est lui le Roi, et moi son sujet, son unique sujet. (Michaux 1998: 422–3)

Incapable de tordre définitivement le cou à son noble souverain, Michaux s'en prendra à une autre institution bien belge et royaliste: le cygne, ce pédant volatile qui arbore un grotesque "port de reine, de reine inapprochable" (Michaux 1963: 153) dans les jardins publics. Or "cet idéal d'élévation au cou altier" (Michaux 1963: 154) ne fascine que les conservateurs, les attachés au maintien et au rite du Dimanche. Aussi Michaux rêve-t-il secrètement de souiller cette blancheur puritaine, immaculée.

L'actuel "entarteur" Noël Godin, Belge cela va sans dire, a quant à lui réussi à convertir ce désir d'insoumission en intervention directe, en prenant d'assaut la tête des rois de notre époque: magnats de l'intelligentsia, potentats du marché mondial etc. Son "Manifeste de l'internationale pâtissière", disponible sur Internet, se passe de commentaire:

> L'internationale pâtissière entend assassiner par le ridicule toutes les célébrités mondiales se prenant spectaculairement au sérieux. C'est ainsi que, ces dernières années, en France et en Belgique, ont reçu des tartes à la crème en pleine figure bon nombre d'illustres baudruches: la romancière creuse Marguerite Duras, le cinéaste mystique Jean-Luc Godard au festival de Cannes, le philosophe nombrillesque Bernard-Henri Lévy, cinq fois, le chanteur

crétinisant Patrick Bruel, le présentateur TV faux-cul number one Patrick Poivre
d'Arvor, en plein jogging, [...] les ministres visqueux Philippe Douste-Blazy et
Nicolas Sarkozy, et bien d'autres. Chaque fois, les terroristes pâtissiers se sont
écriés: "Gloup! Gloup! Gloup! Gloup!" et il ont chanté: "Entartons, entartons
les pompeux cornichons!"[5]

Dans son dernier ouvrage éponyme, Noël Godin (2005: 7), tout en
soulignant qu'il agit "sans dieux ni contremaîtres ni ports d'attache
flibustiers", se revendique néanmoins d'une certaine tradition avant-
gardiste:

C'est l'apothéose (ou plus précisément l'acmé, le point culminant éruptivo-
jouissif) d'une tradition séditieuse fort godante. Comme moultes mauvais
esprits, en effet, nous avons été souvent mis en joie par les lettres d'insultes
assassines que les Dadaïstes et les surréalistes, puis les situationnistes,
expédiaient à d'illustres raclures de vide-poubelles [...]. L'attentat pâtissier,
c'est ma matérialisation dégoulinante de ces lettres d'insultes sans quartier
(Godin 2005: 16).

Or on doit concéder à ce facétieux profanateur, à ce terroriste pâtissier
que "[ses] pâtisseries de combat n'ont jamais blessé que des égos"
(Godin 2005: 53). Son offensive gloupinesque se veut "définitivement
anticulturelle":

L'art n'étant le plus souvent pour nous comme pour Picabia qu' "un produit
pharmaceutique pour imbéciles" [...] nous choisissons de cultiver le "sentiment
exquis d'inadhérence à la norme", de mettre nos vies en aventures, en gags, en
émotion fortes, de les rendre de plus en plus ludiques, de plus en plus dissolues,
de plus en plus inadmissibles gondolantes, de plus en plus inadmissibles pour
les pouvoirs en place" (Godin 2005: 53–4).

Ce "Gloup! Gloup! Gloup! Gloup!" n'est toutefois pas étranger au
poème "Te gri ro ro" avec son "Glü glodül ül" ou au "Glu et Gli" de
Michaux, comme si dans tous ces cas l'action (encore velléitaire chez
Michaux, réelle chez Arp et Godin) était indissociable d'une
intervention directe sur la langue maternelle. Deleuze n'hésiterait pas
à qualifier ces gestes de "mineurs", la littérature mineure relevant
selon lui également d'une politique, d'une machine de guerre, d'une
guérilla, "écrire dans sa langue, comme un juif tchèque écrit en
allemand, ou comme un Ouzbek écrit en russe. [...] devenir le nomade
et l'immigré et le tzigane de sa propre langue?", un geste "orphelin"
une façon de se déterritorialiser et de déterritorialiser ses parents, un
geste "célibataire, qui devance les conditions collectives
d'énonciation" (Deleuze et Guattari 1975: 33, 142, 150):

> et glo
> et glu
> et déglutit sa bru
> gli et glo
> et déglutit son pied
> glu et gli
> et s'englugliglolera
>
> les glous glous
> les sales rats
> tape dans le tas! (Michaux 1998: 110)

Mais Michaux n'a pu, semble-t-il, se satisfaire de velléités d'action ou de jeux de langue. C'est à une action sur sa propre personne, une réelle expatriation volontaire, voire une trahison envers soi-même, qu'il s'est livré. Dans "Qui il est" (1939), autre avatar de l'auto-portrait fictif, Michaux (1998: 75) usurpe une identité autre, il se dit de Paris: "Né le 24 mai 1899. Belge, de Paris". De surcroît, cette dénégation du père et de la patrie, cette expulsion hors de soi de ses ancêtres et de ses chefs va de pair chez Michaux avec une autre déterritorialisation, autrement spectaculaire, en l'occurrence un changement de mode d'expression, le passage de l'écriture à la peinture.

Et c'est encore Deleuze qu'il faut invoquer ici car il a eu le mérite de considérer la déterritorialisation et le devenir comme des formes de trahison eux aussi: "Etre traître à son propre règne, être traître à son sexe, à sa classe, à sa majorité. [...] trahir, c'est difficile, c'est créer. Il faut y perdre son identité, son visage. Il faut disparaître, devenir inconnu" (Deleuze et Parnet 1996: 56). Devenir-peintre au risque d'y sombrer c'est le défi que Michaux a voulu relever.

Or le fameux *Clown* de 1939 réussira, grâce à cette percée dans un autre art, à hypothéquer l'être en général et à faire perdre la face au sujet en particulier. Le texte et la gouache étant réalisés conjointement, l'impact en sera décuplé. Faisant écho à Plume, mais assumé par une première personne, le clown s'érige maintenant en emblème d'une option existentielle à laquelle correspond un nouveau moyen d'expression. Double déterritorialisation dès lors, de la poésie vers la peinture et du moi formé vers la dépossession du moi (à la fois pénible et salutaire). Après avoir vilipendé ses proches, c'est sa propre identité que Michaux fustige ici, bref, il se trahit:

> Un jour
> Un jour, bientôt peut-être.

Un jour j'arracherai l'ancre qui tient mon navire loin des mers.
[…] A coups de ridicules, de déchéances (Qu'est-ce que la déchéance ?) par éclatement, par vide par une total dissipation-dérision-purgation, j'expulserai de moi la forme qu'on croyait si bien attachée, composée, coordonnée, assortie à mon entourage et à mes semblables, si dignes, si dignes, mes semblables. (Michaux 1998: 709–10)

On connaît la suite. Michaux se mettra à peindre de façon effrénée des bouches ouvertes, des cris: ainsi cette gouache intitulée *CRIER*. Michaux s'est rendu compte que sa rage demandait à être montrée faute d'être entendue. Qui plus est sa femme succombe à d'atroces brûlures au visage en février 1948 ce qui fera qu'il redoublera en vigueur avec des visages à l'aquarelle, flous, informes, délavés, cabossés, balafrés au mépris de tout trait de visagéité, trahissant toute la tradition iconographique du portrait, dans un affolement sans précédent, comme pour se déconditionner de l'écriture. Il inaugure d'une certaine façon les esthétiques molles qui ajoutent à l'informe une temporalité de l'écoulement, une horizontalisation par liquéfaction, une irréversibilité entropique.

Cette nouvelle esthétique se transformera encore radicalement sous l'influence de l'expérience hallucinogène en ruissellement de traits, en déferlement de sillons, en "tapis vibratile" (Pacquement 1993: 182), le dessin devenant sismographe de la révolte intérieure.

René Magritte témoigne, à notre sens d'une trahison analogue, perpétrée également en 1948 d'ailleurs. Déjà *Le Viol* de 1934 ne laissait rien présager de bon mais la facture était encore irréprochable. Or en 1948, à l'époque où sa renommée était plus ou moins établie, Magritte n'a pas hésité à renier soudain son style et à bafouer sa réputation avec son exposition "vache" à la galerie du Faubourg Saint-Honoré à Paris.[6] Composée de 17 toiles et de 22 gouaches, celle-ci est exécutée en cinq semaines, entre mars et avril 1948. S'agit-il d'un canular d'un Magritte qui veut s'acoquiner ou s'est-il livré à une expérience plus subtile que de choquer seulement les Parisiens? Il s'agit en tout cas d'un geste de déstabilisation: "déstabilisation par rapport aux techniques consacrées par l'œuvre précédente; déstabilisation par rapport au figuratif magrittien, à son réalisme et à sa façon de provoquer le mystère" (Meurice 1970: 119–21). Cette exposition fit scandale par ses obscénités, ses outrances, et ébranla tant le public parisien bourgeois que le surréaliste orthodoxe. On lui reprocha d'être belge et de ne pas vivre à Paris, la capitale artistique de l'époque. On lui reprocha également la vulgarité de ses tableaux mais surtout d'avoir été bon peintre autrefois. La pipe, multipliée à outrance, devient allusion sexuelle burlesque et provocatrice lorsque Magritte la relie au nez du fumeur. Ce qui n'est pas sans nous rappeler l'invective de Michaux dans son pamphlet *En Belgique*: "Race au nez luisant! race infecte qui pend, qui traîne, qui coule, voilà la race au milieu de laquelle il est né" (Michaux 1998: 269), les caricatures de James Ensor ou encore les portraits-charge de la plume de Baudelaire dans *Pauvre Belgique:*

> Le visage belge, ou plutôt bruxellois.
> Chaos.
> Informe, difforme, rêche, lourd, dur, non fini, taillé au couteau.
> Dentition angulaire.
> Bouche non faite pour le sourire.
> Le rire existe, il est vrai, mais inepte, énorme, *à propos de bottes.* (Baudelaire 1953: 829)

Magritte aurait forgé le terme *vache* lui-même comme parodie du mot *fauve* et voulait se moquer de la nonchalance des Parisiens en faisant un tableau par jour. Magritte écrit encore à son ami poète Louis Scutenaire: "Eluard aime mon exposition mais il préfère acheter le Magritte d'antan" (Gablik 1972: 151–2). En réponse à cette remarque, Scutenaire rédige une biographie provocatrice dans laquelle il réinvente une identité parisienne à Magritte, une espèce de tract explicitement anti-français intitulé *La vie et les actes de René Magritte d'antan peintre universel et parisien*, dont voici quelques clauses:

> 1. Unissant Descartes au Mystère primordial et au Tropique le Bloc occidental, René Magritte d'Antan naît d'un Auvergnat et d'une indienne Apuz au Guatémala, à la Chocolata.
> 2. "Tu seras peintre!" prédit à l'enfant une envoûtante germano-maya, Canakrol, qui le déniaise dans la grotte initiatique du pueblo. Elle taille des statues maléfiques, dessine des talismans et meurt jeune.
> 4. "C'est le premier de nos Primitifs" déclare Jean-Baptiste Bernanos. "Il est l'aboutissement extrême de notre modernisme" proclame Jean-Baptiste Gide. "Il va mourir au pied de la croix", écrit Jean-Baptiste Claudel. "Votre gueule!" rétorque à celui-ci Jean-Baptiste Péret à une interview à "Le Figaro mercenaire".
> 20. Aujourd'hui, toujours debout sur le fumier du Lion de Belfort et des Chevaux de Marly, René Magritte d'Antan oppose à la facilité monégasque, à l'intransigeance tartare et à la lourdeur belge, la bannière claquante des convenances parisiennes. (Gablik 1972: 189–90)

Jacques Lizène, autre irrévérent belge[7] s'attaque lui aussi au visage, par exemple filmant ou photographiant pour son "fun-fichier" (1993)

des visages dont il troque le nez et les yeux entre eux. La "belgitude",
si elle existe, s'accommode bien, semble-t-il, de ces apatrides, de ces
trouble-fête, de ces traîtres sympathiques ou féroces.

Pierre Alechinsky

Chez Pierre Alechinsky, Belge lui aussi, c'est principalement le
démenti de l'anthropocentrisme par Dada qui résonne. Séduit à la fois
par Michaux et par Dubuffet, Alechinsky fait subir au visage une
anamorphose entre l'humain, l'animal et le végétal, par la grâce
d'un magma de lignes sinueuses aux pouvoirs multiples. L'œuvre de
ce benjamin du mouvement Cobra (1948–51) est en effet marquée par
ce côté incontrôlé de peindre qui engendre des formes indistinctes, un
bestiaire étrange, une "population grouillante d'êtres énigmatiques"
(Van den Bussche 2000: 9), un "devenir-animal" de l'humain selon le
concept de Deleuze, un devenir qui n'a ni effet de source ni effet de
cible, une "alliance monstrueuse", "pacte", "union illicite", "symbiose
entre règnes hétérogènes", "communication transversale" (Deleuze et
Guattari (1980: 28–79).[8]
    Il faut sans doute à nouveau la sensibilité aux dessins d'enfants
que possède Henri Michaux pour comprendre Alechinsky. A l'instar
de ce qui se passe dans le dessin d'enfant, la faune goguenarde semble
chez le peintre belge ignorer la séparation des règnes. Alechinsky, qui,
comme James Ensor, était "friand de carnaval, fête de la
transformation par excellence" (Van den Bussche 2000: 11), nous fait
assister à des curieux devenirs comme ces coiffes à longs panaches
des gilles de Binche qui s'éploient en volcans en éruption, mais aussi
en serpents qui se délovent, cobras en mue perpétuelle. Ainsi cette
Cantatrice de 1966, dont une gueule de cobra sortie de l'abondante
chevelure relaie le chant auquel la cantatrice semble rechigner. Tantôt
devenir-serpent de la chevelure, tantôt devenir-chanteuse du cobra, le
devenir-animal ne s'offre à aucune saisie univoque.
    N'oublions pas qu'Alechinsky préfère, à la station debout du
peintre occidental devant le chevalet, la posture penchée du peintre
oriental, la toile posée à même le sol, la Terre, la Gaia que la
mythologie grecque représentait d'ailleurs sous forme de reptile,
serpent ou dragon. C'est encore cette vue surplombante qui donnera
lieu en 1965 à *Central Park*, qui serait né de la phrase entendue par
tout étranger débarquant à New York: "Don't cross Central Park by
night":

> Du cinquantième étage on domine Central Park [...]
> *Don't cross...* En bas, un monstre attendait tapi dans la topographie du parc.
> Méandre de Cobra ? Anamorphose ? Terrible avec sa perruque en fouillis d'arbres,
> son profil indiqué par la découpe des chemins, ses joues glabres coloriées en vrai.
> [...] Central Park, dragonne aux yeux de rochers plats, mère à la peau de prairie un
> peu chauve. Mais décidée, prometteuse. (Alechinsky 1996: 20)

Le titre de l'œuvre annonce la représentation d'un parc. Le témoignage de l'auteur, mais surtout la morphologie du parc, nous dévoile une tête de *cobra*. Toutefois à y voir une tête de cobra, nous aurions déjà affaire à une signature figurative d'un nom *Cobra* qui n'est finalement qu'un homonyme du "serpent à lunettes" car il désigne, comme on sait, l'acronyme inventé par Christian Dotremont, à savoir: *Co*penhague, *Br*uxelles, *A*msterdam. Le devenir-animal du parc et le devenir-animal du poème se chevauchent à nouveau sur fond de carnaval de Binche.

Central Park véhicule évidemment à la fois la tête de cobra, l'allusion au groupe et, de surcroît, un plan aérien de Central Park. On pourrait même y ajouter une allusion à la tête de mort telle qu'elle apparaît en anamorphose à l'avant-plan des *Ambassadeurs* de Holbein, aux taches et coulures d'un test de Rorschach ou, à plus forte raison, à cette fameuse "tache" de Michaux, sous-titrée *Un poulpe ou une ville* offerte en 1926 à Jean Paulhan: une espèce de protubérance cellulaire à l'allure équivoque, qui fait hésiter le spectateur entre la vue d'un plan aérien d'une ville, celle d'un poulpe aux multiples tentacules, ou celle d'un simple crachat informe. Dans ces conditions, le titre *Central Park* n'est là que pour provoquer le sens, creuser la distance entre signifiant et signifié.

Mais qu'est-ce qui autorise en dernier ressort ces lectures alternatives à celle qu'induit le titre? *Central Park* est le premier tableau d'Alechinsky qui présente des "remarques marginales", terme de typographie désignant ces petites gravures en marge de la planche gravée.

Ce qu'il y a de particulier à ces "remarques" c'est que, loin de composer un cadre ornemental, elles sont comme une lecture, une glose dessinée de l'œuvre première, elles resémantisent l'image colorée et peuvent même l'emporter sur ce noyau central. Dans notre cas, elles confirment la lecture animale, monstrueuse du Park new-yorkais: les remarques satellites modulent, font serpenter la figure de cobra dissimulée dans la végétation. Autrement dit, la périphérie désavoue ironiquement ce que le titre nous enseigne à propos du centre. La marge renferme toutes les perspectives possibles sur la figure centrale qui perd ainsi sa prééminence et se laisse évincer par les sémioses alternatives.

Ajoutons à cela le fait qu'Alechinsky était ambidextre, écrivant de la main droite, peignant de la main gauche revendiquant ainsi le droit à la rébellion graphique. On peut alors émettre l'hypothèse peut-être dérisoire mais néanmoins plausible que la tête de cobra est encore un leurre, que *Central Park* représente bel et bien Central Park, vu du haut par la posture penchée, mais surtout peint de la main gauche, tel un îlot de liberté et de spontanéité, parmi le tracé rectiligne des rues et avenues de Manhattan *écrites* de la main droite. Cette hypothèse n'est cependant pas davantage à l'abri d'une ultérieure révision car les remarques, en dépit de la cartographie ordonnée qui les accueille, pullulent déjà d'une tendance au désordre (le devenir-animal des habitants de Manhattan?)

Ce que toutes ces tentatives brutes, vaches, clownesques, gloupinesques, anarchistes ou carnavalesques ont en commun est un désintéressement et une insolence enfantine impensable sans cet antécédent de choc mais cependant déjà établi que constitue le Dadaïsme, comme si les irrévérents de l'après-guerre jouissaient d'un rapport de *fort-da* avec Dada, bref d'un *fort-Dada*.

Notes

[1] "La tête déjà est importante. Dominante, grosse autant et plus que le corps, lequel n'offre rien de particulier, tandis que la tête (qui dans la réalité sait déjà accomplir tant de fonctions, manger, sucer, mordre, voir, entendre, goûter, retirer, embrasser, gazouiller, crier, rire, grimacer, faire peur, faire enrager, parler peut-être), la tête est dans son dessin la maîtresse partie, accapareuse entre toutes les parties corporelles" (Michaux 2004: 1329).

[2] Chez Gaston Chaissac, Ferdinand Cheval, dit le Facteur Cheval, Alexander Lobanov, etc.

[3] www.dubuffetfondation.com/hourloupe.htm.

[4] "Père, Dieu, ou surmoi tyrannique, il incarne l'ensemble des forces coercitives qui le privent de sa propre souveraineté, tant dans le monde qu'à l'intérieur de lui-même" (Maulpoix 1984: 35).

[5] www.gloupgloup.com

[6] "Pour rappel: il avait 50 ans. Jusque-là, il n'avait montré ses œuvres à Paris que dans des manifestations de groupe. L'accueil qui leur avait été réservé avait été mitigé. Il en souffrait et voulait certainement frapper 'un grand coup', quitte à utiliser une méthode plus Dadaïste que surréaliste – Dadaïsme au demeurant, que Magritte et ses amis proches avaient ressuscité dans trois tracts de 1946 ('L'imbécile', 'L'emmerdeur', 'L'enculeur'). En tout cas, "il ne fut pas question une minute de rassembler des peintures exécutées dans l'une ou l'autre manière

qui avaient fait leur preuves". Louis Scutenaire (1947), cité par Meuris (1970: 116). Le peintre peignit donc à neuf. La source: "Quelques caricatures montrées par Colinet, publiées avant 1914 dans un magazine pour enfants, furent les mèches du brûlot", poursuivait le poète-comparse. [...] il voulait mettre 'les pieds dans le plat', termes par lesquels il intitula le catalogue de cette exposition parisienne et 'vache' " (Meuris 1970: 52).

[7] Rappelons que René Magritte, Marcel Broodthaers, E.L.T. Mesens, Marcel Mariën, et Jacques Lizène ont fait l'objet d'une exposition 'Magritte en Compagnie. Du bon usage de l'irrévérence" à Bruxelles, Musée du Botanique (23 mai–3 août 1997).

[8] Trop oedipiens, familiers, familiaux, sentimentaux ou trop archétypiques, les animaux représentés par l'iconographie traditionnelle sont précisément ceux que Deleuze exclut du devenir-animal. Il réserve celui-ci aux "animaux davantage démoniaques, à meutes et affects, et qui font multiplicité, devenir, population, conte" (Deleuze et Guattari 1980: 293).

Bibliographie

Alechinsky, Pierre. 1996. *Hors cadre*. Bruxelles: Labor.

Baudelaire, Charles. 1953. *Oeuvres complètes II*. (éd. C.Pichois). Paris: Gallimard (Collection La Pléiade).

Dubuffet, Jean. 1968. *Asphyxiante culture*. Paris: Minuit.

Deleuze, Gilles et Félix Guattari. 1975. *Kafka. Pour une littérature mineure*. Paris: Minuit.

Deleuze, Gilles et Félix Guattari. 1980. *Mille Plateaux*. Paris: Minuit.

Deleuze, Gilles et Claire Parnet. 1996. *Dialogues* [1977]. Paris: Champs/Flammarion.

Dubuffet, Jean. 1967. *Prospectus et tous écrits suivants I*. Paris: Gallimard.

Dubuffet, Jean. 1968. *Asphyxiante culture*. Paris: Minuit.

Dubuffet & l'Art Brut. 2005. Paris: Editions Cinq continents et Collection de l'Art Brut (catalogue d'exposition, Musée d'Art Moderne de Villeneuve-d'Ascq).

Gablik, Suzi. 1972. *Magritte*. London: Thames and Hudson.

Godin, Noël. 2005. *Entartons, entartons les pompeux cornichons*. Paris: Flammarion.

de Heusch, Luc. 1992. *Ceci n'est pas la Belgique*. Paris: Editions Complexe.

Didi-Huberman, Georges. 1995. *La Ressemblance informe ou le gai savoir visuel selon George Bataille*. Paris: Macula.

Jean Dubuffet. Portraits. 1947. Paris: Galerie René Drouin.

Lyotard, Jean-François. 1988. *L'Inhumain, causeries sur le temps*. Paris: Galilée.

Martin, Jean-Hubert. 2005. "Dubuffet fonde l'art sans le savoir" in *Dubuffet & l'Art Brut*. Paris: Editions Cinq continents et Collection de l'Art Brut: 10–12.

Maulpoix, Jean-Michel. 1984. *Michaux passager clandestin*. Seyssel: Editions du Champ Vallon.

Meuris, Jacques. 1970. *Magritte*. Paris: Casterman.

Michaux, Henri. 1963. *Passages*. Paris: Gallimard.

Michaux, Henri. 1972. *La Vie dans les plis* [1949]. Paris: Gallimard.

Michaux, Henri. 1998. *Oeuvres complètes I* (ed. R. Bellour). Paris: Gallimard (Collection La Pléiade).

Michaux, Henri. 2004. *Oeuvres complètes III* (ed. R. Bellour). Paris: Gallimard (Collection La Pléiade).

Pacquement, Alfred. 1993. *Henri Michaux. Peintures*. Paris: Gallimard.

Prinzhorn, Hans. 1984. *Bildnerei der Geisteskranken* [Berlin: Springer 1922]; *Expressions de la folie. Dessins, peintures, sculptures d'asile* (tr. M. Weber et A. Brousse). Paris: Gallimard.

Scutenaire, Louis. 1947. *René Magritte*, Bruxelles: Libraire Sélection.

Thévoz, Michel. 2005. "Homo démens" in *Dubuffet & l'Art Brut*. Paris: Collection de l'Art Brut: 62–7.

Van Den Bussche, Willy. 2000. "Un voyage dans l'imaginaire" in *Pierre Alechinsky*. Anvers: Fonds Mercator. n.p.

Chapter 11

**The Critical Reception of René Crevel:
The 1920s and Beyond**

Paul Cooke

Born in 1900, Crevel was slightly too young to participate fully in the Dada movement.[1] However, while fulfilling his military service in Paris's Latour-Maubourg barracks, he met a number of young men – including François Baron, Georges Limbour, Max Morise and Roger Vitrac – who shared his interest in Dada's anarchic spirit. On 14 April 1921 Crevel, Baron, and Vitrac attended the *visite-conférence* organized by the Dadaists at the Parisian church of Saint-Julien-le-Pauvre. Afterwards the three of them met up with Louis Aragon, one of the organizers of the afternoon's event. As a result of this meeting the periodical *aventure* was born, with Crevel named as *gérant*. Only three issues would appear, with the editorial team splitting in February 1922 over the preparation of the Congrès du Palais (with Vitrac supporting Breton and the organizing committee, while Crevel and the others refused to abandon Tzara). Crevel would again defend Tzara against the proto-Surrealist grouping during the staging of *Le Cœur à gaz* at the Théâtre Michel in July 1923. At the very start of his career as a writer, therefore, it is clear that Dada was a significant influence for Crevel.[2] However, despite siding with Tzara in the summer of 1923, it would not be long before Crevel was reconciled with Breton, with the latter naming him in the 1924 *Manifeste* as one of those who had "fait acte de SURRÉALISME ABSOLU" (Breton 1988: 328). It is as a Surrealist novelist and essayist that Crevel is remembered in literary history. However, more than seventy years after his death, his status remains problematic: perhaps more than for any other figure associated with Dada and Surrealism, a legend has grown up around the man that has tended to colour awareness of his work.

A good example of the mythmaking surrounding Crevel was provided in the summer of 1999 when *Le Figaro Magazine* ran a series of weekly articles under the heading "Les Perdants magnifiques" dealing with Billie Holiday, F. Scott Fitzgerald, René Crevel, Amedeo Modigliani, Jim Morrison, and Camille Claudel. Whether *juilletistes* or *aoûtiens*, vacationing readers were being reminded that cultural prestige could come at a high cost. The author of the third article in the series, Arnould de Liedekerke (1999: 65), defined his subject as follows: "Crevel, que tout le monde connaît et que personne ne lit". The idea that Crevel enjoyed iconic status had already been articulated seventy years previously. In a review published in 1929, the critic Bernard Faÿ (1929: 301) described Crevel as "une légende vivante", with the context suggesting that this legendary status had more to do with Crevel's public image than with his significance as an author. This public image would become even more powerful six years later when Crevel took his own life. This death (so easily recuperated into the Romantic stereotype of the tormented artist) had the effect of deflecting interest away from his work and of freezing his image in the pose of the-Surrealist-who-committed-suicide, especially as the polemic surrounding his death served to fuel public interest. Hence de Liedekerke's assertion that Crevel's works have sunk without trace. This too is an assertion that receives some support from earlier commentators. As Léon-Gabriel Gros (1935: 606) observed shortly after Crevel's death, his books were "autant de machines de guerre contre la pensée bourgeoise. Jamais la critique ne leur fut indulgente". No wonder then that Crevel went straight to writers' purgatory.

The first concerted attempt to release him from this limbo of neglect was undertaken by the American academic Carlos Lynes. In the mid-1950s Lynes was working on a book entitled *René Crevel ou le quatorzième convive*. Although this never appeared, Lynes (1956: 336) did publish a few articles on Crevel during the period 1956–58 and, in one of these, he refers to the author's works as "quelques livres bouleversants, qui n'ont guère rencontré que l'indifférence, l'incompréhension ou la haine". Here, then, is the other aspect of the Crevel legend (and one that is equally assimilable to the myth of the misunderstood creative genius): not only did he commit suicide, but also his work was either poorly received or ignored. The claim has proved tenacious – de Liedekerke (1999: 66) states that Crevel's books "n'intéressaient guère que ses amis" – but how true is it? This is the question I want to consider in this essay by examining two aspects of Crevel's reception (a subject that has received very little attention to date): firstly the ways in which his work was reviewed during his lifetime and secondly the broad patterns of critical interest in his work since his death.

In relation to the first of these two aspects, it is helpful to examine the data supplied by Bridel (1988: 173-80) in tabular form in his study of the (essentially) interwar reception of Surrealism in various literary periodicals published in France and French-speaking Switzerland. Firstly we have figures for *La Nouvelle Revue française* (the only Parisian periodical included in Bridel's study) showing the number of reviews and articles devoted to authors associated at some point with the Surrealist movement:[3]

Author	No. of reviews & articles, 1922–39	Rank (out of 14)	No. of reviews & articles, 1922–29	Rank (out of 14)
Aragon	9	4th	5	2nd=
Artaud	8	5th=	4	6th=
Breton	14	2nd	4	6th=
Crevel	**6**	**8th**	**4**	**6th=**
Delteil	8	5th=	5	2nd=
Desnos	4	10th=	3	9th=
Eluard	16	1st	5	2nd=
Leiris	0	14th	1	11th=
Limbour	3	12th	1	11th=
Péret	1	13th	0	14th
Ribemont-Dessaignes	4	10th=	3	9th=
Soupault	13	3rd	9	1st
Tzara	5	9th	1	11th=
Vitrac	7	7th	5	2nd=

These figures for the *NRF* are significant since the periodical was the most prestigious of its time, both reflecting and informing literary opinion. Given that the *NRF* published two of Crevel's novels (*Détours* and *Etes-vous fous?*) and that Crevel contributed occasional pieces to the journal, one might have expected the figures to be higher. Based on these statistics alone, one would have to conclude that Crevel was indeed perceived as a relatively marginal figure within Surrealism. However, there are other data to be taken into account. Here, for example, are the figures for periodicals published in the French provinces (Bridel studied a total of 33 titles):

Author	No. of reviews & articles, 1922–39	Rank (out of 16)	No. of reviews & articles, 1922–29	Rank (out of 16)
Aragon	10	5th=	4	6th
Artaud	3	12th=	2	8th=
Baron	6	8th	2	8th=
Breton	18	1st	9	2nd
Char	3	12th=	1	12th=
Crevel	**12**	**4th**	**7**	**4th**
Delteil	10	5th=	8	3rd
Desnos	5	9th	1	12th=
Eluard	15	3rd	2	8th=
Hugnet	4	10th=	1	12th=
Leiris	2	15th=	1	12th=
Péret	4	10th=	3	7th
Ribemont-Dessaignes	8	7th	5	5th
Soupault	16	2nd	14	1st
Tzara	3	12th=	2	8th=
Vitrac	2	15th=	0	16th

From being in the bottom half of the *NRF* figures for 1922–39, Crevel is now in the upper quartile for provincial periodicals, receiving more critical attention during this period than Aragon. His showing in the data for French-speaking Switzerland (based on 23 periodicals) is even stronger:

Author	No. of reviews & articles, 1922–39	Rank (out of 8)	No. of reviews & articles, 1922–29	Rank (out of 8)
Aragon	3	4th	3	3rd
Breton	5	1st=	2	4th=
Crevel	**4**	**3rd**	**4**	**2nd**
Desnos	1	6th=	0	7th=
Eluard	2	5th	2	4th=
Ribemont-Dessaignes	1	6th=	1	6th
Soupault	5	1st=	5	1st
Tzara	1	6th=	0	7th=

Here Crevel receives more attention than either Aragon or Eluard and is only one item behind Breton and Soupault who share joint first place for the period 1922–39. Indeed, Crevel even finishes ahead of Breton for the period up to 1929.

So, despite his relatively poor showing in the *NRF*, it is not true that Crevel's work was ignored during his lifetime. There does seem to have been a decline in the number of separate reviews his work received as one moves chronologically through his production, especially in connection with his essays and his final novel. But there appears to have been a similar pattern for other authors associated with Surrealism, since from about 1930 literary periodicals became increasingly less interested in the movement (Bridel 1988: 24). In the case of *Les Pieds dans le plat* (1933) there was an additional reason for the critical silence: Crevel's scandalous picture of "le prince des journalistes" was clearly modelled on Léon Bailby, owner of the major Parisian daily *Le Jour*, and it would seem that reviewers preferred to ignore the book entirely rather than run the risk of offending an influential press baron (Roditi 1983: 79). Prior to this novel, however, Crevel's work does not appear to have suffered unduly from critical neglect. The question of his sales figures is more difficult to address. His correspondence indicates that he did not make much money out of his work, and, pondering Crevel's suicide, the painter Jacques-Emile Blanche comments in his diary that the young man was "découragé par des insuccès de librairie" (Collet 2002: 210). But the fact that, in 1931, Aragon complained that he and Crevel found it impossible to find a publisher reminds us that Crevel's situation was very similar to that of other potentially scandalous writers (quoted in Harrison 1995: 154).

Ideally the foregoing analysis of the number of reviews devoted to Crevel's work would now be complemented with a detailed consideration of their content. However, given the limitations of space, I shall restrict myself to a brief selection of comments on Crevel's major books. In a review of Crevel's first novel, *Détours* (1924), Albert Thibaudet (1924: 1469), the leading critic of his generation, wrote: "voilà un livre plein de talent, et qui me rendra attentif à la suite de l'œuvre". Another major critic, Bernard Faÿ (1926: 72), said of Crevel's next novel, *Mon Corps et moi* (1925): "Il ne faut point mettre ce livre entre toutes les mains, mais seulement entre les mains des meilleurs". Georges Poupet (1927: 140) then described *La Mort difficile* (1926) as: "Un livre courageux où René Crevel, sans violence affectée, essaie de lutter contre l'hypocrisie qui nous baigne". This was Crevel's most conventional novel, one in which he dramatized the doomed love affair of a semi-autobiographical gay protagonist. He followed it with *Babylone* (1927), a more openly Surrealist text: "Sans doute, reprochera-t-on à ce livre une certaine incoherence", wrote Georgette Camille (1928: 76), "C'est ce qui nous touche". 1927 also saw the publication of Crevel's essay, *L'Esprit contre la raison*, a text which caused Louis Emié (1928: 64) to comment: "La toute-puissance de la poésie trouve enfin un homme qui consent à s'incliner devant elle". According to Pierre Bost (1929: 336), Crevel's next novel, *Etes-vous fous?* (1929), was "presque une parfaite réussite". A second major essay, *Le Clavecin de Diderot* (1932), provoked a very positive review from Léon-Gabriel Gros (1933: 372): "Ce texte extraordinairement vivant écrit dans une langue à la fois précise et truculente, constitue un exposé parfaitement accessible de la thèse surréaliste". And, finally, despite the general lack of reviews for Crevel's last completed novel, it is worth noting Gérard Servèze's comments on *Les Pieds dans le plat* in the organ of the Association des Ecrivains et Artistes Révolutionnaires: "il faut signaler des pages de critique révolutionnaire, [...] qui sont remarquables, tant au point de vue de la vivacité du style, que de l'acuité des idées" (Servèze 1933: 75).

Bearing in mind Bridel's assertion that there was "une tendance générale au rejet du surréalisme et cela partout" (Bridel 1988: 21), I would therefore argue that Crevel's work received a reasonably favourable press. Having consulted about forty-five contemporary reviews, I have only found two that could be described as strongly critical: Georges Bataille's piece on *Le Clavecin de Diderot*[4] and Pierre Minet's on *Les Pieds dans le plat*.[5] Elsewhere, despite a number of criticisms relating to the perceived "disorder" of Crevel's style and structure, there are many positive assessments of his work.

So whether the reviews are considered in quantitative or qualitative terms the evidence generally fails to support Lynes's claim that Crevel's books met with "l'indifférence, l'incompréhension ou la haine". If he makes such a claim, it is perhaps primarily due to the fact that he is considering Crevel's reception from the perspective of the mid-to-late-1950s. For, if Crevel was reasonably well served by the critics during his lifetime, it is true that there was very little critical interest in his work during the twenty years following his death. It is understandable in this context that enthusiasts such as Lynes and Gros, writing in the second half of the 1950s, should project this contemporary neglect back on to the period in the 1920s and 30s when Crevel was producing his work. But, once again, the idea of Crevel as a neglected author has persisted well beyond the 1950s. In studies published within the last decade or so, for example, Lawrence Schehr (1995: 23) describes Crevel as "often forgotten today except by a small group of experts interested in Surrealism", while Garrett Heysel (1997: 155) states that the author's *œuvre* "remains largely unknown and even more rarely studied", and Elizabeth Ezra (2000: 78) comments that "Crevel remains relatively obscure in France and is still virtually unknown in Great Britain and the United States". Such statements sit somewhat uncomfortably with de Liederkerke's description of Crevel as a figure "que tout le monde connaît", though it may well be that Crevel has been particularly neglected by Anglo-American scholars.

Statements about an author's degree of celebrity are difficult to prove; more often than not, one suspects that judgements are made on the basis of experience and general impressions. There are, however, ways in which the statements can be tested. Bibliographical (or more general data) searches are one way in which one can measure the amount of interest in authors. I conducted two such searches for a selection of writers associated with the Surrealist movement to see what conclusions might emerge as to Crevel's visibility. The first involved an electronic search using the Online Computer Library Center (OCLC) FirstSearch facility.[6] Using each author's surname and first name as "Named Person" (na:) terms as part of an "Expert Search", I consulted the WorldCat List of Records. According to its website WorldCat has more than 54,000 contributing libraries, "making it the world's largest, most complete, and most consulted library union catalog".[7] It lists not only printed matter, but also visual and archival materials, sound recordings, internet resources, and computer files. The results for the six authors I selected were as follows:

Author	No. of entries in WorldCat
Artaud	532
Breton	493
Desnos	131
Soupault	61
Péret	27
Crevel	23

Crevel emerges with the lowest number of entries. The WorldCat search results also provide the number of English-language entries for a search term. This information can be shown as follows:

Author	% of English-language entries
Artaud	31.6
Breton	29.4
Desnos	20.6
Péret	18.5
Crevel	17.4
Soupault	14.8

Although Crevel is not quite at the foot of this table, the statistics provide some empirical data to support Ezra's contention that Crevel is "virtually unknown" in Anglophone circles: compared to other writers associated with Surrealism, it does indeed seem as though Crevel is under-exposed in the English-speaking world.

For my second analysis of bibliographical data, I counted the number of entries for Crevel in *French XX Bibliography* for the period from 1940 to 2003 (no electronic search facility was available; the figures have been calculated by working through the entries in the various volumes). Although *French XX Bibliography* is not exhaustive, it is one of the most comprehensive sources of information on international publications and the picture it offers is certainly more detailed than that provided by the previous search.[8]

Author	No. of entries in *French XX Bibliography*
Breton	1627
Artaud	1540
Desnos	408
Soupault	310
Crevel	266
Péret	138

The table shows that although Crevel's figures lag far behind those for Breton and Artaud, he has generated more publishing interest than Péret and is not too far behind Soupault. Overall, and remembering that his writing career was cut short by an early death, one can say that Crevel has received a limited, though not insignificant amount of critical attention. Although there appears to be proportionately less work on him in English than for other French authors associated with Surrealism, it is worth noting that four of his six completed novels have been translated into English over the past twenty-five years.[9] The data does not therefore appear to suggest that Crevel has been particularly sidelined compared to other writers in the Surrealist movement.

However, if one examines in more detail the pattern of publications relating to Crevel since his death, one begins to understand why those writing in the period up to the mid-1990s saw him as a marginalized figure:[10]

	Monographs	Special issues	Articles/chapters	Crevel's writings
1936–45	0	0	2	0
1946–55	0	1	2	0
1956–65	0	2	7	2
1966–75	1	0	13	7
1976–85	3	2	30	6
1986–95	5	0	35	4
1996–2005	3	1	65	5

This table illustrates very clearly the way in which Crevel was almost entirely neglected in the two decades following his death. Interest began to develop in the period 1956–65, led by Carlos Lynes. The years 1966–75 saw a number of reissues of Crevel's work, especially by the publishers Pauvert – a process that continued into the next decade and beyond. In the context of the events of May 68 and associated phenomena such as the growth of the gay rights movement,[11] one can see how Crevel was sensed as having a fresh relevance. No doubt the appearance of the anthology of Crevel's work in the "Poètes d'aujourd'hui" series further helped his rehabilitation in publishing terms (Courtot 1969). The impact of making Crevel's texts available to new generations of readers can be seen in the dramatic rise in the number of articles and chapters on Crevel published between 1976 and 1985. The appearance of a special issue of the journal *Europe* in 1985 to coincide with the fiftieth anniversary of Crevel's death is partly responsible for this increase, but one should also note the launch of the specialist Surrealist periodical *Mélusine* in 1979. The next decade (1986–95) saw the high point of monographs devoted to Crevel, including two substantial biographies published by major French houses (Fayard and Grasset) and in-depth critical analyses by French, Italian, and German scholars. This period also saw the publication of two of Crevel's texts (*Mon Corps et moi* and *La Mort difficile*) in the popular Livre de Poche series, suggesting that Crevel was at last attracting significant sales figures. The most recent decade has seen the publication of a number of volumes of Crevel's correspondence, but the most striking feature of the data is the huge increase in the number of articles and chapters. Once again, special issues have played a significant role here – both with an entire issue of *Mélusine* devoted to the proceedings of a centenary conference held in Bordeaux in 2000 and with the launch of a more modest series entitled *Bulletin René Crevel*. All of this demonstrates very clearly that if Crevel's work was more or less consigned to oblivion for the first thirty-five years following his death, this state of neglect has been steadily remedied on a number of different publishing fronts over the last thirty-five years.

"Crevel, que tout le monde connaît et que personne ne lit". Although de Liedekerke's words constitute a memorably punchy journalistic antithesis, they are inevitably inadequate as an accurate summary of Crevel's reception in the 1920s and beyond. It is, I think, true that the "legend" embroidered around Crevel's death and life (and the legend derives its power from the inversion of the stock phrase) has tended to displace close engagement with his works, but, as we have seen, Crevel does not appear to have been any more neglected overall than writers such as Péret and Soupault. I have also shown that, among the Surrealists, Crevel has been the object of a lower proportion of English-language publications and this has almost certainly fuelled the sense among recent Anglophone critics that Crevel remains under-studied. However, the demonstrable and considerable growth of scholarship devoted to his work over the past two decades, as well as the increased availability of primary material, reveals that Crevel is by no means as marginalized a figure today as during the four decades following his death. Although it may not be true that everyone knows him, it is certainly not the case that nobody reads him.

Notes

[1]   Tristan Tzara, born in 1896, was the youngest of the major Dadaists. Most of the other leading figures associated with the movement were born in the 1880s.

[2]   For further details see Carassou (1989: 35–49) and Buot (1991: 41–66).

[3]   I have modified the presentation of Bridel's data so as to reveal more clearly the degree of critical interest accorded to Crevel's work; the reason for extracting figures for the period 1922–29 and giving these separately is that Crevel's death in 1935 inevitably limited the amount of critical coverage he received in the late 30s. My figures also differ from those of Bridel in that I have not counted creative texts published in the various periodicals by the authors concerned.

[4]   B[ataille] (1933). Given Crevel's enthusiastic endorsement of Breton and Surrealism in his essay, one should perhaps regard Bataille's harsh judgements of Crevel as part of a response to Breton's critique of Bataille's own views in the *Second Manifeste du urréalisme* of 1930 (see Breton 1998: 824–7).

[5]   Minet (1934). Over half a century later Minet would comment: "En principe je n'avais pas tort. [...] Mais j'eusse dû ne pas céder au besoin, inimical et prétentieux, de sabrer son auteur" (Minet 1989: 74).

[6]   http://www.oclc.org/ consulted on 2 January 2007.

[7]   http://www.oclc.org/firstsearch/content/worldcat/default.htm

[8]   The most recent issue (no. 56, covering material published up to 2003) is *French XX Bibliography: Critical and Biographical References for the Study of French Literature since 1885*, ed. by William J. Thompson (Selinsgrove: Susquehanna University Press, 2005). From 1949 to 1953 it was published under the title *Bibliography of Critical and Biographical References for the Study of Contemporary French Literature*, then from 1954 to 1968 under the title *French VII Bibliography. Critical and Biographical References for the Study of Contemporary French Literature*, the long-serving editor-in-chief being Douglas W. Alden. In compiling my figures, I have only included those items listed in full under the author's name (i.e. not those given as cross references). I have not included items completing information given in previous years. In the case of collections of essays, I have counted each contribution separately.

[9]   *Babylon* (tr. K. Boyle), San Francisco: North Point Press, 1985; *Difficult Death* (tr. D. Rattray, San Francisco: North Point Press, 1986; *Putting My Foot in It* (tr. T. Buckley, Normal, IL: Dalkey Archive Press, 1992; and *My Body and I* (tr. R. Bononno, Brooklyn, NY: Archipelago Books, 2005.

[10] The figures in the following table are drawn from the full range of my bibliographical research (no exhaustive bibliography of Crevel criticism has ever been published). The figures include certain items not listed in *French XX*, but I have not included items such as brief journalistic pieces, personal reminiscences or reviews. This accounts for the fact that only 196 items have been counted in the following table, whereas there are 266 entries in *French XX*.

[11] André Clair (1975) sees in Crevel a precursor of the nascent gay rights movement (*Arcadie* was published by the "Mouvement homophile de France"). It is noteworthy that in Gregory Woods (1998) – a book that spans the period from classical antiquity to the present and that engages with works originally written in

a multiplicity of languages – only Balzac, Proust, Gide, and Genet receive more coverage than Crevel among French writers.

Bibliography

B[ataille], G[eorges]. 1933. "René Crevel: *Le Clavecin de Diderot*" in *La Critique sociale* 7: 50.

Bost, Pierre. 1929. "Les Livres" in *Jazz* 1(7): 333–7.

Breton, André. 1988. *Œuvres complètes I*. Paris: Gallimard (Collection la Pléiade).

Bridel, Yves. 1988. *Miroirs du surréalisme. Essai sur la réception du surréalisme en France et en Suisse française (1916–1939)*. Lausanne: L'Age d'homme.

Camille, Georgette. 1928. "*Babylone*, par René Crevel" in *Les Cahiers du Sud* 97: 75-7.

Carassou, Michel. 1989. *René Crevel*. Paris: Fayard.

Clair, André. 1975. "Pour René Crevel" in *Arcadie* 22: 479–81.

Collet, Georges-Paul. 2002. "René Crevel et Jacques-Emile Blanche. Une amitié intermittente" in *Mélusine* 22: 193–211.

Courtot, Claude (ed.). 1969. *René Crevel*. Paris: Seghers.

Ezra, Elizabeth. 2000. "Cannibals in Babylon. René Crevel's Allegories of Exclusion" in *The Colonial Unconscious. Race and Culture in Interwar France*. Ithaca: Cornell University Press: 75–96.

Emié, Louis. 1928. "*L'Esprit contre la raison*, par René Crevel" in *Les Cahiers du Sud* 103: 64–5.

Faÿ, Bernard. 1926. "*Mon Corps et Moi*, par René Crevel" in *La Revue européenne* 38: 71–2.

——. 1929. "*Etes-Vous fous* [sic], par René Crevel" in *La Revue européenne* 9: 300–01.

Gros, Léon-Gabriel. 1933. "*Le Clavecin de Diderot*, par René Crevel" in *Cahiers du Sud* 151: 372–4.

Gros, Léon-Gabriel. 1935. "René Crevel" in *Cahiers du Sud* 174: 605–07.

Harrison, Nicholas. 1995. *Circles of Censorship. Censorship and Its Metaphors in French History, Literature, and Theory*. Oxford: Clarendon Press.

Heysel, Garrett R. 1997. "René Crevel's Body Algebra" in D. D. Fisher and L. R. Schehr (eds). 1997. *Articulations of Difference: Gender Studies and Writing in French*. Stanford: Stanford University Press: 155–66.

Liedekerke, Arnould de. 1999. "Les Perdants magnifiques (3). René Crevel, l'ange
      déchu du surréalisme" in *Le Figaro Magazine* (31 juillet): 64–66.

Minet, Pierre. 1934. "*Les Pieds dans le plat*, par René Crevel" in *Cahiers du Sud* 165:
      652–3.

Lynes, Carlos. 1956. "Tel qu'en lui-même…" in *Cahiers du Sud* 337: 336–44.

Minet, Pierre. 1989. "Portraits" in *La Nouvelle Revue française* 441: 69–80.

Poupet, Georges. 1927. "*La Mort difficile*, par René Crevel" in *Les Cahiers du mois*
      25–26: 140–1.

Roditi, Edouard. 1983. "*Les Pieds dans le plat*. Histoire d'une publication" in
      Masques 17: 78–82.

Schehr, Lawrence R.1995. "Heterosexual Surrealism and the Problem of René
      Crevel" in *Alcibiades at the Door. Gay Discourses in French Literature.*
      Stanford: Stanford University Press: 23–67.

Servèze, G[érard], 1933. "René Crevel, *Les pieds dans le plat*" in *Commune* 1: 75.

Thibaudet, Albert. 1924. "Débuts" in *L'Europe nouvelle* 350: 1468–9.

Woods, Gregory. 1998. *A History of Gay Literature. The Male Tradition.* New Haven:
      Yale University Press.

Chapter 12

Enfants naturels ou filles spirituelles ? À propos de quelques réflexions sur l'esprit de filiation Dada dans les pratiques "autographiques" des auteures-artistes surréalistes

Andrea Oberhuber

Bruissements d'un héritage Dada

> Mais voilà qu'elle entend quelque chose: piaillant, grognant, aboyant, miaulant, imitant joliment les coin-coin du canard, une joyeuse bande de Dadaïstes semble s'approcher, en bas, dans la rue qu'elle ne peut pas voir, pour la libérer. Tous les anciens Dadaïstes qu'elle a connus à Paris seront là et cette compagnie va l'emmener en triomphe à la fête si longtemps attendue. (Zürn 1971: 66)

C'est au cours de ses pérégrinations hallucinées à travers les rues d'un Berlin nocturne que, après son arrestation par deux policiers, la narratrice de *L'Homme-Jasmin* évoque les Dadaïstes parisiens dans un scénario de performance publique. Cette référence au passé Dada dans le récit d'Unica Zürn mise à part, le legs d'une avant-garde à l'autre en ce qui concerne des pratiques artistiques et des principes poétiques n'a que rarement trouvé une expression écrite dans les textes et les créations de celles que l'on a l'habitude d'appeler "femmes surréalistes".[1] Si, d'office, aucune des auteures-artistes surréalistes (Belen, Claude Cahun, Leonora Carrington, Lise Deharme, Valentine Hugo, Frida Kahlo, Joyce Mansour, Gisèle Prassinos, Valentine Penrose, Kay Sage ou Unica Zürn) ne s'est inscrite *expressis verbis* dans la lignée d'Elsa von Freytag-Loringhoven, de Claire Goll, d'Emmy Hennings, de Hannah Höch, de Mina Loy ou de Sophie Taeuber, certains liens de fil(l)iation entre les premières et les secondes, à bien y regarder, deviennent visibles, et ce, à divers niveaux. En effet, nul doute, ce qui reste de l'héritage des artistes Dadaïstes dans les pratiques scripturaires et artistiques des créatrices surréalistes, c'est avant tout le goût performatif aboutissant à une théâtralisation de l'autoreprésentation par la voie de l'écriture de soi ou de l'autoportrait (en photographie et en peinture). Cette propension à la performance se retrouve, variée chaque fois différemment, dans les œuvres protéiformes de Cahun, de Carrington et de Zürn, par exemple. D'un autre côté, l'esprit de provocation et l'ironie typique de Dada, comme stratégies de mise à distance d'une certaine conception "romantique" de l'œuvre d'art, du génie artistique et de l'acte créateur, sont portés à leur apogée par Belen après avoir été modulés par Prassinos et Deharme. Toutes cependant se caractérisent – et, par là, se démarquent de leurs prédécesseures – par la volonté de *s'écrire*, de créer des œuvres d'art et non des performances éphémères, bref de *se (re)créer* à travers l'écriture, la photographie, le dessin, la peinture, le cinéma. Leur projet "autographique" – tel est le terme convenable pour circonscrire une myriade de récits de soi – consiste donc en l'épanouissement, par l'usage créatif des formes textuelles et iconiques, d'un désir de parler de soi dépassant le simple vécu, le *bios*. Dans cette optique, elles sont nombreuses à opter résolument pour une démarche à la croisée de différents arts et médias: à une praxis intermédiale s'associe le plus souvent une transfrontalité générique.

Dans le contexte des réflexions suivantes sur le passage des générations, la transmission d'un imaginaire et l'incorporation d'un legs esthétique, ce que j'entends par "filiation", ou plutôt par "esprit de fi(l)liation", c'est l'inscription de bon nombre d'auteures-artistes surréalistes, sur le plan symbolique et sous les auspices du féminin, dans une lignée de pratiques scripturaires et picturales Dadaïstes. À peine cette idée d'une généalogie possible formulée, il faut s'interroger sur la légitimité d'une telle conception "traditionnelle" à propos de deux mouvements contestataires ayant conclu le pacte de rompre radicalement avec les valeurs culturelles, artistiques et littéraires des époques précédentes. D'un point de vue historique, surtout dans le contexte plus général des "avant-gardes historiques", comme les a désignées Peter Bürger dans *Theorie der Avantgarde* (1982) il paraît cependant légitime de penser le Dadaïsme et le Surréalisme en des termes de filiation poétique et esthétique: entre le premier et le second s'établit le lien généalogique d'une transmission-réception entre deux générations d'artistes et d'auteurs. La question plus particulière d'une fi(l)liation implique, outre la construction identitaire, celle d'une *memoria* au feminine. Pour les critiques littéraires et les historiens de la literature, cette mémoire fragmentaire et hétéroclite, pas toujours aisée à reconstituer, prend appui dans une conscience auctoriale certaine.[2] S'ajoute, à cette tentative de penser les lignes de convergences et de différences entre le Dadaïsme et le Surréalisme comme une élaboration fictionalisante, un roman familial, donc, construit à partir de la mémoire à la fois individuelle et collective, le fait historique que pour plusieurs artistes, dont Sophie Taeuber, Hannah Höch et Mina Loy, le mouvement Dada ne marqua qu'une étape dans leur carrière et que plusieurs membres des divers groupes Dadaïstes furent emportés par le nouveau courant du milieu des années 1920, soit le Surréalisme.

Des portraits de groupe avec dame, dans lesquels les principales représentantes des divers groupes Dada occuperont le premier plan, me permettront de faire apparaître les deux leitmotivs de ma réflexion sur les liens généalogiques d'une transmission de modèles poétiques et esthétiques – la mise en scène de soi et la transgression générique. Suivra une partie à visée conceptuelle qui a pour but de lancer des pistes de réflexion sur des pratiques d'*écriture de soi* et les stratégies médiatiques que celles-ci mettent à l'œuvre entre les années 1930 et 1970.

Dada et ses figures de proue... féminines: Elsa von Freytag-Loringhoven, Hannah Höch, Sophie Taeuber et Emmy Hennings

Par ces quatre cas de figure d'une création Dadaïste au féminin sont évoqués simultanément les trois grands centres du mouvement: New York avec Elsa von Freytag-Loringhoven, Berlin avec Hannah Höch et Zurich avec Emmy Hennings et Sophie Taeuber. Elles réunissent à elles seules les principales caractéristiques Dada: la préoccupation performative et l'aspect théâtral de toute manifestation artistique, l'esprit collectif en opposition avec l'idéal romantique prônant l'artiste comme génie individuel, la charge ironique animée par une volonté de provoquer le spectateur.

La Baroness Elsa ou Dada incarné dans un corps de femme
Figure à la fois centrale et marginale de Dada New York, la Baroness Elsa – tel fut le pseudonyme qu'adopta l'exilée allemande après son troisième mariage en 1913 avec le baron Leopold von Freytag-

Loringhoven, de douze ans son cadet –, cette *performance artist* avant
la lettre témoigne de l'esprit activiste de la femme artiste moderniste.[3]
Elle s'expose dans les rues de New York, lieu de rassemblement de
bon nombre d'expatriés européens, où elle était arrivée en 1910, cinq
ans avant Gabrielle Buffet-Picabia, en se transformant elle-même en
œuvre d'art:

> silhouette souple, gracieuse comme une panthère, yeux turquoise et cheveux
> teints rouge […], la Baronne arbor[e] un chapeau d'aviateur orné d'une plume,
> le corps enveloppé d'un costume si ajusté qu'il semble peint directement sur son
> torse, la tête relevée, les bras tendus tels des ailes aérodynamiques, véritable
> fusée qui s'apprête à décoller. (Gammel 2007: 186)

À un autre moment, dans la posture de l'artiste provocatrice, la
Baronne se promenant avec un pénis postiche, phallus performatif et
symbole de l'adoption d'attributs phalliques par la *New Woman*
androgyne.[4] Durant sa carrière new-yorkaise, de 1913 à 1923,
l'ancienne actrice de vaudeville puis modèle d'artiste transfère son
expérience de la scène et du studio d'artiste, à travers des
performances hautement théâtralisées, dans la vie de tous les jours.[5]
Elle projette ses images d'un corps orné, décoré, assorti de divers
objets – le plus souvent utilitaires (boîtes de conserve, cuillers à thé,
timbres américains, le phare d'une voiture, entre autres) et détournés
de leur contexte habituel, plusieurs années avant Duchamp – dans des
lieux publics et privés, expérimentant une nouvelle mascarade à
chaque nouvelle apparition. Ces performances axées sur le corps et
excessivement sexualisées effraient souvent les Dadaïstes masculins,
sans parler du public spectateur malgré lui, lors des mises en scène de
soi de la Baronne. Son art corporel raconte l'histoire du mouvement
Dadaïste: confondre l'art et la vie, illustrant sans cesse une déroutante
esthétique transgressive – de l'entre-deux, du grotesque et du
difforme; se mettre en avant comme sur une scène de théâtre, engager
son corps là où les artistes hommes préfèrent les objets-machines ou
les *ready made*, tels semblent être les principes créateurs de la
Baronne. Il est vrai qu'Elsa, comme le souligne Amelia Jones (1998:
156), au lieu de *représenter* les concepts Dada (par exemple l'objet
érotique de la femme-machine), les *vit* à travers son propre corps, bref
elle incarne Dada même. Ou comme l'exprime Jane Heap au
printemps 1922 dans l'un de ses nombreux rapports pour *The Little
Review:* "the first American Dada […] she is the only one living
anywhere who dresses Dada, loves Dada, lives Dada", avant de la

proclamer "première Dada américaine" (Jones 2005: 156).[6] Retenons de ces expérimentations, enrichies à certains moments de sa carrière d'une collaboration originale avec Duchamp, Man Ray et Berenice Abbott, que l'autoreprésentation, telle que pratiquée par la Baroness Elsa sous forme d'un art visuel qui implique la *physis* du sujet au même titre que des objets de consommation, anticipe sur le questionnement du genre sexuel et les préoccupations dada en matière d'un art avant-gardiste empreint d'érotisme. En même temps, cette conception esthétique "révolutionnaire" atteint l'objectif dada de "désautomatisation" du regard: le spectateur se voit contraint de concevoir autrement l'objet d'art, de réfléchir à sa façon de le contempler-consommer, d'adopter de nouvelles modalités d'intégrer le quotidien et le familier au sublime artistique, à l'original et à l'unique. Rappelons ensuite que, telle une étoile filante, après la mort de la Baronne en 1927, son nom disparaît aussi rapidement qu'elle-même était apparue comme artiste-poétesse sur la scène new-yorkaise, que son art visuel est exposé sous le nom d'autres artistes et que ses performances éphémères tombent dans l'oubli.[7] Constatons finalement avec Amelia Jones que des artistes lancent des défis plus grands à leur réception-perception (à l'époque autant qu'aujourd'hui) lorsqu'ils choisissent de performer la sexualisation (féminisation/ homosexualisation) du sujet moderne dans un système capitaliste plutôt que de l'*illustrer*.[8] Les *self-performances* d'Elsa se trans-formeront chez les auteures-artistes surréalistes en des mises en théâtre de soi profondément intériorisées; restera la conception de soi comme œuvre d'art inspirée d'une nette volonté de brouiller les frontières entre l'art et la vie, de remettre en cause la morale bourgeoise et de se situer toujours par delà les frontières, autrement dit dans une permanente "transfrontalité" générique, sexuelle et éthique.

Hannah Höch, la collaboration interartistique et la pratique du photomontage

Le slogan: "Dada est politique, l'Art est mort" et la devise plus personnelle de Hannah Höch: "Ich möchte die festen Grenzen verwischen, die wir Menschen selbstsicher um alles uns Erreichbare zu ziehen geneigt sind" [J'aimerais effacer les frontières fixes que nous, êtres humains sûrs de nous-mêmes, avons tendance à établir autour de tout ce que nous pouvons toucher] (Lavin 1993: 340) résument bien la visée générale du travail artistique de cette Dadaïste berlinoise, notamment en ce qui concerne ses photomontages qui détournent la fonction documentaire de la photographie tout en leur attribuant un côté féérique (Riese Hubert 1998a: 27).[9] Dès 1917, elle est associée au mouvement et participe en 1920 à la *Erste Internationale Dada-Messe* à Berlin. Höch illustre, sans aucun doute plus que la Baronne, l'esprit de collaboration prôné par les avant-gardes. Ainsi collabore-t-elle avec Raoul Hausmann[10], le "Dadasophe", puis avec Johannes Baader, le "SurDada", comme les appelle Marc Dachy (1994: 153) – les deux étant également ses compagnons de vie –, avant de rencontrer en 1919 Kurt et Emma Schwitters avec qui elle travaillera plus étroitement, comme plus tard, au milieu des années 1920, avec le couple Taeuber-Arp, les artistes du Bauhaus et du cercle néerlandais De-Stijl, de même qu'avec la poétesse Til Brumann, de 1926 à 1935 sa compagne de vie. Par le biais du collage et du photomontage, Hannah Höch s'inscrit dans le groupe politisé allemand qui focalise ses activités sur l'utilisation "anarchique" des mass médias et le montage de différentes sources iconiques (images d'objets mécaniques et industriels). En effet, à ses débuts, Dada Berlin trouve plus urgent de réfléchir aux possibilités d'une révolution sociopolitique qu'à l'avènement d'une nouvelle esthétique; les membres oscillent entre communisme et anarchisme, privilégiant une vision politique au détriment d'une investigation artistique. Si Dada Berlin a pour vocation première celle de décomposer et de détourner de l'autocratisme une société régie par Guillaume II et son chancelier Hindenburg afin de la fragmenter, et que, dans cette perspective, le photomontage devient la pratique qui tient le mieux compte de cette volonté, l'activité poétique s'immisce rapidement, avec Salomon Friedlaender dit Mynona notamment, sous forme de la performance lors des séances de lectures-récitations publiques (Valabrègue 2000).

Ce qui distingue le travail de Hannah Höch de ses collègues artistes et collaborateurs masculins, ce sont l'humour et l'ironie, allant parfois jusqu'au cynisme et à la parodie de certaines formes picturales, par lesquels elle s'attaque, comme par une *Schnitt mit dem Küchenmesser,*[11] à des questions sociales et politiques.[12] Outils principaux des femmes, le couteau de cuisine et la paire de ciseaux se transforment en armes. Elle coupe et découpe, monte et colle des fragments d'images, souvent recyclés de cartes postales, d'affiches publicitaires, de patrons de couture ou d'autres supports visuels quotidiens propres à une société de consommation en émergence, en y intégrant également des matériaux quotidiens associés généralement à la femme (rubans, boutons, morceaux d'étoffe, passementerie), les déformant jusqu'à ce que l'ensemble prenne des allures grotesques et menaçantes.[13] Le photomontage réalisé en 1919-1920, *Coupe-au-couteau-de-cuisine-Dada-dans-la-panse-à-bière-allemande-de-la-dernière-des-époques-culturelles-de-Weimar*, traduit toute la violence des figures monstrueuses, en exposant des créatures hybrides et souvent bouffonnes. Après la Première Guerre mondiale, de nouveaux monstres peuplent la ville et hantent l'imaginaire des artistes et des écrivains; aussi de nouveaux monstres de papier naissent-ils des ciseaux de Hannah Höch, tout comme elle engendre, dans une perspective plus féministe, une série d'images de la *New Woman*, autre phénomène social corollaire de la guerre, pour propulser ces icônes du modernisme dans l'espace public.[14] Höch explore la question du "gender politics within the wider socio-political realm" (Meskimmon 1997: 699) et démontre, à l'instar de la peintre Käthe Kollwitz, l'accès des femmes à la sphère publique. Résumons donc la démarche Dadaïste de Hannah Höch comme suit: elle collectionne et récupère des images publiques (tirées de journaux, magazines, affiches, tracts, etc.) qu'elle garde dans ses journaux et ses *scrapbooks* pour en proposer dans chaque nouvelle œuvre un surprenant assemblage d'éléments disparates. Elle interroge également une certaine représentation "fétichisante" ou mythique de la femme (comme dans *Da Dandy* ou, plus tard, dans *Trauer*) et, finalement, elle confronte directement le spectateur avec *sa* vision du désordre de la société de l'entre-deux-guerres, de ses lieux communs sur la différence sexuelle (*Bürgerliches Brautpaar – Streit*) et sur l'Autre excentrique, androgyne ou ethnique (*Dompteuse* ou *Fremde Schönheit II*).[15] Tous ces éléments se trouvent réunis grotesquement au sein d'un même espace pour que le regardant-lisant, étant donné que surtout au début de sa carrière, Höch adhère à une pratique profondément intermédiale en mariant volontiers, tels deux moyens d'expression équivalents, textes et images dans ses photomontages, se rende compte de l'impossibilité à ressaisir un sens global dans la vie, pour que les œuvres gardent un caractère de boîte de Pandore renversée. Apparaît alors une esthétique de l'espace visuel qui fonctionne comme un espace poétique, c'est-à-dire un espace où le sens se voit constamment différé, voire menacé ou suspendu temporairement grâce à des lectures multiples. C'est par la stratégie du *Verfremdungseffekt* au sens brechtien, par le détournement ironique des images et des mots de leur contexte habituel que Höch a contribué à provoquer chez le lecteur une distance critique face à l'œuvre et, par là, à l'inciter à redéfinir ses modes de réception-perception de l'art. Vers la fin de sa carrière, Höch révèle dans son œuvre une tendance dans *Lebensbild/Lebenscollage* (1970–72), bien que l'expérimentation prenne le dessus sur la représentation de soi pour dériver vers l'onirique et le fantastique (Riese Hubert 1994: 302–3).[16] Inutile de dire qu'elle s'avère ainsi une voie de transmission entre, d'un côté, la conception Dadaïste de la subversion-transgression des arts et des genres, des moyens de représentation et du rôle conventionnel du spectateur et, de l'autre côté, l'esthétique surréaliste au féminin liée intrinsèquement à l'autoréflexivité et à la transfiguration (parfois ironique) de soi, tel le phénix qui renaît de ses cendres.

Emmy Hennings et Sophie Taeuber ou l'art du pas de deux

D'office, les membres du groupe Dada Zurich, qui, chronologiquement, a lancé le mouvement de révolte et de protestation, souscrivent à une esthétique du spectaculaire et du *happening* au même titre qu'au travail de collaboration interartistique. Comparé à Dada New York et à Dada Berlin, l'esprit de collaboration entre artistes, surtout entre femmes et hommes fait partie intégrante d'une démarche artistique autre, propre à Dada Zurich; une collaboration qui, dans certaines œuvres, atteint l'effacement des apports respectifs au profit de la création d'un *Gesamtkunstwerk* avant-gardiste.[17] Les couples d'artistes les plus prolifiques sont, tout au long de leur vie, Emmy Hennings et Hugo Ball, Sophie Taeuber et Hans Arp. Dans les deux cas, ni l'un ni l'autre ne semblent connaître la compétition, l'un et l'autre faisant foi d'un double rapport entre artiste pratiquant et critique, entre "performant" et spectateur.[18] En effet, lors des spectacles interdisciplinaires organisés au Cabaret Voltaire et à la Galerie Dada, la chanteuse-danseuse-poète Emmy Hennings[19] et la peintre-danseuse-plasticienne Sophie Taeuber[20] occupent des places de premier ordre, tout comme elles créent des œuvres en étroite collaboration avec leurs conjoints.[21] Elles incorporent littéralement l'art performatif cher aux Dadaïstes de Zurich, au-delà des traditionnels codes de représentation des arts occidentaux, faisant souvent preuve d'une maîtrise de la scène qui leur permet de passer du chant et de la danse à la récitation de poèmes pour Hennings (les siens ou ceux de ses amis) et, pour ce qui est de Taeuber, de jongler entre la danse abstraite, la fabrication de marionnettes et la conception du décor pour le spectacle *Le Roi cerf*, entre la peinture, la broderie et les *Têtes Dada*.

À Zurich, la théâtralité des événements sert de filtre pour déréaliser la réalité: d'abord celle de la Première Guerre mondiale, puis celle, nouvelle, de l'entre-deux-guerres. Si, en effet, la performance est le moyen privilégié du groupe Dadaïste de Zurich pour attirer l'attention du public sur une esthétique transgressive, à la croisée des arts et des médias, mais loin d'un programme politique ou d'un manifeste philosophique, les deux femmes artistes contribuent incontestablement à la mise en place d'une *praxis* intermédiale qui se verra portée à son apogée par la majorité des auteures-artistes surréalistes: à travers la mise en scène de soi impliquant le corps féminin réel et la projection d'une série de *personae* imaginaires (récitation, chant, danse, théâtre de marionnettes), d'une part, et par le biais d'une tendance certaine à l'autoréflexivité teintée d'humour et parfois d'absurdité, d'autre part. Hennings, notamment dans ses écrits autobiographiques (Hennings 1990),[22] et Taeuber, sous forme d'un rapport spéculaire entretenu avec certaines sculptures des *Têtes Dada*,[23] de même que dans ses danses multimédia, mariant chorégraphie, costumes, poésie et masques,[24] amorcent un mouvement vers le déploiement d'univers plus intériorisés: ceux de l'imaginaire et du fantaisiste. De plus, Sophie Taeuber se fera concrètement figure de relais entre le Dadaïsme et le Surréalisme, car elle participera à la grande exposition surréaliste de Londres (1936), à celles de New York (1936), de Paris (1938) et d'Amsterdam (1938).

De manière générale, les traces de certains liens généalogiques entre artistes Dadaïstes et auteures-artistes surréalistes sont visibles dans l'activité artistique plurielle de ces dernières. Elles recourent quasi toutes à différents médias pour interroger les limites et les normes d'une mise en scène de soi par la voie de l'autoportrait ou de l'écriture du moi.

Pratiques autographiques des auteures-artistes surréalistes

S'il est vrai que l'incontestable legs Dadaïste consiste, primo, dans le parti pris de la performance au sens d'une *autoreprésentation* multimédia et, secundo, dans la *représentation* fragmentée sous forme de collage et de photomontage, les auteures-artistes surréalistes intègrent ces deux grands principes de création pour y ajouter souvent la question de l'identité sexuelle, des identités sexuelles en pleine redéfinition depuis l'entre-deux-guerres, et, dans ce même ordre d'idées, le regard oblique de la femme créatrice sur le centre du Surréalisme, à forte domination masculine. Si, d'autre part, l'écriture spéculaire ne semble pas avoir occupé chez les Dadaïstes tant d'espace dans la création d'images de soi, souvent par ailleurs en rapport avec l'Autre, chez les surréalistes, la pratique scripturaire précédera ou accompagnera parallèlement l'expression artistique, ou alors viendra s'y ajouter. Ainsi, Gisèle Prassinos, femme-enfant par excellence, stylisée en enfant prodige par les surréalistes hommes, écrit des poèmes longtemps avant de commencer à illustrer ses récits de soi, comme *Le Temps n'est rien* (1958), *Brelin le frou* (1975) ou *Mon cœur les écoute* (1982), par ses propres dessins. Quant à Leonora Carrington, elle ponctue, à l'occasion, sa carrière de peintre de textes auto(bio)graphiques, comme ce fut le cas d'*En bas* (écrit en 1945 et publié seulement en 1973) et du *Cornet acoustique* (traduit en français par Henri Parisot en 1974). La cinéaste Nelly Kaplan choisit d'écrire les *Mémoires d'une liseuse de draps* (1974) plusieurs années après avoir réalisé ses films, dont *La Fiancée du pirate*, et la peintre Bona de Mandiargues publie son récit de soi, *Bonaventure*, seulement en 1977. Tandis que chez Claude Cahun, pratiques scripturaires et photographiques sont intimement liées dès le début de sa carrière, si l'on pense à ses poèmes en prose, *Vues et visions*, publiés en 1914 dans le *Mercure de France*, et à ses premiers autoportraits datant des années 1910; elle recourut simultanément aux deux médias dans son grand projet autobiographique, voire autofictionnelle, *Aveux non avenus* (1930), dans lequel se trouvent insérés dix photomontages oniriques. On peut constater le même usage parallèle des arts et des médias par Unica Zürn pour qui l'écriture et le dessin (ou la peinture) sont des formes d'expression complémentaires, bien que les médias alternent, correspondant à des états d'esprit et de santé mentale différents.

Le but principal des "autographes" surréalistes n'est pas de *raconter* la vie de l'auteure au sens propre, mais de proposer un temps d'arrêt, une réflexion intimiste sur certaines expériences du passé ou sur l'à-venir du "je" narrant, et d'imaginer une façon de *se dire* autrement face à soi-même, certes, mais aussi devant autrui. Ces écrits semblent répondre de manière kaléidoscopique à la quête identitaire originelle du "Qui suis-je?" surréaliste. Or, chez ces femmes qui s'écrivent, le choix du genre "auto(bio)graphique" en cache souvent un autre. Car, dans ces récits de soi, le choix du genre fonctionne comme un filtre qui polarise les éléments du texte d'une façon particulière. On sait que le genre, annoncé habituellement dans le paratexte, crée chez le lecteur des attentes précises au point de guider son intellection du texte. À la lecture des œuvres de Belen, de Cahun, de Carrington, de Prassinos ou de Zürn, par exemple,[25] on constate que le choix du genre implique le "je" féminin dans un jeu avec le genre traditionnel de l'écriture intime, de plus associée traditionnellement à l'écriture des femmes.[26] Plusieurs des textes cités ci-dessus se trouvent en effet à l'intersection du récit, du drame et de la poésie: romans par leur forme extérieure, tenant du (psycho)drame par l'effacement de la voix narrative homogène et authentique au profit de celles d'une *persona*, des *personae* fragmentées, les écrits des auteures surréalistes sont profondément poétiques dans leur inspiration et dans leur réalisation. Poésie de mots et poésie des images, tragédie des tranches de vie remémorées, ironie et humour noir face à soi-même et à son propre destin s'assemblent pour, dans un jeu de registres génériques et d'optiques autoréflexives, faire entendre différentes voix, faire résonner ces voix intérieures autrement.[27] Aussi cet *autrement* passe-t-il par l'hybridation des genres, mais également par la fragmentation du regard porté sur soi, qui, en outre, adopte des points de vue changeants, par le recadrage des épisodes et des événements du passé selon une mémoire volontairement sélective, par l'insertion de photographies, de photomontages ou de dessins. Le souvenir s'inscrit, certes, dans l'idée d'un devoir mémoriel, l'écriture autographique est toutefois conçue comme une tentative de *reconstruire* des traces mémorielles, sans forcément vouloir se souvenir "réellement" de soi et de son passé. En résultent des textes littéraires autographiques qui élaborent le sujet comme une fiction; de là, nous ne sommes qu'à quelques pas d'une écriture appelée par Doubrovsky en 1977 "autofiction". La nouvelle poétique des genres, plus précisément celle de l'écriture autographique telle que mise à l'épreuve par les auteures-artistes surréalistes obéit à l'idée du bouleversement et du dépassement d'une écriture du moi traditionnelle. La narration dévoile un "je" pluriel favorisant allègrement un rapport spéculaire entre le sujet (féminin, masculin, indéfini ou variant entre les sexes selon certaines "tranches de vie", comme c'est le cas dans *Aveux non avenus* et *Confidences au miroir* de Cahun et aussi dans *L'Homme-Jasmin* de Zürn) et l'objet du récit mémoriel. Ce faisant, elle fonctionne comme un miroir tendu au lecteur, où se révéler et se perdre sont les deux versants d'une prodigieuse machine à provoquer des lectures en boucle. Dans ces écritures autographiques au féminin, la vérité sur soi (et les autres) n'est qu'une tentation fascinante, un enjeu illusoire, et le sens, un refuge provisoire aussitôt dénoncé comme insupportable. Contrairement à des autobiographies plus traditionnelles – de Colette, de Catherine Pozzi ou même d'Emmy Hennings,[28] par exemple, pour citer quelques prédecesseures ou contemporaines –, les textes surréalistes se situant de l'autre côté de l'authenticité, de la chronologie des événements et d'une narration linéaire ne basculent guère dans le piège de l'illusion de vérité.

De plus, les frontières entre le texte et les images sont poreuses chez la plupart des auteures-artistes, c'est-à-dire que l'écriture contient l'image et que l'image est toujours là dans l'écriture. Le recours à divers médias par les artistes Dadaïstes tout au long de leur carrière, mais souvent utilisés indépendamment l'un de l'autre ou correspondant à différentes étapes de leur création se transforme chez les surréalistes en une véritable conception novatrice de l'écriture qu'il conviendrait d'appeler des "stratégies intermédiales de l'écriture de soi avant-gardiste". Autrement dit, souscrivant à une poétique de la transgression générique pour les uns (Belen, Carrington, Deharme, Peignot, Penrose) et à une esthétique de l'intermédialité au sein d'une même œuvre pour les autres (Bona, Cahun, Kahlo, Prassinos, Zürn), les auteures-artistes appartenant à la seconde ou à la troisième génération du surréalisme choisissent la vision fragmentaire sur soi au détriment d'une rétrospective linéaire, qui joue délibérément avec les instances narratives, énonciatives et actantielles, qui déjoue volontiers l'horizon d'attente du lecteur, qui se moque du pacte autobiographique. La plupart des œuvres autographiques privilégient l'hétérogène et l'insaisissable en réfutant tant le conformisme du centre que la confusion du chaos. Ils démontrent que leurs auteures détournent, adaptent, renversent ou réécrivent les données surréalistes en les recentrant sur les questions de l'altérité et de l'autrement, d'une "transfrontalité" générique et de perspectives culturelles plurielles (Béhar 1997).

Adaptation et transformation d'un legs

Nous avons pu constater, à partir de la *praxis* de l'autoreprésentation par le biais de différents médias, caractéristique des quatre artistes Dadaïstes évoquées – la Baronne Elsa, Hannah Höch, Emmy Hennings et Sophie Taeuber –, que les pratiques d'écriture, de création et d'invention de soi (au sens d'une autogenèse) de bon nombre d'auteures-artistes surréalistes sont redevables à l'esthétique Dadaïste au féminin ayant inauguré de nouvelles postures autoréflexives. Le legs des "mères symboliques" aux "filles spirituelles" semble avoir trouvé *naturellement*, à quelques années d'intervalle, des voies d'expression – textuelles et visuelles – axées plus délibérément sur le "comment (s')écrire". Ce nouveau parti pris de *s'écrire* et d'entretenir des rapports spéculaires avec son *alter ego* réel (le collaborateur/la collaboratrice) ou fictif (par des voix narratives polyphoniques) s'est opéré un véritable déplacement de la mise en théâtre de soi Dadaïste vers une autoreprésentation polymorphe surréaliste: l'extériorité théâtrale a progressivement cédé le pas à une introspection décentrée, plus subjective, autrement spectaculaire.

Notes

[1] C'est le terme employé par Georgiana M. M. Colvile (1999). Je préfère cependant le terme binomial "auteure-artiste" ou celui de "créatrice surréaliste" à l'expression générique de "femme surréaliste", étant donné la double, voire la triple, orientation de leur travail de création au croisement des arts et des médias – j'y reviendrai plus loin.

[2] Le mérite de s'être penché sur une filiation entre auteures-artistes Dadaïstes et surréalistes revient incontestablement à Renée Riese Hubert (1998a), qui jette des passerelles entre Sophie Taeuber et Meret Oppenheim, entre Hannah Höch et Toyen, entre Mina Loy et Joyce Mansour.

[3] Résumant son activité artistique protéiforme, Rudolf Kuenzli (1998: 442) parle de la Baroness Elsa comme poétesse, sculptrice, artiste multimédia, protopunk et modèle d'artiste.

[4] Est ici évoqué l'objet *Limbswish* créé environ en 1920: ressemblant à un fouet, constitué d'un ressort métallique et d'un gland de rideau, cet 'appareil' constituait un ornement que la Baronne portait aux hanches, attachée à sa ceinture. Déambulant dans les rues de New York, elle créait de la musique corporelle Dada à chaque mouvement.

[5] La performance de soi au sens moderne du terme et qui emprunte souvent le médium photographique commença à émerger dans les années 1870. Associée

pour cette époque aux incessantes séances chez le photographe de la comtesse de Castiglione et à ses mises en théâtre de soi à la cour et dans les salons, de même qu'à celles de Robert de Montesquiou, cette nouvelle perception du sujet kaléidoscopique prit son envol à l'époque moderniste, comme en fait foi, par exemple, la démarche de Claude Cahun. Pour plus de détails à ce propos, voir Oberhuber (2005b et 2007c).

[6] Signalons que c'est grâce à Jane Heap que la poésie dada d'Elsa et une partie de sa correspondance purent être conservées. Ainsi, à partir de 1918, furent publiés les poèmes d'Elsa parce que la journaliste avait pris soin de les envoyer régulièrement à *The Little Review;* pour cette poésie, voir Freytag-Loringhoven (2005).

[7] Certes, le propre de la performance est de ne pas survivre au moment présent, comme nous le rappelle justement Peggy Phelan (1993: 146–53): la performance ne peut être sauvegardée, ni enregistrée, ni documentée, ou autrement participer dans la circulation de représentations de représentations: dès qu'elle le fait, elle se transforme en autre chose qu'une performance. Mais comment se fait-il que tant d'artistes et d'auteures des avant-gardes de l'entre-deux-guerres aient été si souvent et pendant plusieurs décennies "oubliées" par les historiens de l'art et de la littérature ? Le caractère éphémère de certaines performances, œuvres ou autres traces peut avoir sa part de responsabilité; l'oubli d'Elsa dans la lignée des Dadaïstes new-yorkais, malgré les publications constantes de ses poèmes dans des revues d'avant-garde, s'explique toutefois, selon Rudolf Kuenzli, par le parti pris de l'histoire culturelle en faveur d'artistes masculins comme Duchamp, Picabia et Man Ray (Sawelson-Gorse 1998: 446–7). Susan Rubin Suleiman (1990) avaient déjà circonscrit la place et le rôle des femmes artistes dans les mouvements d'avant-garde par le trope de la "double marginalité" par rapport au centre masculin

[8] "[A]rtists who *performed* rather than *illustrated* the sexualization (feminization/homosexualization) of modern subjectivity in capitalism pose more intense challenges […] we might begin to rethink how these most extreme sexualizations of the artistic subject have permeated contemporary artistic practice" (Jones 1998: 162).

[9] Malgré cette orientation politique du travail de Hannah Höch, signalons, en accord avec Marsha Meskimmon (1997), qu'on aurait tort de réduire son œuvre à la seule pratique du photomontage. Elle a également fait du dessin, de la peinture, de la photographie, tout comme elle a fabriqué des collages et des poupées, les célèbres *Dada-Puppen*. Si les historiens de l'art discutent et étudient le plus souvent les photomontages de Höch, c'est parce qu'elle peut se disputer l'honneur, avec George Grosz et Raoul Hausmann, d'avoir inventé cette technique avant-gardiste.

[10] C'est à ce premier travail de collaboration qu'est consacrée l'étude de Renée Riese Hubert (1994). Pour une revalorisation du travail de Höch, dans le contexte d'une esthétique féminine, voir Christine Battersby (1989: 11–14).

[11] Tel est le début du titre de l'un des photomontages les plus étudiés de Höch. Pour la technique du photomontage höchien, on consultera Dech (1981).

[12] Renée Riese Hubert (1994: 294) note que "instead of preaching against male exploitation, Höch institutes through irony a rupture of social and aesthetic

conventions". À propos des enjeux esthétiques, psychologiques et politiques dans l'œuvre de Höch, en comparaison avec celle de Claude Cahun, on lira avec intérêt Adamowicz (2007).

[13] Pour la technique de recyclage-récupération, voir Vergine (1982: 190–2).

[14] On reconnaît souvent sur ces photomontages des icônes féminines de l'époque, c'est-à-dire des danseuses ou des patineuses artistiques faisant la une des magazines féminins comme par exemple Niddy Impekoven, Asta Nielsen et Pola Negri.

[15] L'aspect ethnique, en combinaison avec une dimension *gender*, est particulièrement exploité dans la série de photomontages *Aus einem ethnographischen Museum* (1924–34). Voir à ce sujet Lavin (1998).

[16] Au sujet d'une vision intériorisée dans les œuvres post-Dada de Hannah Höch, jouant avec l'iconographie primitiviste ou, plus généralement, exotique (*Negerplastik; Indische Tänzerin; Fremde Schönheit*, entre autres), Lavin (1998: 345) note que l'on y décèle une tension entre l'autoreprésentation ("one that follows the patriarchal standards by which women must redefine their bodies as commodities or by which men must embody the phallus-power") et la dépossession de soi ("according to European myths about African religion as embodied in their art objects").

[17] Signalons toutefois que, malgré cette visée esthétique autoproclamée d'une création à quatre mains, l'histoire culturelle a eu tendance jusqu'à il y a une dizaine d'années à retenir de ces couples d'artistes plutôt les membres masculins, soit Hugo Ball et Hans Arp, et moins leurs *alter ego*, Emmy Hennings et Sophie Taeuber. Le même constat s'impose pour les couples d'artistes surréalistes.

[18] Le rôle fondateur pour Dada Zurich et le travail des deux couples d'artistes ont été brillamment mis en évidence par Riese Hubert (1994 et 1998b). Elle insiste sur la différence entre Berlin et Zurich en ce qui concerne l'inclusion des femmes artistes dans le mouvement, le respect et l'appui mutuels si caractéristiques des couples d'artistes de Zurich: "Moreover Hennings and Taeuber played crucial roles during the vibrant months of the Cabaret Voltaire and the Galerie Dada, participating in various forms of entertainment sponsored by the group" (Riese Hubert 1998b: 517).

[19] Outre les pages consacrées à Hennings par Riese Hubert (1998c), on consultera les présentations bio-bibliographiques proposées par Le Bon (2005: 482–3) et Dickerman (2006: 473–4).

[20] Pour une présentation générale de la carrière, du travail artistique et de l'enseignement de Sophie Taeuber, voir Vergine (1982: 219–21), Brown (1997: 1349–50), Le Bon (2005: 924–35) et Dickerman (2006: 488).

[21] Citons à titre d'exemple le magnifique livre surréaliste *Muscheln und Schirme* (1939) qui fait dialoguer les dessins de Taeuber avec les poésies d'Arp.

[22] À retenir surtout, suivant la lecture proposée par Riese Hubert (1998b: 522–3) la partie "Aus dem Tagebuch", dans laquelle Hennings propose une réflexion quelque ironique sur sa performance d'Arachne, notamment en ce qui concerne son triple rôle de femme, d'amante et d'artiste de performance.

[23] Pensons précisément à cette photographie de Nic Aluf datée de 1920 et montrant un tête-à-tête entre Sophie Taeuber et l'une de ses *Têtes Dada*.

²⁴ Pour plus de détails sur la mise en scène de l'intériorité et de l'art primitif dans ces spectacles de danse, de même que sur la collaboration entre Taeuber et Arp, voir Dachy (1994: 91–9), ainsi que le chapitre de Jill Fell dans le présent volume.

²⁵ Pour une lecture plus approfondie et des réflexions conceptuelles sur l'écriture "autographique" avant-gardiste, voir Oberhuber (2005b et 2007b).

²⁶ Voir à ce propos Planté (1989: 227–37). La question d'une écriture sexuée vient d'être abordée dans l'ouvrage collectif Mavrikakis et Poirier (2006).

²⁷ Susan Rubin Suleiman (1990: 26) rappelle la position précaire des sujets féminins au sein du groupe surréaliste dominé par Breton, Aragon, Éluard et Péret, en soulignant la difficulté de s'affirmer par delà les images fantasmées d'une certaine féminité: "A woman Surrealist, in other words, cannot simply assume a subject position and take over a stock of images elaborated by the male imaginary. In order to innovate, she has to invent her own position as subject and elaborate her own set of images – different from the image of the exposed female body, yet as empowering as that image is, with its endless potential for manipulation, disarticulation and rearticulation, fantasizing and projection, for the male colleagues".

²⁸ Je pense notamment au texte de prose *Gefängnis* (1918). Outre la correspondance, et le journal *Das Brandmal* (1920), il s'agit là du principal texte en prose autobiographique de Hennings, généralement plus connue pour ses poèmes d'inspiration expressionniste pour l'essentiel, de facture Dadaïste toutefois pour certains, écrits sous l'influence de Hugo Ball, bien sûr, mais aussi des autres membres du groupe de Zurich.

Bibliographie

Adamowicz, Elza. 2007. "Je(u) masqué(e): Claude Cahun et Hannah Höch" in A. Oberhuber (2007a): 201–16.

Arp, Jean and Sophie Taeuber. 1939. *Muscheln und Schirme*. Meudon: Val Fleury.

Battersby, Christine. 1989. *Gender and Genius: Towards a Feminist Aesthetics*. London: The Women's Press.

Béhar, Henri. 1997. *Cultures, contre-cultures*. Lausanne: L'Âge d'homme.

Brown, Betty Ann. 1997. "Sophie Taeuber" in D. Gaze (ed.). *Dictionary of Women Artists II*. Londres: Fitzroy Dearborn Publishers.

Bürger, Peter. 1982. *Theorie der Avantgarde*. Frankfurt am Main: Suhrkamp.

Colvile, Georgiana M.M. 1999. *Scandaleusement d'elles: trente-quatre femmes surréalistes*. Paris: Jean-Michel Place.

Dachy, Marc. 1994. *Dada et les Dadaïsmes: rapport sur l'anéantissement de l'ancienne beauté*. Paris: Gallimard.

Dech, Jula. 1981. *Schnitt mit dem Küchenmesser DADA durch die letzte Weimarer Bierbauchkulturepoche Deutschlands: Untersuchungen zur Fotomontage bei Hannah Höch*. Münster: Literatur-Verlag.

Dickerman, Leah (ed.). 2006. *DADA*. Washington: National Gallery of Art.

Freytag-Loringhoven, Elsa von. 2005. *Mein Mund ist lüstern - I Got Lusting Palate: Dada-Verse* (tr. and ed. I. Gammel). Berlin: Ebersbach.

Gammel, Irene. 2002. *Baroness Elsa: Gender, Dada, and Everyday Modernity*. Cambridge Mass.: MIT Press.

——. 2007. "La Baronne chauve: Elsa von Freytag-Loringhoven: une trajectoire vers Claude Cahun" in A. Oberhuber (2007a): 186–200.

Hennings, Emmy. 1990. *Betrunken taumeln alle Litfass-Säulen. Frühe Texte und autobiographische Schriften 1913–1922* (ed. B. Merkelbach). Hannover: Postskriptum.

——. 1985. *Gefängnis* [1918]. Frankfurt, Berlin, Vienne: Ullstein.

Jones, Amelia. 1998. "Women in Dada: Elsa, Rrose, and Charlie' in Sawelson-Gorse (1998): 142–72.

——. 2005. "New York Dada: Beyond the Readymade" in *The Dada Seminars* (ed. L. Dickerman). Washington: National Art Gallery: 151–71.

Kuenzli, Rudolf. 1998. "Baroness Elsa von Freytag-Loringhoven and New York Dada" in Sawelson-Gorse (1998): 442–75.

Lavin, Maud. 1993. *Cut with the Kitchen Knife. The Weimar Photomontages of Hannah Höch*. New Haven and London: Yale University Press.

——. 1998. "Hannah Höch's *From an Ethnographic Museum*" in Sawelson-Gorse (1998): 350–9.

Le Bon, Laurent (ed.). 2005. *Dada*. Paris: Éditions du Centre Pompidou.

Mavrikakis, Catherine et Patrick Poirier (eds). 2006. *Un Certain Genre, malgré tout. Pour une réflexion sur la différence sexuelle à l'œuvre dans l'écriture*. Québec: Nota bene.

Meskimmon, Martha. 1997. "Hannah Höch" in *Dictionary of Women Artists I* (ed. D. Gaze). Londres: Fitzroy Dearborn Publishers: 697–701.

Oberhuber, Andrea. 2005a. " 'J'ai la manie de l'exception': illisibilité, hybridation et réflexions génériques dans *Aveux non avenus* de Claude Cahun" in R. Ripoll (ed.). *Stratégies de l'illisible*. Perpignan, Presses universitaires de Perpignan: 75–87.

———. 2005b. "Mise en scène et autoreprésentation chez la Contessa di Castiglione et Claude Cahun" in C. Bauer-Funke et G. Febel (eds) *Der automatisierte Körper. Literarische Visionen des künstlichen Menschen vom Mittelalter bis zum 21. Jahrhundert*. Berlin: Weidler Buchverlag: 109–29.

——— (ed.). 2007a. *Claude Cahun: contexte, posture, filiation. Pour une esthétique de l'entre-deux*. Montréal: Paragraphes.

———. 2007b. "S'écrire à la dérive: du plaisir, de la souffrance et de la complaisance chez Claude Cahun, Leonora Carrington et Unica Zürn" in J.-M. Devésa (ed.). *Plaisir, souffrance et sublimation*. Bordeaux: Pleine Page: 133–48.

———. 2007c. "La théâtralité de la comtesse de Castiglione comme préfiguration des mascarades de Claude Cahun. Entre vanité et désir d'immortalité" in Oberhuber (2007a): 161–83.

Phelan, Peggy. 1993. *Unmarked. The Politics of Performance*. London: Routledge.

Planté, Christine. 1989. *La Petite Sœur de Balzac. Essai sur la femme auteur*. Paris: Seuil.

Riese Hubert, Renée. 1994. *Magnifying Mirrors: Women, Surrealism, and Partnership*. Lincoln and London: University of Nebraska Press.

———. 1998a. "Femmes Dada, femmes surréalistes" in G. M. M. Colvile and K. Conley (eds) *La Femme s'entête: la part du féminin dans le surréalisme*. Paris: Lachenal & Ritter: 19–39.

———. 1998b. "Zurich and Its Artist Couples" in N. Sawelson-Gorse (1998): 516–45.

Sawelson-Gorse, Naomi (ed.). 1998. *Women in Dada: Essays on Sex, Gender and Identity*. Cambridge Mass. and London: MIT Press.

Suleiman, Susan Rubin. 1990. *Subversive Intent: Gender, Politics, and the Avant-Garde*. Cambridge-Mass. and London: Harvard University Press.

Valabrègue, Frédéric. 2000. "Les photomontages d'Hannah Höch" in M.-H. Dumas (ed.). *Femmes et art au XXe siècle: le temps des défis*. Évreux: Lunes: 38–41.

Vergine, Lea. 1982. *L'Autre Moitié de l'avant-garde: 1910-1940*. Paris: Des femmes.

von Freytag-Loringhoven, Elsa. 2005. *Mein Mund ist lüstern – I Got Lusting Palate: Dada-Verse* (tr. and ed. I. Gammel). Berlin: Ebersbach.

Zürn, Unica. 1971. *L'Homme-Jasmin. Impressions d'une malade mentale*. Paris: Gallimard.

Chapter 13

"The Rimbaud of Cwmdonkin Drive": Dylan Thomas as Surrealist

John Goodby

"Very little idea what Surrealism is ..."?

During the 1930s Dylan Thomas was often associated with Surrealism, and, equally often, vehemently repudiated it. "I have not, never have been, and never will be, or could be for that matter, a Surrealist", he informed his editor at Dent, Richard Church, in December 1935, "and for a number of reasons: I have very little idea what Surrealism is; until quite recently I had never heard of it; I have never, to my knowledge, read even a paragraph of Surrealist literature" (Thomas 2000: 231–2). At the time, however, Church, who had written to Thomas to deplore signs of what he called this "abhorrent" and "pernicious" trend in his work, was threatening to stall the publication of his second collection *Twenty-Five Poems* (1936), and Thomas's response was nothing if not disingenuous.[1] Church, evidently unable to spot a tongue in a cheek, was not fully convinced; but in April 1936 he bluffly informed him: "Still cannot understand the meaning of the poems, but in this matter I have decided to put myself aside and let you and the public face each other" (Ferris 1978: 145). With apparently more conviction, Thomas would tell Henry Treece in March 1938 that "the comparison [of my work] with the Surrealists should give you a lot of scope, especially if, as I'm sure you do, you think it little more than a highbrow parlour game. I haven't, by the way, ever read a proper Surrealist poem" (Thomas 2000: 39). But the same letter contradicts that last claim by describing the poems of David Gascoyne, the one British Surrealist poet of note, as "worthless" – an opinion Thomas could only have formed had he read them.[2] The same is true even of his most unambiguous dismissal of Surrealism, made in 1950, which is dismissive, but curiously knowledgeable about some of the details of "the credo of the Surrealists".[3]

The truth is that Thomas was viewed as a Surrealist in the 1930s, and has been since, with good reason. His claims of innocence certainly did not fool all of his contemporaries, and have not always fooled literary historians: Paul Ray (1971: 277), indeed, claims in his *The Surrealist Movement in England* that "of the major poets of our time, Dylan Thomas was the one most influenced by Surrealism".[4] Indeed, the vehement and often self-contradictory nature of the denials leads one to suspect that Thomas was playing an elaborate game of hide and seek, or *fort-da*, with his critics, perhaps even with himself. The New Testament (with Peter's triple disavowal of Christ), the Hegelian-Marxist dialectic (and its "negation of the negation") and Freudian psychoanalysis (based on the notion of repression), all important sources for Thomas's writing, are reminders that the vehemence of a rejection is often in inverse proportion to the importance of what is being denied. That denial was, of course, also clearly tactical: Thomas was making his way in the literary world at a time after the experimentation of High Modernism, when British poetry had settled for the plain-style, political discursiveness of the Audenesque New Country poets. He was also, evidently, concerned to emphasise the deliberated and highly-wrought structures of his work. Stephen Spender's description of his first collection, *18 Poems* (1934), as "just poetic stuff with no beginning or end, or intelligent and intelligible control" which could be "turned on and off like a tap", shows just how the New Country discourse acted to obscure the elaborate rhyme and metrical schemes, even though these now seem obvious enough (Kershner 1976: 121–2). In this way Thomas's work was shoehorned into a polarised schema in which it featured as the instinctual, irrational, feminine Other to New Country's rational, masculine, neo-classicism, to be linked with Surrealism, which was new, vaguely threatening, and fulfilled the criteria.[5] Since it was known that Surrealism was nothing more than automatism, Thomas was, naturally, an "automatic" writer. Few were aware that even Breton's first *Manifesto on Surrealism* (1924) offered two definitions of Surrealism, one concerning modes of expression, the other relating to the dimensions of reality, and that the dichotomy was paralleled in the British reception of Surrealism and Thomas's response to it (Preminger and Brogan 1993: 1234–5).[6] But none of this can be said to invalidate Thomas's links to, and similarities with, Surrealism.

Timing had much to do with the shallow association of Thomas with Surrealism which it is necessary to challenge before the deeper similarities can be explored. His first collection had appeared in December 1934, just before Surrealism arrived in Britain in 1935 in the form of a series of publications and a home-grown group of Surrealist practitioners. David Gascoyne's *A Short Survey of Surrealism* was published in 1935, and by 1936 there was a English Surrealist group which also included Humphrey Jennings, Hugh Sykes Davies and Herbert Read, these associated with visual artists (who had been rather quicker on the uptake than writers), such as Roland Penrose and Ithell Colquhoun. Sykes Davies' Surrealist novel *Petron* also appeared in 1935, and Gascoyne's Surrealist poems in *Man's Life Is This Meat* in 1936; in that year, too, Read's essay "What is Revolutionary Art?" and his book *Surrealism* appeared. At this point Surrealism could be said to have become the main avant-garde literary fad of literary London, maintaining its grip (although it remained a weak one: Surrealism was never widely-emulated) until 1939. And while the claim is often made that it disappeared with the outbreak of the war, it can be argued that Surrealism enjoyed a revival in Blitz writing and an afterlife as an element of the neo-Romantic, Apocalypse style, as well as in popular culture, with far-reaching, if little-investigated consequences for British culture.

The problem is, of course, that Thomas's work is highly wrought. But because it is not "automatic" in some obvious sense does not mean that it has nothing to do with Surrealism. Thomas insisted, in the letter to Church, that "every line [of mine] is meant to be understood; the reader is meant to understand every poem by thinking and feeling about it, not by sucking it in through his pores, or whatever he is meant to do with Surrealist writing", is true insofar as some "meaning" can, finally, be worked out for even the obscurest passages in the poetry (Thomas 2000: 232). But, of course, Surrealist poetry can be understood by "thinking and feeling about it", even if it is not always possible to easily turn a Surrealist image into prose sense. Automatism does not mean vagueness or incomprehensibility. Moreover, Thomas is being deliberately misleading to the degree that he suggests that non-Surrealist poetry is trying, in all places equally, to be understood. His own work, to the contrary, not only resists paraphrase, but exhibits wide *degrees* of in/comprehensibility. Often it generates obscurity to prevent easy translation into discursive sense. Thus, Thomas told Vernon Watkins that the poem "Now", "so far as he knew [...] had no meaning at all", but rejected Watkins's suggestion that it be left out of *Twenty-Five Poems* on the grounds of "unwarrantable obscurity". Watkins's point was that the poem would give a handle to critics wishing to convict him of Surrealism, at the expense of the book's more lucid pieces. Thomas's response was "give them a bone", and "Now" remained in, as did the equally tough obscure "How soon the servant sun" (Thomas 1957: 16). The real issue here is the desire to baffle, to force the reader to be content with the materiality of the words and a narrative which has no external reference. The five similarly-shaped stanzas all, disturbingly, open with the same three words: this is the first:

> Now
> Say nay,
> Man dry man,
> Dry lover mine
> The bedrock base and blow the flowered anchor,
> Should he, for centre sake, hop in the dust,
> Forsake, the fool, the hardiness of anger. (Thomas 1993a: 45)

But it can be construed, despite appearances. The key, as so often, lies in deceptive syntax; we must read "mine" in line four as a verb not as the possessive pronoun it seems. The poem then becomes a critique of "mine" in that possessive sense, a kind of soliloquy urging rejection of a self-centred (male) sterility and the thoughts of violence it engenders ('the hardiness of anger"). As well as courting incomprehension, the poem's difficulty also mocks avant-garde practice. As his friend Trevor Hughes guessed, the poem is, among other things, Thomas's "burlesque" (or parody) of Gertrude Stein, and it is typical that the form used is cryptically conservative: for all its strangeness, the stanza's first four lines (of one, two, three and four syllables) add up to an iambic pentameter (Thomas 1993a: 200–1).[7]

Such pranksterism marked most of Thomas's dealings with Surrealism, and they were extensive, for all his denials. He knew Edgell Rickword (author of the first English life of Rimbaud published in 1924) and Norman Cameron (who showed him his translation of "Le Bateau ivre" in 1935), and was a member of the

Parton Books coterie which included Gascoyne, usually taken to be the one English Surrealist poet of note. He read and contributed to *New Verse*, which carried Surrealist material. Thomas, too, participated in the International Surrealist Exhibition, held in London in June 1936, at which he circulated among the crowds carrying a tray which bore a teapot of boiled string and a cup, and accosted visitors with the words: "Weak or strong?"[8] At a related event, on 26 June 1936, he also read his poetry with Paul Eluard; and there were Surrealist encounters later in his career (Lycett 2003: 132).[9] More significant, was Thomas's encounter with Eugene Jolas's Paris-based journal *transition* (1927–38), the main anglophone conduit for Surrealism and "the Revolution of the Word", a Joyce-inspired "Proclamation" carried in the June 1929 issue. Thomas was a fascinated *transition* reader possibly as early as 1930, certainly by 1933, and he avidly sought out back issues (Ray 1971: 278). This activity coincided with the formative phases of his style in 1932–34.[10] He would go on to publish "Then was my neophyte" and the story "The Mouse and the Woman" in *transition* in 1936. Dougald McMillan's contention that *transition* had a hand in Thomas's densest phase, in 1935–37, is justified, as is his claim that Thomas's descriptions of his writing method, and avoidance of Modernist "distrust of language", link him with the Surrealists. It might also be added that Thomas also contributed to the only English Surrealist journal, Roger Roughton's *Contemporary Prose and Poetry* of 1936–37.[11]

Still, evidence of an interest in Surrealism, contradicting the denunciations, does not fianlly tell us very much. In isolation, indeed, it is little more than an exercise in source-spotting; an inadvertent contribution, even, to the Dylan Thomas legend (adding contrariness to the other charges) which has hampered past criticism. Rightly understood, however, the contradictions point beyond biography to more substantial reasons why Thomas might have flirted with Surrealism even as he disavowed it. Given Thomas's general importance, this in turn promises to shed new light on literary Surrealism in Britain as whole.

Showing Surrealism: body, psyche, language

It is at the level of aesthetic priority and style that Thomas's affinities to Surrealism ultimately have to be demonstrated. There are several ways, I think, by which this can be done. Briefly, these include his extensive use of the human body and the related "process metaphysic", his treatment of religious and psychoanalytic material, and the attitude the writings show towards language.

The body is crucial to Thomas and is the primary ground of figuration in his work. As early as 1933 he was rebuking Pamela Hansford Johnson's accusations that his work was "hideous":

> I fail to see how the emphasizing of the body can, in any way, be regarded as hideous. The body, its appearance, death, and disease, is a fact, sure as the fact of a tree. It has its roots in the same earth as the tree. The greatest description I know of our own "earthiness" is to be found in John Donne's *Devotions*, where he describes man as earth of the earth, his body earth, his hair a wild shrub growing out of the land. All thoughts and actions emanate from the body. Therefore the description of a thought or action – however abstruse it may be – can be beaten home by bringing it onto a physical level. Every idea, intuitive or intellectual, can be imaged and translated in terms of the body, its flesh, skin, blood, sinews, veins, glands, organs, cells, or senses. (Thomas 2000: 57)

But his treatment of the body is not problematic in the usual way; that is, in contrast with soul, spirit or intellect. Like Surrealism (and in contrast to the cerebral-social New Country poets) Thomas's bodily emphasis is intended to counter dualist thinking.

By treating the human body as a microcosm, Thomas was able to present both it and the cosmos as interconnected in space and simultaneous in time, with conventionally distinct spirit and matter viewed as different forms of the same "force":

> The force that through the green fuse drives the flower
> Drives my green age; that blasts the roots of trees
> Is my destroyer. (Thomas 1993a: 13)

The body in Thomas is traversed by desire – that is, by ineluctable biological drives which terrify even as they overwhelm the subject. The scenario is thoroughly Darwinian, and the poems acquire their universalising authority from a knowledge that our sense of unique subjecthood is a cheat, since the meaning of the individual is ultimately merely as a transmitter of genetic material (what Richard Dawkins, more recently, has theorised as the "selfish gene"). Sex, then, is central to this poetry. It may be thwarted (masturbation is the subject of "My hero bares his nerves"), or be the source of unreal appetites created by film (in "Our eunuch dreams"), but even if it does take place the moment of orgasm will be a kind of séance attended by all the ancestors whose genetic material is being passed on (thus, the womb is a "town of ghosts" in "The seed at zero"). Sexual desire is inscribed in the forms of its repression, but unlike the New Country poets, Thomas does not directly indict these forms which, in Wales, are largely those of Nonconformism. Rather, the socio-ideological codes responsible for distortion inform the genetic textures of the poems themselves as pulpit rhythms, Biblical references and an apocalyptic imagery of striving, ruin, death, and darkness. There is to be no facile isolation and "treatment" of repressions; on such issues Thomas is close to a Bataillean-Foucauldian notion of desire as produced by repression.

In Thomas's metaphysic of "process", all entities are interlinked and subject to perpetual change; post-Darwinian biology is subject in its turn to the physics of the Theory of Relativity, and a universe in which creation *is* destruction, birth *is* the beginning of death (a "green age"), and so on.[12] Noun so often becomes verb in Thomas that it is tempting to read this form of wordplay as an expression of Einstein's theorum that all matter is energy, and vice versa ("the brawned womb's weathers", "cargoed apples", and so on) (Thomas 1993a: 7). In accordance with this, Thomas's con/fuses states in which the body is undergoing maximum physical transformations – the foetal phase and birth itself, hormonally-charged adolescence, orgasm, and death – which may be presented in the poems in ways which make them indistinguishable from each other. Yet for all the continuities, the body itself is always fragmented, itemised in a kind of modernist-Gothic blazon of blood, bone, hair, veins, heart, nerve, head, gland, brain, "worm" (penis), "fig" (vagina), skull, muscle, eye, hand ('The hand that signed the paper" imagines a hand as an autonomous, tyrannical agent). This is more significant, I think, than the standard point made about Thomas's work, that human beings tend to be reduced to their sexual organs. Such bodily fragmentation is also a Surrealist characteristic, of course: "[l]ike Bakhtin's grotesque body, predicated on excess, mutability and the "violation of natural bodies", as Elza Adamowicz (2005: 183) writes of Ernst's collages, "these body parts exceed their anatomical limits and become other". Thus, "Light breaks where no sun shines" anatomises "thighs", "eyes", "rod", "sockets", "bone", "skinning gales", "lids" (Thomas 1993a: 23–4). The body is a Frankenstein-like assemblage of parts: "hair and bone [...] sewn to me by nerve and brain", a mere "flask of matter" (Thomas 1993a: 9). Body parts are defamiliarized, distanced from any controlling subjectivity, by euphemism and grotesquerie: this, for example, is sexual congress:

> A stem cementing, wrestled up the tower,
> Rose maid and male,
> Or, masted venus, through the paddlers bowl
> Sailed up the sun. (Thomas 1993a: 47)

Inexorably gripped by process, these parts are nevertheless not discontinuous. Like the Freudian unconscious, they are timeless and contradictory. Thomas, too, understands experience as "essentially *continuous*", as Peter Nicholls notes of the work of the Surrealists, and he shares their delight in "unbroken contiguity [which] distinguishes [their work] not only from fictional realism but also from forms of modernist montage [...] which [...] seek to make the space between elements the key to some mysterious plenitude" (Nicholls 1995: 284-5). Thomas's often contorted, but always continuous syntax does not permit such spaces, and its "plenitudes" are "mysterious" in different, grosser, ways.

In addition, although his work can be viewed in a Freudian matrix – figures of confinement, castration, explosion and so on, continually hint at it – Thomas is by no means a Freudian as such. That is, while invoking classical Freudian scenarios, the poems continually frustrate them; their circularity prevents therapy, let alone cure. If he may be said to have made a "Freudian exemplar of himself", in Stewart Crehan's phrase, the move was tactical, a form of subaltern mockery rather than a strategic positioning (Crehan 2001: 58). So, we encounter imagery which is blatantly Freudian – maternal or sexually fecund seas, phallic towers of the male ego, *doppelgänger*-like "doubles" and "fellows" – and yet this is countered elsewhere by a refusal to play the game. If for Freud, as Elder Olson (1954: 6) notes, "fruit symbolizes the female breast and definitely does not symbolize offspring, it is generally a child-symbol for Thomas"; similarly, the equation of "caves, churches and chapels" with "the female genitalia" is overlooked in Thomas who uses these, respectively, to symbolise the inner self and lost, pristine faiths. Although Crehan, in a particularly insightful essay, works hard to substantiate a rivalry between Thomas and his father, the poems speak not of murderous Oedipal rivalry and resentment so much as gratitude for a gift inherited and pity for the father's failure: "An old, mad man still climbing in his ghost, / My father's ghost is climbing in the rain"

(Thomas 1993a: 25). (If there is a mother's body whose possession is contested in Thomas's work, it is the material body of language itself; on this territory, the poet has always-already triumphed over the fathern, and this may be one reason why Thomas's attitude to language is so playfully exultant.)

Typically, the scenarios of the early poems echo *Hamlet*, as "Now" and a title such as "If I were tickled by the rub of love" suggests. But they do so through the figure of the malcontent tempted to suicide, not as revenger against the father-usurper and incestuous mother (this incest fixation being the unresolved "objective correlative" which Eliot felt flawed Shakespeare's play). When Thomas takes up the motif of the Oedipal triangle, it is as a pretext for one of his personal symbolic clusters; refusing its abstract, geometric form, it is at the heart of an "Egyptian" group, signifying deathliness, which include mummies, scarabs, crocodiles, and deserts. The dynamic of "My world is pyramid" is un-Oedipal, despite a primal scene complete with Freudian phallus-snakes:

> The patchwork halves were cloven as they scudded
> The wild pigs" wood, and slime upon the trees,
> Sucking the dark, kissed on the cyanide,
> And loosed the braiding adders from their hairs;
> Rotating halves are horning as they drill
> The arterial angel. (Thomas 1993a: 27)

The offspring here is "the arterial angel" being "drilled" into existence in the sexual act, which inscribes him within a world of division, of male and female parent "halves" who are "patchwork", "cloven", and the narrative is gloatingly gothic, rather than traumatised.

Freudian discourse, then, enters the poems as it "enters Surrealism" in Adamowicz's phrase, that is as "fragmented, distorted or displaced" (Adamowicz 2005: 22), in powerful, but calculatedly incoherent, form: Egyptian belief systems and motifs mingle promiscuously with Christian, pagan and wholly personal ones. This is a reminder that Thomas differed from his English contemporaries in living in a rather more religious world; the social glue of Welsh society in the 1920s and 1930s was Nonconformism. Indeed, the intensity of Nonconformism could be said to resemble Catholicism in France, Spain and Italy in certain key respects, linking the anti-clerical tone of Thomas's earliest poetry to Surrealism's rabid antipathy to the Catholic Church. Part of Surrealism's appeal would have lain in this;

and Nonconformism is treated in "Altarwise by owl-light", for example, in a manner reminiscent of *L'Age d'or*. Similarly, Dalí's "The Great Masturbator" can be read in conjunction with poems such as "My hero bares his nerves". Thomas undermines the Word through the word, however; this is what generates his poetry's subversive imagery and hypnotic rhythmic power, subjecting its metanarrative materials to "ludic manipulations". As Adamowicz (2005: 22) notes of Surrealist collage the "aesthetic or sublimatory recodings" of psychoanalytic and religious materials are best considered as "the dynamic reworkings of the 'signe ascendant' rather than the fixed traces of a trauma, in a juggling with fragments which are signifiers unhinged from earlier meanings and exposed to the play of difference".

The freedom and ability to subject such material to the "signe ascendant", his rejection of Modernist linguistic scepticism, its "distrust of language", is of the essence of Thomas's use of Surrealism. His visceral and dream landscapes and narratives proceed by a logic unleashed by verbal play and autonomy, Jolas's "Revolution of the Word" slyly and knowingly invoking Freudian motifs and verbal parapraxes but never endorsing psychoanalysis as a method. If Thomas rejects automatism it is because he felt confident in his verbal ability to evade the censor through the logic of breeding language, believing this to be a more dynamic critique of hyper-rationalism than the inert image-chains of, say, Gascoyne's most Surrealist poem, "And the Seventh Dream is the Dream of Isis".

It is, then, Thomas's surrender to language's innate slippage, pun, parapraxis and polysemy which ultimately establishes his Surrealist credentials. The first three stanzas of "When, like a running grave" offers a typical example of Thomas's logo-surreal method, as associative wordplay and image interact:

> When, like a running grave, time tracks you down,
> Your calm and cuddled is a scythe of hairs,
> Love in her gear is slowly through the house,
> Up naked stairs, a turtle in a hearse,
> Hauled to the dome,
>
> Comes like a scissors stalking, tailor age,
> Deliver me who, timid in my tribe,
> Of love am barer than Cadaver's trap
> Robbed of the foxy tongue, his footed tape
> Of the bone inch,

> Deliver me, my masters, head and heart,
> Heart of Cadaver's candle waxes thin,
> When blood, spade-handed, and the logic time
> Drive children up like bruises to the thumb,
> From maid and head. (Thomas 1993a: 34, 19)

Typically, Thomas piles appositive clauses upon each other in order to arrest syntactical temporal flow (there are no less than thirty-four separate clauses in this opening sentence, which extends over a further two stanzas), while at the same time generating a sense of urgency, even threat, in his noun-verbs, forceful idioms and startling collocations. This in itself produces a dreamlike arrest familiar to us from Surrealist literature and visual art. Even more strikingly surreal are images such as a "running grave", a "scythe of hairs", or "scissors stalking". However, pun – the master-trope in Thomas's early work – is more important still, and can be seen at work in "running" (as of matter from a sore, as well as motion), "gear" (clothes, but turned by "hearse" into a vehicle's gears), "turtle" (marine animal and turtle-dove), "candle waxes thin" (candle-wax, but, as the verb, giving a candle which grows ("waxes") as well as becoming "thin", burning up rather than down), "maid and head" (maidenhead), and so on. This is Thomas's generative method as he attempted to describe in a letter of 1938 to Treece ("image" here means "polysemous word" or "word-cluster", as well as having its usual sense):

> I make one image, – although "make" is not the word, I let, perhaps, an image be "made" emotionally in me and then apply to it what intellectual & critical forces I possess – let it breed another, let that image contradict the first, make, of the third image bred out of the other two together, a fourth and contradictory image, and let them all, within my imposed formal limits, conflict. Each image holds within it the seed of its own destruction, and my dialectical method, as I understand it, is a constant building up and breaking down of the images that come out of the central seed, which is itself destructive and constructive at the same time.
> Reading back over that, I agree it looks preciously like nonsense. To say that I "let" my images breed and conflict is to deny my critical part in the business. But what I want to try to explain – and it's necessarily vague to me – is that the life in any poem of mine cannot move concentrically round a central image; the life must come out of the centre; an image must be born and die in another; and any sequence of my images must be a sequence of creations, recreations, destructions, contradictions. I cannot either [...] as others do [...] – make a poem out of a single, motivating experience. (Thomas 2000: 238)

This is a good description of Thomas's oscillation between an urge to conscious control ("I make one image") and the necessary surrender to the unconscious ("I let, perhaps, an image be 'made' "), which asserts the primacy in the final instance of "my critical part in the business". Thus, the "running grave" leads to "tracks", because runners run on running-tracks, for example, although "tracks" is used as a verb, rather than a noun. This fortuitous association is then extended in the "footed tape" that runners breast (but it is also an undertaker's for measuring a body, developing the pursuit-by-time theme), and so on. By the final verse, the association-cluster / image re-appears in the form of "time on track / Shapes in a cinder death", with Cadaver (time, death) as a figure who races after the speaker around the cinder-covered running-track of life. As Ray (1971: 279) has noted, there are similarities between Thomas's "dialectical method" and Pierre Reverdy's definition of the image:

> The image is a pure creation of the mind [*esprit*] [...] The characteristic of the strong image is that it is born of the spontaneous bringing together of two very distant realities of which the mind alone has seized the connection [...] If the senses completely approve of the image, they kill it in the mind.

Thomas's Surrealist images and metaphors do just this, squirming to avoid such fatal "approval", often resmbling the Metaphysical yoking of heterogeneous objects (Donne's lovers and a pair of compasses, for example) and Lautréamont's famous chance meeting on a dissection-table of a sewing-machine and an umbrella (Ducasse 1994: 14, 23). In Thomas's version – as in "scythe of hairs" – two terms are juxtaposed so as to create a third which is more weirdly potent than the sum of its parts. Surrealist metaphor does this, as Geoff Ward has argued, by flaunting rather than smoothing over (by context or familiar usage) the different sources of tenor and vehicle: "a Surrealist metaphor is a collage in miniature [...] Strength comes from the shock-effect of encountering in poetic language something we could never meet elsewhere" (Ward 2001: 73-4).[13] As Ward adds, a feature of Surrealist metaphor is its "militant literalism" (recalling Thomas's frequent insistence that his poetry be read 'literally': thus, "spade-handed" blood means that we must imagine a personified figure of blood with spade-shaped, gravedigger hands). Ward illustrates his case with "white curtains of infinite fatigue", the opening line of "And the Seventh Dream is the Dream of Isis", in which, as he notes, it is impossible to determine "whether the windows of cries are basically strange-sounding windows, or transparent cries"; it behaves, that is, "as if its attachments were not metaphorical but metonymic" (Ward

2001: 74). In the same way it is impossible to tell whether the "scythe of hairs" is a scythe made from hair, or hairs which cut like a scythe (Thomas is alluding to the *vagina dentata* / castration fear implicit in the Surrealist association of hair with the female genitalia). Thus, the third term which is the metaphor itself "forces an equality of attention onto the two originating terms [...] by the equal weighting of the component nouns". Thomas uses this "equal weighting" effect to problematise image and symbol as well as metaphors; "turtle in a hearse" can be taken, albeit after deliberation, as a symbol of the death of love ("turtle" as turtle-dove). This does not, however, explain why the initial sense conveyed, militantly literal in its grotesque-surreal effect, of "turtle" as the marine animal, should be so forceful. I would argue that in such cases Thomas is playing off Modernist-derived close reading techniques (as exemplified by the then-recently published *Seven Types of Ambiguity*) against a Surrealist effect. That is, if Surrealist figuration "achieves its strange resonances by oscillating undecidably between metaphor and metonymy", as Ward claims, Thomas's image gains something of its own "strange resonance" by oscillating meta-discursively between our perception of what is Surrealist and what can be rationalised by more orthodox, if hyper-sensitive, means.

There are other ways, it seems to me, in which Thomas drew on the Surrealists' example. Not all can be dealt with here – I note, in passing, the fact that (to cite Nicholls) Thomas's texts "constantly show [the Surrealist characteristic whereby] one trope [is] be inhabited by its opposite" – indeed, such "inhabiting" is the basis of the first chapter of Ralph Maud's 1963 study of Thomas – as well as the suggestiveness, in this context, of Nicholls's description of how, in Breton's *Mad Love*, the "intricate chain of images constantly displac[es] a point of origin which is somehow double, containing both life and death" (Nicholls 1995: 299-300). Despite what Nicholls rather dismissively says elsewhere, Thomas's "rich talk of blood and bone and [...] quest for a knowingly archetypal language of "clay" and "shroud" is almost always subjected to linguistic slippage and displacement, its chthonic, primitivist and "natural" aspects undercut and deferred by its delighted immersion in verbal play and *jouissance* (Nicholls 1995: 299). In fact, precisely this process of undermining is a typical Thomas theme: "How shall my animal", for example, explores the impossibility of any such "archetypal" ground in language; recent misreadings reflect the extent to which the Thirties are still seen through Audenesque lenses, even by Modernist critics.

Perhaps the best example of such "undercutting" at a local level – it is certainly the most Surrealist-resembling – is Thomas's penchant for cybernetic conjunctions. Annis Pratt (1970: 130) has argued that "[t]he most striking trait of Surrealist art was a weird mingling of object and subject, of machine and flesh in an expression of both acceptance and distaste for the modern age", adding that "Thomas struggled throughout his early and middle years with the relationship between metal and flesh, the modern age and poetic lyricism". That is, social surfaces are not so much expelled by Thomas's union of the micro- and macrocosmic, as fused with them. His ur-vocabulary of "bone", "blood", "flesh", nerve" and so on, cited as proof of irredeemable organicism, is supplemented by a fondness for items which are at least ambiguously mechanical, such as "worm" (a kind of gear), "gear", "lever", "drill", "iron", a host of film terms, and even the blatantly contemporary "subway" and "macadam". Flesh, spirit (as "ghost" or phantom) and metal fuse everywhere in "I, in my intricate image", for example, where the self is a "half ghost in armour", "man-iron", "ghost in metal", and "metal phantom", and a similar body-and-mechanism fusion is a theme of "When once the twilight locks", "My hero bares his nerves", and "I dreamed my genesis", in which "I dreamed my genesis in sweat of sleep, breaking / Through the rotating shell, strong / As motor muscle on the drill, driving / Through vision and the girdered nerve" (Thomas 1993a: 33, 25). Whatever else it is, this isn't some neo-Romantic fantasy lacking "inherited distrust of the merely 'natural' ", as Nicholls avers. On the contrary, it borders on science fiction in "All all and all", which apotheosises Thomas's queasy cybernetic concerns in an imagined sexual-revolutionary transfiguration:

> Fear not the working world, my mortal,
> Fear not the flat, synthetic blood,
> Nor the heart in the ribbing metal.
> Fear not the tread, the seeded miling,
> The trigger and scythe, the bridal blade,
> Nor the flint in the lover's mauling. ...
>
> Flower, flower, the people's fusion,
> O light in zenith, the coupled bud,
> And the flame in the flesh's vision.
> Out of the sea, the drive of oil,

> Socket and grave, the brassy blood,
> Flower, flower, all all and all. (Thomas 1993a: 29-30)

Typically, this is enacted most thoroughly at a fundamental linguistic level. John Bayley (1957: 193) found Thomas's "petrol face" to be "implacably opaque", but it is simply one of many such yokings by him of organic and inorganic. The first dozen poems in the *Collected Poems* alone yield "chemic blood", "milky acid", "seaweeds" iron", "worm of my finger" (a worm-screw operating lock-gates), "ghostly propellors", "leaden stars [...] rainy hammer", "flesh's armour", "green fuse" (where "fuse" is the kind found in a fuse box, and an explosives-timer, as well as an archaic word for a plant stem), "nerves [...] wired to the skull", "box of nerves", "photograph [...] married to the eye", "cemented skin", "oils that drive the grass", "brain [...] celled and soldered", "the gushers of the sky" (a metaphysical image comparing tear-ducts and oil-wells, which produce "the oil of tears'). Such examples could easily be multiplied.

Hybridity, parody and surr(egion)alism

I have argued that Thomas's writing draws on Surrealism in a manner which combines endorsement and rejection; it is a slyly subaltern appropriation of it, a kind of parody which, out of its own marginalised position, part-embraces that which is parodied. The poems abound with Surrealist-style images ("the candle shows its hairs", or the brilliant, Magritte-like "bearded apple"), and there are even specific Surrealist allusions – the shocking climax of *Un Chien andalou*, for example, became "Splitting the long eye open" (in "I, in my intricate image"), while the "lionhead" of "How shall my animal" derives from "Le Lion de Belfort" of Max Ernst's *Une Semaine de Bonté*. For all their arbitrary-seeming flow, such images can invariably be shown to have been generated by the "dialectical method" of composition. Yet, just as invariably, Thomas problematised the reading process by impeding the straightforward detection of such development: "when logics die", as 'Light breaks where no sun shines" has it, poetic syntax must enact social irrationality and paralysis rather than simply reflecting or commenting upon it (Thomas 1993a: 24). Ever distrustful of metropolitan fashions, Thomas simultaneously guyed avant-garde pretensions even as he used them; and just as he had rejected New Country and modernist myths of themselves – perhaps the strongest and most lasting of all the myths they created – so he was not prepared to take Surrealism wholly seriously either.

The outcome was surrealis*tic*, not Surreal*ism* as it would have been understood in Paris. Indeed, we might call it "surre(gional)ism" given its origins as a response from the margins. The form it took in Thomas was characterised, above all, by hybridity. Although this was unclear to his contemporaries, the "process metaphysic" and the associative-generative linguistic method which embodied it arose out of Thomas's hybridising of elements of the then-current New Country style and the High Modernism of Eliot, Joyce, Pound and Lawrence which had preceded it as the period styles of modernity. Developed by Thomas in just a few months over the summer of 1933 (as his astonishing *Notebooks* reveal), this entailed a combination of Eliotic "difficulty" and the New Country embrace of traditional forms. The Audenesque poets had displaced Modernism's formal radicalism into a socio-political register, a *thematics* of modernity and revolution: for such writers, as Marjorie Perloff (1998: 53) notes, social crisis had made formal experimentation an indefensible luxury: " '[M]ake it new!' could hardly be the watchword of a poetic generation that came of age in the Great Depression, a generation that understood that the 'new' was by no means equivalent to the true, much less to the good and the beautiful".[14] But Thomas's geographical and cultural liminality (lower-middle class, non-university educated, Welsh), as well as the size of his talent, meant he did not have to follow this course. To carve out hs own stylistic space, he imploded modernism into New Country's retro forms: pun, heaped-up appositive clauses, abstruse metaphysical conceits, and wordplay replicated the "difficulty" of modernist parataxis and collage within the constraining traditional stanza frames. Lawrence's blood-worship is undercut by Joycean "dislocat[ion] [...] of language into meaning" informed by a parodic-reverential appropriation of Eliot's modernist primer, "The Metaphysical Poets".

Thomas's Welshness – or better, his Anglo-Welshness – was crucial because it provided the context for a more thoroughgoing and imaginative use of Surrealism than could occur in England. Thomas was unsympathetic to Welsh nationalism's fetishization of the rural, the language and community, not to mention its Maurrassian politics, but this made him no less of a "Celtic" outsider in England. His Welshness was a highly studied performance of a conflicted identity which could only ever be provisional. Although he occasionally drew on Welsh legend, then, the Welshness of his pre-1938 work arose from his reaction to a religious and sexual repressiveness which has been internalised, and so is more tonal than thematic, and hardly ever foregrounded in thematic, identitarian terms. Similarly, Thomas was able to exploit – particularly in his stories – the Welsh tradition of the Gothic-grotesque, but without the folkloric and essentialist baggage these things could carry in 1930s writing, as well as drawing also on other genres, such as horror and thriller (in film as well as literature).[15]

While the hybrid elements are sometimes irrecoverably blurred and buried in the poems, they are very clear in the short stories written before Thomas's turn to a more realistic prose style in 1938. Prose unpacks the poems' radical ellipses – although it should be said that these stories contain some of Thomas's most experimental writing, and are among the most innovative prose of their time, redolent of his affinities with (and fondness for, in all but the last case) the work of Djuna Barnes, Henry Miller, Flann O'Brien and Samuel Beckett. Annis Pratt's discussion of one of the best of them, "The Orchards", is suggestive in regard to what I have been saying about Thomas's relationship to Surrealism. Marlais, the tale's narrator, attempts at one point to write down, to verbalize, a dream he has had; for Pratt (1970: 137), the passage displays "what Kenneth Burke calls the 'gargoyle thinking' of Surrealism" and is "an example of automatic writing" which Thomas is, in fact, presenting as a "[parody] of the Surrealist method as a style which drives the hero to despair that 'the word is too much with us' ":

> Put a two-coloured ring of two women's hair around the blue world, white and coal-black against the summer-coloured boundaries of sky and grass, four-breasted stems at the poles of the summer sea-ends, eyes in the sea-shells, two fruit-trees out of a coal-hill; poor Marlais's morning [...] spins before you. Under the eyelids, where the inward night drove backwards through the skull's base, into the wide, first world on the far-away eye, two love-trees smouldered like sisters. Have an orchard sprout in the night, an enchanted woman with a spine like a railing burn her hand in the leaves, man-on-fire a mile from a sea have a wind put out your heart. (Thomas 1993b: 44)

This convinces, up to a point, although Pratt does not say that it is difficult to tell parody from "real" Surrealism in these stories, and their plots and characters (insofar as these exist) are not as clear-cut as she seems to think, albeit the writing is certainly visionary and dream-like. What can be said is that the instability of hybridity necessarily involves a writer in parody, and that Thomas was well aware of this, as well as of the dangers it posed. Replying in 1936 to Glyn Jones's claim that his increased density was verging on self-parody, he bullishly asserted: "I'm not sorry that, in that Work in Progress thing ['Altarwise by owl-light'], I did carry 'certain features to their logical conclusion'. It had, I think, to be done; the result had to be, in many of the lines & verses anyway, mad parody; and I'm glad that I parodied these features so soon after making them, & that I didn't leave it to anyone else" (Thomas 2000: 272). In truth, parody (and so, inevitably, a degree of self-parody) were part of Thomas's project, and shaped his use of Surrealism as another, if peculiarly appealing fashion to be negated, buried, flaunted and absorbed. In "In the direction of the beginning" and "An adventure from a work in progress", the last two prose pieces he completed before his 1938 realist turn, unprecedented risks are taken, reaching a near-paranoid verbal clottedness in their exploration of the trope of sexual encounter-as-voyage: the style could go no further (Thomas 1993b: 117–23). It seems to me that the extremist trajectory of Thomas's prose between 1934 and 1937 belies Pratt's New Critical and Jungian claims that a story such as "The Orchards" resolves its tensions with Marlais' renewal of the "flames of death and rebirth" within his own "personality". Rather, these stories trace the effects of submission to unconscious promptings, fusing sexual encounter, language and the unconscious: as already argued, Thomas's response to Surrealism was not simply to *invert* passive realism, or transcribe dream-images, but to provoke encounters with the unconscious at a linguistic level: "how shall my anima(l)?" was the question it continually put to itself.

Thomas's marginality and his exploitation of it determined the form his Surrealism took – pranksterism, parody, a poetry which assumes language to be innately excessive, processual and liberatory. It was informed by Jolas's "Revolution of the Word", which claimed that Breton was wrong not to "see that the expression of the unconscious demanded new means. It was not enough to whirl the unaccustomed realities of the dream-state together", because what was now required was "a means of creating the a-logical grammar which alone can mirror the new dimension" (Ray 1971: 78). Unmediated representations of the unconscious, untouched by the ego and conscious thought, were, as Jolas argued, an impossibility: the conscious mind would inevitably interfere in the selection and ordering of material from the unconscious, no matter how spontaneously it seemed to arise. It is a mistake to confuse this extension of Surrealism (however much it is an apologetic for Joyce's *Work in Progress, transition*'s prize exhibit) with the English neo-Romantic Surrealism advocated by Read. Read took his cue from Breton's praise for the English Romanticism, Gothic, nonsense writing and so on, in order to concoct a nativist pedigree for Surrealism (or "superrealism", as he called it): "under another name, or no name at all, it is already indigenous [...] Webster, Peele, Donne, Young, Blake, Beddoes, Poe, Swinburne [...] might all be regarded as precursors".[16] In doing so, he elided the avant-garde character of Surrealism and so misunderstood many of its most basic aims, particularly in the claim that, in creating a Surrealist poem, "the conscious mind of the poet" worked over dream-thoughts, using "order" and "craft" "to disguise any gaps or incoherency [...] and [give] it [the poem] that smooth façade which is generally demanded by the literary conventions of an age" (Read 1936: 76). But Thomas, who mocked Read, had as troubled a relationship with neo-Romanticism as he ostensibly had with the Surrealists, even after he came to be seen as its leader, around 1940. It is, I would argue, simply impossible to equate Read's bland neo-Surrealism with Thomas's hugely energetic, erotic and blasphemous version as found in, say, "Altarwise by owl-light".

Far more unsettling than anything by Gascoyne or Sykes Davies, this is a sequence of ten inverted sonnets Surrealistically presenting a *Bildungsroman* whose decentred, composite protagonist (Adam, Odysseus, Rip Van Winkle, Tutankhamen, Christ) moves through various trials and travels – he is the embryo who "took my marrow-ladle / Out of the wrinkled undertaker's van" of his dead forebears, "a dog among the fairies" determinedly "[biting] out the mandrake [penis]" of his progenitor "with tomorrow's scream", currishly falling into language, childishly throwing out questions which confound adults, encountering the archangel Gabriel cast as a Western gunslinger and card-sharp, together with "Jonah's Moby", "the frozen angel" of the Inferno and "waste seas where the white bear quoted Virgil / And sirens singing from our lady's bedstraw" before being decoyed by "bagpipe ladies in the deadweed" and displaying a twice-'lopped "minstrel's tongue" (Ernst's Loplop, perhaps?) before witnessing a crucifixion staged like Picasso's or Dalí's at which "the three-coloured rainbow from my nipples / From pole to pole leapt round the snail-waked world". The clarity and strangeness of this hallucinatory, yet always concretely-realised journey are no more apparent than in the visionary arrival:

> Let the tale's sailor from a Christian voyage
> Atlaswise hold halfway off the dummy bay
> Time's ship-racked gospel on the globe I balance:
> So shall winged harbours through the rockbirds' eyes
> Spot the blown word, and on the seas I image
> December's thorn screwed in a brow of holly.
> Let the first Peter from a rainbow's quayrail
> Ask the tall fish swept from the bible east,
> What rhubarb man peeled in her foam-blue channel
> Has sown a flying garden round that sea-ghost?
> Green as beginning, let the garden diving
> Soar, with its two bark towers, to that Day
> When the worm builds with the gold straws of venom
> My nest of mercies in the rude, red tree. (Thomas 1993a: 63)

The "Christian voyage" seems orthodox, but it is also that of Fletcher Christian, the *Bounty* mutineer, a model of rebellion, and it is upheld by one who knows his charts (or a pagan god, Atlas, or both). The bay which might promise rest is, in either case, a "dummy" one – false, for fools, and a child's soother – and the "tale's sailor" (or "sail's tailor') is called upon to hold "time's ship-racked gospel" "halfway" off it. This is a densely impacted scenario of not-quite arrival where the harbours have wings, the founder of the Church is also slang for penis, the "brow of holly" is pagan as well as Christ-like, "rockbirds" fly in from from *A Thousand and One Nights* (Aladdin's roc), and the "rhubarb man", the actor-poet Thomas himself, makes an appearance. If there is any English poem of the time, apart from others by Thomas, which presents "life and death, the real and the imaginary, the past and the future, the communicable and the incommunicable, the high and the low" as things that have "cease[d] to be perceived as contradictory" with similar intensity, it is hard to think of them. In imagining "the worm", creation's necessary satanic principle, building in venom and gold, on the "Day" of some resolution of contradictions, the poem concludes with a genuine, unsentimental utopian vision fusing the "mercies" of a "red" socialist millennium, domesticated ("nest") phallic energy and the restored Garden of Eden, what William Empson called a "ragingly good" fusion of Marx, religion and Freud (Empson 1988: 394).

If there is a marked contrast between the dynamism and riskiness of Thomas's 1930s poetry and the solemn lists of bizarreries of the self-proclaimed Surrealists, then taking Thomas into account involves redefining English Surrealism. It is no longer simply a question of *either* the real (non-English) thing *or* an ersatz (English) "neo-Surrealism" if we accommodate Thomas as the belated, liminal and hybrid Welsh modernist who employed the "Revolution of the Word" and parody to forge "an aesthetics of the unprecedented" (perhaps one way of understanding the function of Surrealism in this case would be to think of its use by Aimé Césaire) (Connor 1995: 206). This, in turn, requires a reading of the 1930s which steps outside of the "Auden decade" discourse which has dominated English criticism since the 1970s. Like Joyce, but without opting for the more thoroughly associational, portmanteau-and-pun dream-language of the *Wake*, Thomas explored the movements of the unconscious not in visual imagery but in the workings of language itself. "Dream and language here", to use Nicholls's more general description of Surrealism, "were intersecting worlds we inhabit rather than merely vehicles of self-expression'; and, despite what he claims elsewhere, Thomas was one of very few British writers to answer the challenge of the avant-garde, however partially. His simulacrum Surrealism is "the real thing" because British circumstances – the dominance of irony, plain-style discursivity, a narrowly-defined "political" writing, and traditional forms – set such severe limits to the degree to which Surrealism could develop. Neither an exile, nor gifted with Joyce's intellectual or cultural resources, Thomas nevertheless made a seedily heroic stand against the conservative pressures of English poetry. He attempted, and frequently in the 1930s succeeded, in forging a version of the most advanced artistic practice of the time, even if his self-mocking description as "the Rimbaud of Cwmdonkin Drive" reveals that he understood from the start the banal limitations of his suburban surre(gion)alist revolt.[17]

Notes

[1] Thomas had confessed to Edith Sitwell in January 1936 that he had believed that Church had disliked his "Surrealist imitations so strongly that he'[d] be willing to break the contract" (Thomas 2000: 232, 238).

---

² The denigration of Gascoyne as "worthless" was not new; Thomas used it in a letter of five years earlier to his then fiancee, Pamela Hansford Johnson, in which he had quoted extensively from Gascoyne's "And the Seventh Dream is the Dream of Isis" (Thomas 2000: 45–6).

³ "The Surrealists wanted to dive into the subconscious mind ... and dig up their images from there without the aid of logic and reason, and put them down, illogically and unreasonably, in paint and words [...] One method [they] used was to juxtapose words and images that had no rational relationship; and out of this they hoped to achieve a kind of subconscious, or dream, poetry that would be truer to the real, imaginative world of the mind, mostly submerged, than is the poetry of the conscious mind, that relies upon the rational and logical relationship of ideas, objects, and images.

This is, very crudely, the credo of the Surrealists, and one with which I profoundly disagree. I do not mind from where the images of a poem are dragged up [...] but before they reach paper, they must go through all the rational processes of the intellect. The Surrealists [...] put their words down together on paper exactly as they emerge from chaos; they do not shape these words [...] the Surrealists imagine that whatever [...] they put down [...] must, essentially, be of interest or value. I deny this" (Thomas 1971: 159–60).

⁴ It is no accident that Thomas is cited under entries on Surrealism in literary glossaries. See, for example, Abrams (1985: 205).

⁵ For the 1930s contexts of Thomas's writing, see Goodby and Wigginton (2000).

⁶ Breton's first definition advocated psychic automatism to manifest the repressed activities of the mind; however, he also described what he called 'encyclopaedic" Surrealism; namely, a more complex (and inevitably mediated) practice based on the awareness of previously neglected forms of association, one said to be particularly immanent in dream states, sexual attraction, and the free play of thought and language. In his *Second Manifesto* (1929), Breton added that Surrealism represented that level of reality where "life and death, the real and the imaginary, the past and the future, the communicable and the incommunicable, the high and the low, cease to be perceived as contradictory". Like the stress on immanent forms of association, this can be compared with Thomas's "process poetic" and its sense of micro- and macrocosmic identity, although if Thomas's poems turn on a recognition of contradiction it should be added that they are more concerned to exacerbate than abolish it.

⁷ Davies and Maud, Thomas's editors, think the poem's significance "comes from its form and its insistence on form", but they fail to explain the nature of the formal game Thomas is playing here.

⁸ Of the organisers and those associated with the show, Thomas knew Roland Penrose, Henry Moore, Bill (S. W.) Hayter, Herbert Read, Humphrey Jennings and George Reavey.

⁹ In 1950 Thomas acted the part of The Stage Manager Who Gives the Clues in a production at the ICA of Picasso's Surrealist play *Le Désir attrapé par la queuel*, and in 1952, while he was on his second US tour, both he and Caitlin Thomas were guests of Max Ernst and his wife in Arizona.

¹⁰ *transition* ran from 1927 to 1938, and enjoyed wide influence and prestige: through it Thomas would have been exposed to work by, among others, Hugo

Ball, Salvador Dalí, Paul Eluard, Robert Desnos, Georges Ribemont-Dessaignes, André Lhôte, Phillipe Soupault, James Joyce, Herbert Read, Léon-Paul Fargue, Louis Aragon, Kurt Schwitters, Gertrude Stein and Hans Arp. Thomas referred to *transition* in his correspondence, and Daniel Jones, a reliable witness, confirms the earlier date (McMillan 1975: 157–66).

[11] Roughton published three Thomas short stories ("The Burning Baby", "The School for Witches" and "The Holy Six") and four poems (VIII, IX and X of "Altarwise by owl-light" and "Foster the light").

[12] The title "process poetry" and the label "process metaphysic" to describe Thomas's philosophy, can be traced to the criticism by David Aivaz and early critics which was given its fullest exposition in Maud (1963). The label comes from Thomas's poem "A process in the weather of the heart".

[13] That is, no one will ever see a "scythe of hairs", only read of one (although it is possible to conceive of it as a Surrealist sculpture, like Meret Oppenheim's fur teacup and saucer, or Dalí's lobster telephone).

[14] Thomas's 1930s style can also legitimately be seen as a version of the 'mannerist modernist" style Perloff persuasively identifies in this essay.

[15] A specifically Welsh tradition of the Gothic runs from the mid-nineteenth century through to the work of Arthur Machen and Caradoc Evans. Machen, who "took up Darwinian anxieties as the basis for terror", was the author of what has been described as "the most deacdent book in English", *The Hill of Dreams* (1907), which mixed Huysmans, Pater, *La Queste del Sante Graal* and Sherlock Holmes. In the earlier *The Great God Pan* (1894), a doctor operates on a young girl to open her "inner eye" to the existence of Pan. The resulting visionary power eventually drives her insane, and when the "hell-child" born of her coupling with Pan dies, its body passes through all the stages of biological species reversion, ending up as "primal slime". See Punter (1996: 22-5). For a discussion of Evans and Thomas, see Goodby and Wigginton (2000: 98-102).

[16] In "Surrealism Yesterday, To-Day, and To-Morrow", published in *This Quarter* in September 1932, Breton acknowledged Surrealism's debt to Swift, the Horace Walpole of *The Castle of Otranto*, Mary Radcliffe, "Monk" Lewis, Maturin, Edward Young and Synge (Ray 1971: 81, 93).

[17] "At a very early age Dylan was referring to himself as the Rimbaud of Cwmdonkin Drive" (Fitzgibbon 1965: 61).

Bibliography

Abrams, M. H.. 1985. *A Glossary of Literary Terms*. Cornell University: Harcourt, Brace, Jovanovich.

Adamowicz, Elza. 2005. *Surrealist Collage in Text and Image: Dissecting the Exquisite Corpse*. Cambridge: Cambridge University Press.

Bayley, John. 1957. *The Romantic Survival: A Study in Poetic Evolution*. London: Constable.

Connor, Steven. 1995. "British Surrealist Poetry in the 1930s" in G. Day and B. Docherty (eds) *British Poetry 1900-50: Aspects of Tradition.* Houndmills: Macmillan: 169–92.

Crehan, Stewart. 2001. 'The Lips of Time" in Goodby and Wigginton (2001): 46–64.

Ducasse, Isidore. 1994. *Maldoror and the Complete Works of the Comte de Lautréamont* (tr. and ed. A. Lykiard). Cambridge: Exact Change.

Empson, William. 1988. *Argufying* (ed. J. Haffenden). London: Hogarth Press.

Ferris, Paul. 1978. *Dylan Thomas*, London: Penguin.

Fitzgibbon, Constantine. 1965. *The Life of Dylan Thomas.* London: Plantin Publishers.

Gascoyne, David. 1994. *Selected Poems*, London: Enitharmon Press.

Goodby, John and Chris Wigginton. 2000. " 'Shut, too, in a tower of words': Dylan Thomas' Modernism" in A. Davis and L. Jenkins (eds). *Locations of Literary Modernism: Region and Nation in British and American Modernist Poetry.* Cambridge: Cambridge University Press: 89–112.

—— (eds). 2001. *Dylan Thomas: New Casebook.* London: Palgrave..

Kershner, R. B. 1976. *Dylan Thomas: The Poet and His Critics.* Chicago: American Library Association.

Lycett, Andrew. 2003. *Dylan Thomas: A New Life.* London: Weidenfeld & Nicolson.

McMillan, Dougald. 1975. *transition: The History of a Literary Era.* London: Calder and Boyars.

Maud, Ralph. 1963. *Entrances to Dylan Thomas's Poetry.* Pittsburgh: Pittsburgh University Press.

Nicholls, Peter. 1995. *Modernisms: A Literary Guide.* Basingstoke: Macmillan.

Olson, Elder. 1954. *The Poetry of Dylan Thomas.* Chicago: The University of Chicago Press.

Perloff, Marjorie. 1998. " 'Barbed-Wire Entanglements': The 'New American Poetry', 1930–32" in *Poetry On & Off the Page: Essays for Emergent Occasions.* Evanston, Ill.: Northwestern University Press: 51–82.

Pratt, Annis. 1970. *Dylan Thomas' Early Prose: A Study in Creative Mythology.* Pittsburgh: University of Pittsburgh Press.

Preminger, Alex and T. V. F. Brogan (eds). 1993. *The New Princeton Encyclopaedia of Poetry and Poetics.* Princeton: Princeton University Press.

Punter, David. 1996. *The Literature of Terror: A History of Gothic Fictions from 1765 to the Present Day III, The Modern Gothic.* London: Longman.

Ray, Paul C. 1971. *The Surrealist Movement in England.* Ithaca: Cornell University Press.

Rickword, Edgell. 1924. *Rimbaud: The Boy and the Poet.* New York: Haskell House Publishers.

Thomas, Dylan. 1957. *Letters to Vernon Watkins* (ed. and intro. V. Watkins). London: J. M. Dent and Faber and Faber.

——. 1971. *Early Prose Writings* (ed. and intro. W. Davies). London: J. M. Dent.

——. 1993a. *Collected Poems 1934–1953* (eds W. Davies and R. Maud). London: J. M. Dent.

——. 1993b. *Collected Stories* (ed. W. Davies). London: J. M. Dent.

——. 2000. *The Collected Letters* (ed. P. Ferris). London: J. M. Dent.

Ward, Geoff. 2001. *Statutes of Liberty: The New York School of Poets.* London: Palgrave.

BEYOND DADA

Chapter 14

Tararira de Benjamin Fondane et l'héritage subversif du Dadaïsme

Olivier Salazar-Ferrer

Toute interprétation cinématographique, esthétique, philosophique du film *Tararira*, réalisé en 1936 à Buenos Aires par Benjamin Fondane, est soumise à des hypothèses imposées par la disparition de toutes les copies du film. Nos analyses relèvent donc d'une archéologie cinématographique fondée, d'une part, sur une trentaine de photographies de tournage et une quarantaine de photogrammes retrouvés complétant le lot des quinze photographies du film publiées par Michel Carassou en 1984 (Fondane 1984: hors textes) et republiées par nous-même dans la nouvelle édition des *Ecrits pour le cinéma* (Fondane 2007: 167–74) et, d'autre part, sur notre découverte d'une partie de la partition musicale du film en 2005. La question qui orientera nos réflexions est celle-ci: *Tararira* est-il un film en accord avec la conception fondanienne du cinéma? Je propose de répondre en examinant les écrits théoriques, pour savoir si Fondane était resté fidèle à ses exigences, en dépit des contraintes industrielles et économiques qui s'exerçaient à ce moment sur la réalisation d'un tel film. De fait, on imagine difficilement Fondane, qui s'était présenté comme le représentant du cinéma d'avant-garde en 1929 en Argentine, recourir aux facilités du cinéma commercial qu'il avait dénoncées. Il est vrai que la situation internationale, la possibilité d'une guerre imminente et la montée des fascismes en Europe, le conduisaient aussi à envisager une installation en Amérique du Sud avec sa famille, possibilité suspendue au succès commercial du film. Mais un certain nombre d'indices nous permettent de penser que le film intégrait des caractéristiques subversives représentatives de l'univers poétique fondanien. C'est cette hypothèse que je voudrais défendre ici.

De Dada à *Tararira:* la théorie cinématographique

Dans un texte publié par Michel Carassou (Carassou/Raelanu 1999: 76–82): "Signification de Dada" (1930–33), Fondane réinterprète la signification du Dadaïsme d'une part en fonction de la crise ontologique du rationalisme induite par la Première Guerre mondiale, et d'autre part en fonction des catégories du scepticisme chestovien qu'il vient d'adopter sans réserves: anti-idéalisme féroce, irrationalisme, ontologie de la discontinuité, éloge de l'accidentel et du périssable, vitalisme, valorisation de l'individuel et du singulier, apologie du hasard et de l'absurde, subversion de la morale sociale, pratique systématique de l'humour. Les éléments constitutifs de la subversion Dadaïste excluent toute finalité sociale, intellectuelle ou esthétique. Dada représente donc pour lui une manifestation "catastrophique", catégorie qui deviendra essentielle dans son univers philosophique et poétique. Autrement dit, Dada est "convulsionnaire" et implique dans le cadre d'une crise de réalité une anti-création, une anti-œuvre où du "vide ne peut engendrer que du vide" (Carassou/ Raelanu 1999: 82). Cette autodestruction inhérente au Dadaïsme, qu'il oppose aux récupérations intellectuelles et politiques du surréalisme de Breton, est illustrée dans le même texte de Fondane par l'image paradigmatique de "l'œil coupé au rasoir" du film *Un Chien andalou* de Buñuel. Lorsqu'il s'agit d'interroger les véritables possibilités du cinéma, l'œuvre de référence est *Entr'acte* (1924) de René Clair et Francis Picabia dont il fait l'éloge en 1925 dans le premier numéro d'*Intégral*: "Il n'est donc pas surprenant si le monde, à l'instant même, perdit dimensions, épaisseur, opacité et position verticale; dans ce voyage à travers la vieille création des six jours déjà ranci, nous vîmes le Tout, bousculé, brouillé, emmêlé à force de vitesse, d'une vitesse que le vacarme de Satie rendait étourdissante" (Fondane 2007: 60) écrit-il, en parlant de "transsubstantiation". L'univers cinématographique implique une ontologie du fluide et du continu qui se retrouvera dans sa philosophie (*La Conscience malheureuse*: 1936) et dans sa poésie. Mais il porte aussi en lui une subversion sociale; jusqu'en 1933, Fondane ne cessera de regretter cette période héroïque du cinéma: "Où êtes-vous à présent James Cruze, Walter Ruttmann, Man Ray, René Clair de l'*Entracte?* Où êtes-vous Luis Buñuel? Où êtes-vous soirées des Ursulines, couvertes de cris, de sifflets, de vociférations, où le sang se sentait vivre au milieu d'une chose vivante, explosive" (Fondane 2007: 60).

Ce texte est à mettre en parallèle avec la "Présentation de films purs" prononcée à Buenos Aires en 1929 (Fondane 2007: 63–78). Invité par Victoria Ocampo, Fondane était allé y présenter, en juillet 1929, une série de films d'avant-garde, probablement *Entr'acte* (1924) de René Clair, *L'Étoile de mer* (1928) de Man Ray à partir d'un poème de Desnos, *La Coquille et le clergyman* (1928) de Germaine Dulac, et sans doute aussi *Un Chien andalou* de Buñuel et *Le Cabaret épileptique* de Henri Gad (Virmaux 1998). Après la publication des *Ciné-poèmes* en 1928 avec deux photographies de Man Ray, ses articles théoriques soulignent, comme le font aussi Chaplin, Poudovdine ou Alexandrov, la nécessité de ne pas céder à un cinéma parlant réaliste et de dissocier le son et l'image pour réduire au maximum la structure logique de la syntaxe des dialogues dans un cinéma sonore (Masson 1989: 20). C'est en ce sens que Fondane peut faire l'éloge de *La Mélodie du monde* de Walter Rutmann dans *Bifur* en 1930 (Fondane 2007: 91). Le son dissocié, voire arbitraire, attire le jeune théoricien du cinéma qui a pu réfléchir sur la réalisation de *Rapt* (1934) de Dimitri Kirsanoff dont il a été le scénariste et qui a utilisé un montage expérimental de A. Hoérée et A. Honegger. En travaillant sur la bande sonore avec Kirsanoff qui était aussi musicien, ces derniers avaient utilisé l'improvisation, le son synthétique, les bruitages et les ondes Martenot (Honegger et Honérée: 1934). Nous retrouvons aussi cet intérêt pour le matériau sonore dans l'adhésion de Fondane à un manifeste sur la musique moderne lancé à l'initiative du groupe surréaliste belge constitué autour d'André Souris et E.L.T. Mesens en octobre 1936 (Fondane 1996: 141).

Les *Ciné-poèmes* de 1928 et le scénario retrouvé "Une journée d'ivresse" publié par Michel Carassou (Carassou/Raelanu 1999: 23-6) empruntent beaucoup au cinéma muet burlesque en se présentant comme des séries de courses poursuites. En effet, n'oublions pas que Fondane partage avec l'avant-garde une admiration pour Chaplin et les grands comiques du muet. Dans une séquence de *Tararira,* les quatre principaux personnages apparaissent déguisés avec des draps de lits comme des fantômes, marchant en file indienne, scène qui évoque les gags des Marx Brothers. C'est le mot d'ordre d'une pleine liberté qui gouverne les admirations fondaniennes:

On s'évade de n'importe quel bagne, le mieux gardé. Les quatre ou cinq évadés du cinéma, un Chaplin, un Stroheim, les Marx Brothers, témoignent de l'excellente humeur d'être libres et de l'affreuse angoisse d'être reconnus et repris. Bien d'autres, au cours d'une longue détention, ne se sont évadés qu'une fois ou deux et ont immédiatement été coffrés: un Murnau, un Pabst, un King Vidor avec *La Foule* et cet extraordinaire *Hallelujah*. (Fondane 2007: 109)

Genèse du film

Après avoir été le scénariste de *Rapt* (1936), Fondane avait sollicité Victoria Ocampo et Paco Aguilar pour l'aider à réaliser un film en Argentine. De leur côté, les membres du Cuarteto Aguilar, qui seront les acteurs de *Tararira,* avaient déjà envisagé de faire un film avec Carlos Gardel qui était mort peu après dans un accident d'avion. Le troisième projet envoyé à Paco Aguilar: *A Little Musical Night*, allait déterminer Victoria Ocampo. Dans une lettre à Fondane du 10 avril 1936, elle souligne que l' "espèce de génie du comique" des Aguilar pouvait convenir à merveille au scénario proposé (Fondane 2007: 176).

Le projet est bouclé très rapidement et Fondane s'embarque fin avril 1936 sur le Florida à destination de Buenos Aires. Un télégramme de Victoria Ocampo arrivé à Cadix le 21 avril lui demande de "fondre scénarios tous deux en profitant grand film" (Fondane 2007: 177). Il s'agit probablement de réunir les scénarios de *La Tocatina* inspiré probablement de la *Tocatina en si majeur* composée par Paco Aguilar et celui de *A Little Musical Night*. La maison de production Falma Film, dont le gérant est Juan José Barcia et le directeur l'espagnol Miguel Machinandiarena, propriétaire de casinos soucieux d'investir dans une industrie cinématographique qui est en plein essor en Argentine, va apporter les fonds nécessaires. Aujourd'hui, le casting de ce film disparu ne laisse pas d'étonner ; on y trouve en premier lieu le Cuarteto Aguilar, alors mondialement célèbre, composé des quatre membres d'une famille espagnole en exil en Argentine: Ezequiel (laudín ou bandurria), Pepe Aguilar (luth contralto), Elisa Aguilar (luth tenor) et Paco Aguilar (laudón). Puis viennent des artistes célèbres du Théâtre national de Buenos Aires, comme Delfina Fuentes ou Iris Marga (1901–97), qui avait obtenu un triomphe en 1935 dans *Miss Ba*, et des acteurs déjà connus qui feront carrière au cinéma: Leopoldo Simari, Orestes Caviglia, Miguel Gómez Bao ou Guillermo Battaglia. Les souvenirs de Chola Ascensio, une actrice du film qui interprétait la directrice d'une école de danse, font état d'un tournage festif et plutôt désordonné qui va durer de début juin au 24 septembre 1936 à Buenos Aires (entretien inédit de Chola Ascensio avec Eve Griliquez). La correspondance de Fondane fait état de nombreuses difficultés techniques et matérielles dues au manque d'équipement (caméras, projecteurs), à son inexpérience en tant que réalisateur, mais aussi à la hâte avec laquelle le projet a été conçu.

Du point de vue technique, *Tararira* était un long métrage tourné en noir et blanc sur une pellicule Eastman Kodak ou Afga Pankine munie d'une piste sonore optique à double élongation. Le film fut apparemment tourné aux studios Rayton de Buenos Aires. La production changea plusieurs fois de titre: si le film apparaît d'abord sous celui de *La Nariz de Cleopatra* [Le Nez de Cléopâtre], il devient rapidement *Tararira*, du nom de la *tararira*, un poisson de rivière assez commun en Argentine, pour être parfois appelé plus tard *La Bohemia de hoy* [La Bohème d'aujourd'hui], peut-être à cause d'un réajustement du producteur soucieux de commercialiser son film sous un titre moins absurde. Le choix apparemment immotivé du terme (mis à part le "rira" pour une oreille française) revendiquait peut-être déjà implicitement une filiation avec le cinéma d'avant-garde; il indique en tout cas que le film ne s'inscrivait pas dans une volonté simplement commerciale.

En arrivant en Argentine, Fondane s'était assuré l'aide d'un jeune assistant, Enrique Cahen Salaberry, futur réalisateur argentin et du chef-opérateur John Alton (1901–96), de son vrai nom Jacob Altman (1901–96) qui deviendra un des plus célèbres directeur de la photographie des films noirs américains: *T-Men* (1948), *He Walked by Night* (1951) et *The Big Combo* (1955). D'origine juive hongroise, émigré aux Etats-Unis en 1919, puis en France où il avait travaillé avec Dimitri Kirsanoff pour *Les Nuits de Port Saïd* à la Paramount, il avait été mandaté en Argentine pour y introduire les techniques américaines. Il avait déjà été le réalisateur de *El Hijo de papa* (1933) et dirigé la photographie de plusieurs films à Buenos Aires. Son manuel de photographie au cinéma, *Painting with Light* (1949), deviendra un classique. Or sa participation est probablement d'une extrême importance pour comprendre le style de la photographie du film, remarquable, avec son travail sur les ombres, ses forts contrastes entre les noirs et les blancs, ses perspectives inattendues, ses atmosphères nocturnes et un traitement expressionniste des lumières qui renforcent le caractère dramatique, conformément aux principes de *Painting with Light*.

Si le script du scénario a disparu aujourd'hui, plusieurs de ses feuillets ont été réutilisés par Fondane pendant l'Occupation pour écrire des poèmes et ont ainsi été conservés au Fonds Doucet à Paris. Nous ne possédons donc plus aujourd'hui que quelques fragments des dialogues écrits en espagnol qui accompagnaient les aventures des musiciens Cleo, Agapito, Perico et Curro. D'autres personnages: Obdulio et Pancracia, une vieille duchesse, un ministre, des policiers, des danseuses, font probablement partie d'un monde qui résiste à leur fantaisie délirante et subversive. Fondane résume l'intrigue dans une lettre à sa sœur:

> Ce sera la caricature de la société d'aujourd'hui, un monde où l'art n'est plus [...] Les Aguilar ne pourront être engagés pour un concert qu'uniquement parce qu'on les prend pour de célèbres bandits et, vers la fin du film, se révolteront contre la condition que leur fait le cinéma, refuseront le mariage et le baiser final et préféreront, en jouant sans instrument le *Boléro* de Ravel, mettre en pièces le salon d'une vieille duchesse qui les avait fait jouer – par pitié. (Fondane 2007: 179)

Plusieurs séries de photogrammes représentent des hommes en uniformes qui devaient incarner les forces de l'ordre. Le cadre de l'action était presque exclusivement constitué d'une cour intérieure avec ses appartements, dont une chambre de musique (appelée "atelier"), qui apparaît par exemple dans la photographie de tournage 34. Enfin, l'intrigue était censée se dérouler dans une ville ultramoderne, ce qui explique la présence d'une salle de conférence au décor "cubiste" qui évoque certains décors de *L'Inhumaine* (1924) de Marcel Lherbier, d'une salle de danse étrangement sillonnée de câbles verticaux, équipée par ce qui ressemble à un appareillage de "télévisions" ou d'écrans miniatures, et surtout d'un cinéma "olfactif" à propos duquel nous avons retrouvé la photographie de tournage n°6, très instructive puisqu'elle montre un homme sortant d'une "cabine de l'odeur" dont la porte est surmontée d'un panneau avertissant en espagnol: "prise: ceux qui ont l'estomac délicat sont priés de retenir leur respiration". Apparemment, les musiciens ont été recrutés comme acteurs pour tourner un film total capable d'intégrer les odeurs.

Certaines comédies de science-fiction de l'époque, par exemple *Just Imagine* (1930) ont pu influencer ce cadre futuriste. Quoi qu'il en soit, cette dernière photographie indique bien que dans le scénario les quatre musiciens faisaient du cinéma, ce qui permettait peut-être au réalisateur d'introduire une réflexion ironique du cinéma sur lui-même.

L'univers poétique de *Tararira*

"Si j'étais libre, vraiment libre, je tournerais un film absurde, sur une chose absurde, pour satisfaire à mon goût absurde de liberté", avait écrit Fondane en 1933 (Fondane 2007: 116). Le tournage de *Tararira* lui en offrit-il la possibilité? Un certain nombre de convergences thématiques de *Tararira* avec ses essais critiques apparaissent: le film, musical sans être une comédie musicale, est favorable à un cinéma

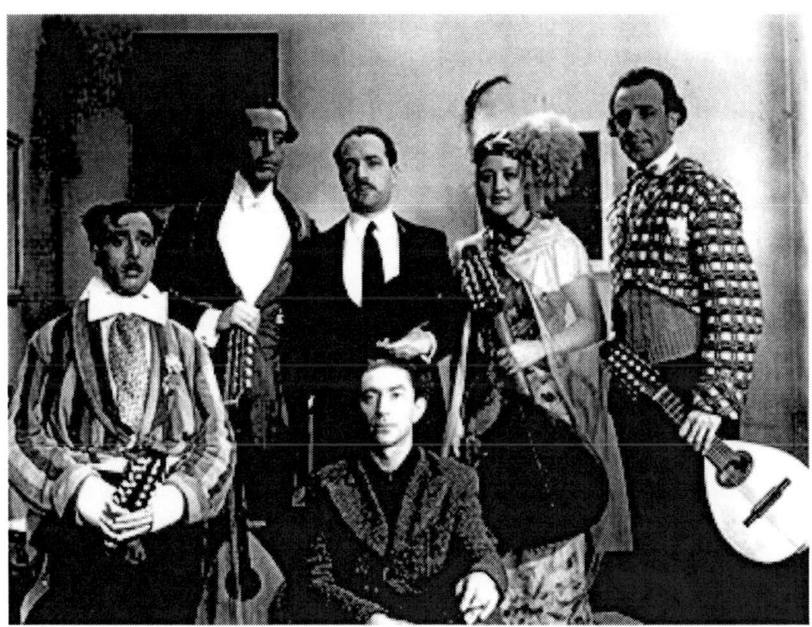

Figure 8. Photographie du tournage de *Tararira* avec Fondane
au premier plan

sonore plutôt que parlant. Il est vrai que le genre musical et dansant abondait au début des années trente, notamment avec la comédie musicale hollywoodienne, telle que le film *Broadway Melody* (1929) de Harry Beaumont, admiré par Fondane. Les photogrammes de ce qui ressemble à un mariage avec une mariée en blanc, portant un chapeau haut de forme, entourée de fleurs et d'enfants, reflètent sans doute le style de ces comédies flamboyantes. Par ailleurs, nous sommes aussi en pleine période de gloire de Carlos Gardel et des comédies musicales à succès basées sur le tango. Toutefois, il ne faut pas oublier que la musique du film était composée d'adaptations musicales réalisées par Paco Aguilar, sur des pièces de Mozart, Haydn, Albéniz, Ravel, Brahms, et interprétées par le Cuarteto Aguilar.

Le climat poétique du film devait s'inspirer assez largement du comique du cinéma muet. De son propre aveu, Fondane devait inventer "2400 mètres de gags" (Fondane 2007: 180). Chez les Marx Brothers, le personnage muet d'Arpo permettait le recours direct à la pantomime et à des gags sonores obtenus au moyen des divers instruments de musique pratiqués en virtuose par les frères Marx dont *A Night at the Opera* (1935) venait de sortir sur les écrans et dont *Monkey Business* (1931) avait enthousiasmé Artaud. De fait, les photographies de *Tararira* représentent de nombreuses scènes comiques. Les partitions retrouvées de la musique du film indiquent également un recours à la pantomime et aux percussions. Un des exemples les plus significatifs est une séquence comportant une interprétation "catastrophiste" du *Boléro* de Ravel. Cette dernière, sous-titrée "pantomime" sur la partition pour luth datée de 1936 par Paco Aguilar avec des indications sur le jeu théâtral de la musicienne Cleopatra (Cléo), devait être interprétée par Elisa Aguilar: "en pleurant"; "en pleurant comiquement"; "en pleurant désespérément", "en beuglant" [berreando]. L'accélération du *Boléro* était rythmée avec des percussions improvisées selon des indications précises sur la partition: "bois", "chaises", "métal", permettant ainsi de signifier une décomposition symbolique de l'ordre et de l'espace bourgeois représenté par un salon de style néo-classique. La photographie de tournage n°130 [figure 9] correspondant à cette fameuse scène finale aurait été tournée selon Edgardo Cozarinsky (2006) dans la Confiteria Ideal de Buenos Aires, un célèbre établissement de tango de Buenos Aires, mais il ne s'agit probablement que d'une reconstitution en studio.

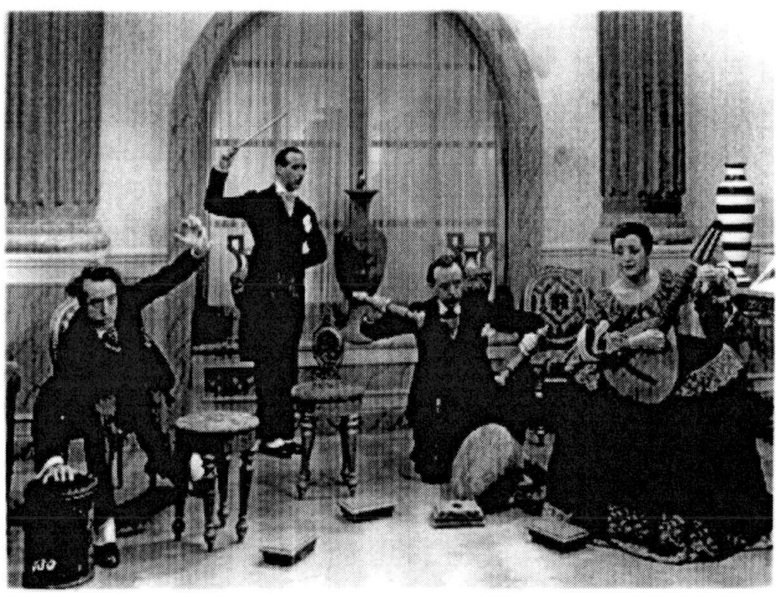

Figure 9. Concert final de *Tararira* joué sur l'air du *Boléro* de Ravel

Elle montre les musiciens marquant le rythme avec les pieds de
tabourets qu'ils ont brisés. Le chef d'orchestre fait sonner un gong
métallique et Pepe Aguilar frappe les tabourets avec ses mains. Bref,
la matière du décor a été transformée en potentialité sonore. Cet
orchestre catastrophique, selon une rare spectatrice du film, Gloria
Alcorta (1997: 53), constituait une scène finale au cours de laquelle,
invités par une vieille duchesse, les musiciens se révoltaient contre
l'ordre imposé. Si le thème du désastre est une catégorie poétique
fondanienne, par exemple dans *Titanic* (1937), il se retrouve aussi
dans les premiers court métrages de Chaplin et dans les scénarios des
Marx Brothers où l'étranger figure un perturbateur social qui
désorganise l'environnement où il est arrivé par hasard et auquel il ne
parvient pas à s'adapter. Notons que *A Nous la liberté* (1931) de René
Clair et *Les Temps modernes* (1936) de Chaplin utilisent également ce
thème de l'inadaptation sociale des personnages comme moyen
burlesque et subversif. Il est aussi probable que des éléments

clownesques participaient au comique de *Tararira*. Le fragment de la
page 404 du scénario est particulièrement significatif à cet égard:

> *SCEN. 404*
> SEMI CLOSE UP
> Agapito et Perico (Perico lui arrache un second poil. Il se tourne vers la
> duchesse. Il lui arrache un autre poil.)
> Perico: Ce poil est appelé "Grand Guignol" parce qu'il a la faculté de vous
> hérisser les cheveux
> *CLOSE UP*
> La Duchesse fait un bond pendant qu'on entend le cri d'Agapito….

Ces composantes scéniques sont certainement à rapprocher à la fois de
l'expérience théâtrale du théâtre *Insula* fondé par Fondane en
Roumanie et peut-être des conventions du théâtre juif, ce théâtre du
geste inspiré de la *commedia dell'arte*, ainsi que le rappelle Nina
Gourfinkel (1950: 375), que Fondane avait été amené à connaître avec
les spectacles du théâtre Habima et la mise en scène du *Dybouk*. La
partition de la musique du film utilisait aussi la mélodie d'une
chanson juive: *A Brivele der Mamen* de Salomon Shmulewitz, adaptée
pour luth par Paco Aguilar. La partition porte en sous-titre les
mentions: "Chant populaire hébreu" et "Chant populaire Iris", dernier
terme qui est probablement la transcription erronée de "Yiddish". Ces
marqueurs de l'identité juive ne sont pas étonnants chez ce poète qui
s'était décrit comme un "Ulysse juif", qui avait consacré de nombreux
poèmes aux émigrants juifs pourchassés par les pogroms et qui, avec
le durcissement de l'antisémitisme fasciste en Europe, affirmera de
plus en plus nettement sa filiation judaïque, en particulier dans le
poème *L'Exode* (1932–44). De leur côté, les membres du Cuarteto
Aguilar semblent avoir partagé cette revendication: "J'ai écrit une
lettre à la Société hébraïque de Buenos Aires pour leur demander, au
nom de leur Dieu, qu'ils me considèrent comme un des leurs, et leur
dire que, dès que l'on m'a dit pour la première fois qu'il y a
différentes races d'hommes, j'en ai aimé une, la tienne, par-dessus
toutes les autres", écrit Paco Aguilar à Fondane en 1939 (Carassou
1996: 161). Enfin, il faut souligner que le Cuarteto affichait nettement
ses choix républicains et anti-franquistes. Il n'est pas étonnant que
Paco Aguilar, après le naufrage du film, ait continué seul à jouer du
luth dans un spectacle poétique et musical itinérant en collaboration
avec le poète Rafael Alberti.

D'autres aspects du film semblent fidèles à l'univers poétique de
Fondane. Notamment le thème de l'errance, homogène aux poèmes

"Ulysse" (1933) ou "Le Mal des fantômes" (1943). Il se retrouve dans la bohème des musiciens, cette "bohème d'aujourd'hui" qui constitue un des titres du film car *Tararira* retrace les aventures de "quatre bohèmes fous de musique" dans "une ville ultramoderne" explique Fondane le 29 janvier 1937 au journal *L'Intransigeant* (Carassou 1996: 140). La notion de bohème recouvre aussi un élément d'improvisation, de bricolage, de juxtaposition d'éléments hétérogènes que nous retrouvons dans le décor de certaines scènes, par exemple dans la photographie de tournage n°56. La pièce de l'atelier où à lieu un des concerts est constituée d'un paravent japonais ou chinois, de marionnettes posées sur une armoire qui elle-même est posée sur un lit. Quelques tableaux et des meubles encombrés: ce décor illustre bien le principe d'hétérogénéité d'une poétique du "marché aux puces" qui laisse une place à la fantaisie et à l'irrationnel. Les costumes bricolés en hâte répondent encore mieux à ce principe d'hétérogénéité qui évoque les émigrants, ces "ressemeleurs de mots" et ces "bijoutiers d'accidents", cités dans "Ulysse" (Fondane 1996: 109). Sur une photographie de tournage, Ezequiel Aguilar est habillé de manchettes sans doute fabriquées avec du carton blanc, d'une robe de chambre tenue à la taille par une corde, d'un double col clownesque fait de la même matière, d'un foulard de soie et d'une rose à la boutonnière. Pepe Aguilar, pour sa part, porte un pullover de laine blanche sous son gilet. Une autre série de photogrammes montre ce groupe ainsi costumé tentant de délivrer un chat suspendu à une corde. Certains films se déroulant dans le milieu du cirque, tel que *Laugh, Clown, Laugh* de Herbert Brenon (1928) ou *Le Cirque* de Chaplin (1928) ont peut-être impressionné Fondane. Une série de photogrammes en extérieur sur un parvis montre Paco Aguilar en mendiant loqueteux aveugle et sourd que l'on aperçoit ensuite jouant du luth sur ce même parvis. Il est probable que le groupe de musiciens s'augmente d'un (faux) aveugle et sourd à l'aide d'un épisode tragi-comique. Improvisation, jeu, bohème, pathétique inadaptation d'artistes marginaux dans une société oppressive: ces composantes semblent anticiper parfois sur l'exubérance et la provocation de certains films de Fellini.

Tararira est-il un film subversif?

La subversion semble donc bien réelle dans *Tararira*. "Ce sera la caricature de la société d'aujourd'hui, un monde où l'art n'est plus", précise le poète (Fondane 2007: 179) dans une lettre à sa soeur (19 mai 1936). C'est l'usage de plusieurs travestis montrant des hommes déguisés en femmes qui illustre le mieux cette composante subversive.

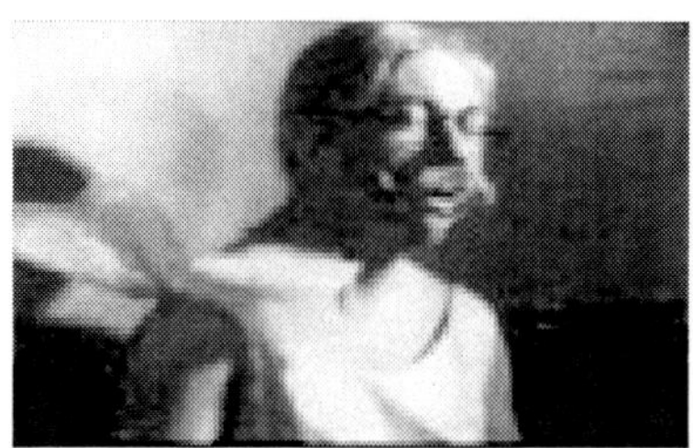

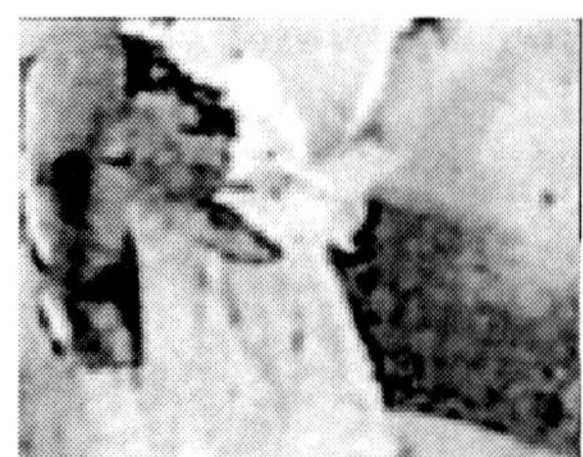

Figure 10. Scène de Tararira - personnage masculin habillé en danseuse

Fondane réalise probablement une satire sociale de la bourgeoisie avec une bonne place faite à l'absurde. Le scandale avait commencé dès le tournage lorsqu'il avait remplacé par un homme une vieille duchesse que devait interpréter "la première actrice du théâtre national", sans doute Iris Marga (1901–97) et qui ne s'était pas présentée (Fondane 2007: 195). On imagine mal en effet la star du théâtre argentin qui avait obtenu un succès retentissant en 1935 en interprétant dans *Miss Ba* un rôle mélodramatique, accepter un rôle burlesque. Il est probable qu'elle se retira du casting. Elle ne fera d'ailleurs aucune mention du tournage de *Tararira* dans ses mémoires intitulés *El Teatro mi verdad* (1983). Une série de photogrammes montre cette scène comique: un homme travesti, ganté et portant perruque à bouclettes semble engagé dans une conversation assez précieuse avec les musiciens déguisés en chirurgiens. Une autre série de photogrammes montre un homme portant moustache et lunettes ressemblant de façon frappante à Paul Valéry qui réapparaît ailleurs dans le rôle d'un sérieux conférencier, dansant en tutu, les bras levés dans une sorte d'extase [figure 10]. Or Fondane, dénonçant la confusion entre célébrité et talent au cinéma, avait écrit: "Supposez que 'l'Empire' engage Paul Valéry pour y danser en Tutu, sous prétexte qu'il est de l'Académie" (Fondane 2007: 113). Or, un examen attentif des photographies permet de voir que ce personnage porte des jarretelles. Le transfert des sous-vêtements féminins, apte à bouleverser l'identité sexuelle des personnages, semble donc acquis comme principe subversif. Or, un tel élément rapproche *Tararira* par exemple des audaces de *L'Age d'or* de Bunuel. Si nous revenons en arrière, l'esprit du film avait été annoncé par Victoria Ocampo elle-même dans une lettre à Fondane: "A exploiter le grand naturel avec lequel ils [les frères Aguilar] se foutent des convenances, des conventions, etc." (Fondane 2007: 176). Le message avait été sans doute parfaitement reçu par Fondane qui ne se priva pas d'une certaine provocation. Enfin, les déguisements baroques et le burlesque de situation semblent être complétés par le recours à des dialogues absurdes. Par exemple, à la page 80 du scénario nous trouvons l'échange suivant:

> Duchesse: Je comprends !…il pourrait y avoir un obstacle sérieux. Il / elle ne jouera pas trop bien, je veux dire avec une parfaite maîtrise ?
> Curro: Soyez tranquille, Madame la Duchesse. Sur 100 personnes opérées par le docteur, 99 d'entre elles perdent leurs facultés.
> Duchesse: (tranquille) Vraiment !…
> Ecoutez ! J'organise cette semaine une fête de charité au profit des orphelins de la guerre des gaz asphyxiants. Mais avec un seul instrument, même si elle en joue mal…
> Curro: Ne vous en faites pas pour ça, Madame la Duchesse, à force de soigner le malade, j'ai appris à jouer du luth.
> Cleo: et moi aussi. A force de le soigner. (tr. O. Salazar-Ferrer avec R. Nirenberg)

Fondane n'avait pas cessé dans ses écrits sur le cinéma de louer "la pure création de types, d'un rythme, d'un allant, d'un humour, délicieusement arbitraires, je veux parler de la comédie qui va de Mack Sennet à Charlot, à travers un Buster Keaton, un Harry Langdon" (Fondane 2007: 69). Il n'est donc pas surprenant que comique de *Tararira* rappelle les effets du muet et s'inspirent des procédés de la *commedia dell'arte* que Fondane avait jadis tenté d'appliquer au théâtre: "Je me suis efforcé d'y introduire l'esprit et la fantaisie de la *comedia dell'arte*", affirme t-il lui-même à *L'Intransigeant* le 29 janvier 1937 (Carassou 1996: 140). La description du plan 238 de l'atelier, indiqué en médium shot, illustre ce burlesque:

> Le gendarme se rapproche lentement d'une porte – un homme derrière lui qui le suit. Le gendarme écoute à la porte et l'ouvre lentement. Au moment d'ouvrir, l'homme qui était derrière lui donne un coup de pied qui le fait tomber dedans. Il ferme la porte à clef et dit d'un air satisfait: "maintenant, je suis sûr d'obtenir le divorce".

Une autre série montre Pépé Aguilar subissant une "opération" pratiquée avec une grosse pince extrayant ce qui ressemble à une corde d'instrument par l'un des musiciens, habillé en chirurgien et accompagné d'une sœur en cornette blanche qui rappelle une scène du film futuriste *Le Tunnel* (1934) de Kurt Bernhardt. Sans doute est-il important de rappeler que le comique cinématographique, dont Chaplin est l'exemple type, représente pour Fondane un comique tragique. L'alternance de comique et de tragique est citée en 1929 comme "la pierre de touche du tragique moderne" (Fondane 2007: 78). L'humour participe aussi d'un "sentiment violent du néant humain à portée de notre esprit d'aujourd'hui" (Fondane 2007: 77). D'autres extraits de la partition de *Tararira*, par exemple "l'hymne au ministre" montre que le film faisait alterner pathétique et comique: par exemple, la partition "Brivele der Mame" correspondait probablement au fragment pathétique de la page 8 du scénario où le groupe pleure autour de la lettre envoyée par une mère à l'un des membres du Cuarteto. Un autre exemple de pathétique photographique est fourni par la photographie de tournage représentant Paco Aguilar en aveugle et sourd (n°125) avec une prise de vue calquée sur un tableau du Gréco. De nombreuses photographies de tournage de *Tararira* sont empreintes d'une gravité dramatique, en particulier certains visages de femmes éclairés sur un fond obscur qui rappellent aussi la photographie des visages dans *La Marche nuptiale* (1928) de Stroheim, admiré par Fondane. Les scènes comiques, elles, sont nombreuses. La photographie de tournage n°46 montre une double sérénade parodique offerte par Pepe et Ezequiel de leurs fenêtres à une voisine d'en face (Elisa Aguilar), tandis que les plantes qui poussent dans les pots de fleurs sont réduites à des tiges rachitiques sans doute fabriquées avec du fil de fer. Sans cette relation du comique au tragique, nous ne pourrions probablement pas comprendre le style cinématographique de *Tararira*.

La disparition du film

Le 24 septembre 1936, le tournage était terminé et le montage "bien avancé" (Fondane 2007: 196). La correspondance de Fondane laisse percevoir un découragement progressif et une impatience grandissante de rentrer en France, quitte à laisser le film à peine monté. "Je sais que je quitterai l'Argentine, le film à peine terminé, sur un essai de montage, abandonnant tout" (Fondane 2007: 197). Cette hâte et ce découragement annoncent une série de difficultés qui conduiront à la non-distribution du film par le producteur. Fondane et son équipe avaient visionné une première version du film. Après que Fondane fut rentré en France, John Alton, pourtant chef-opérateur, effectua un autre montage, mais celui-ci fut désapprouvé par Fondane: "Comme si je n'avais pas assez crié que je ne reconnaissais pas précisément ce film-mutilé, détruit, sans tête", écrivit-il à Fredi Guthmann en février 1938. (Fondane 2007: 204). Le début du film avait-il été coupé ou censuré? Quoi qu'il en soit, cet aveu laisse supposer que Fondane avait vu en Argentine ou en France le montage final de John Alton. Les démarches pour récupérer le film vont s'enliser peu à peu. On s'explique mal ce désastre final que rien ne semblait annoncer lors du départ festif du réalisateur. Certaines audaces du film furent-elles censurées après son départ par le producteur, Miguel Machinandiarena, qui refusa de le distribuer? D'autres facteurs ont pu conduire à une rupture: le fort engagement en faveur de l'Espagne républicaine des frères Aguilar, l'esprit subversif du film et ses composantes absurdes et burlesques. Une autre hypothèse avancée par Hector Kohen se rapporte aux difficultés techniques présentées par le montage du film musical. Machinandiarena soutiendra pour sa part que le film n'avait pas été terminé.

Les tentatives de Fondane pour récupérer son film, après son retour au début du mois de novembre 1936, avec l'aide de son ami Fredi Guthmann et pour en refaire un montage à Paris conforme à ses conceptions échoueront (Fondane 2007: 204). La Seconde Guerre mondiale achèvera de couper toute possibilité de communication entre la France et l'Argentine et Fondane sera déporté et assassiné à Birkenau. Quelques projections privées du film eurent lieu pourtant en Argentine à la fin des années trente mais toutes les copies négatives et positives disparaîtront après la guerre à la fois en Argentine et à la cinémathèque française où le film aurait été déposé par Geneviève Fondane. Etrangement, Victoria Ocampo, qui avait été l'instigatrice du projet, disparaît presque aussitôt dans la correspondance de *Tararira* et ne fera aucune mention du film dans son autobiographie. Paco Aguilar ne l'évoque pas non plus dans ses souvenirs (Aguilar 1944) et Elisa Aguilar n'en parlera jamais à ses amis. Un étrange silence recouvrira donc ce film. Pourtant, tout laisse penser que *Tararira*, en métamorphosant les multiples effets du cinéma muet, s'inscrivait dans un héritage de la subversion post-Dadaïste et exprimait pleinement l'univers poétique fondanien.

Bibliographie

Aguilar, Paco. 1944. *A orillas de la musica*. Buenos Aires: Losada.

Cozarinsky, Edgardo. 2006. "Benjamin Fondane en la Argentina" in *La Nacion* (25 juin).

Alcorta, Gloria. 1997. "Du nouveau sur *Tararira*" in *Cahiers Benjamin Fondane* 1: 53.

Fondane, Benjamin.2007. *Ecrits pour le cinéma. Le muet et le parlant* (eds M. Carassou, O. Salazar-Ferrer and R. Fotiade). Lagrasse: Verdier poche.

———. 1936. *La Conscience malheureuse*. Paris: Denoël et Steele.

Carassou, Michel et Patrice Beray. 1996. *Le Voyageur n'a pas fini de voyager*. Paris-Méditerranée/L'Ether Vague-Patrice Beray.

Carassou, Michel et Petre Raelanu. 1999. *Benjamin Fondane et l'Avant-garde*. Paris: Fondation culturelle roumaine/Paris Méditerranée.

Gourfinkel, Nina. 1950. "Le théâtre du geste" in *Aspects du génie d'Israël*. Marseille: Cahiers du Sud.

Honegger, Arthur et Arthur Hoérée. 2002. "Particularités sonores du film Rapt" in "Le film sonore". *Revue musicale* 151 (décembre 1934). Repr. in *Revue de l'AFRHC* 38: 211–14.

Marga, Iris. 1983. *El Teatro mi verdad*. Buenos Aires: Ediciones tres tiempos.

Masson, Alain. 1989. *L'Image et la parole, L'Avènement du cinéma parlant.* Paris: La Différence.

Virmaux, Alain. 1998. "Un article pugnace" in *Cahiers Benjamin Fondane* 2: 81–6.

Chapter 15

Dada and its Afterlife in Czechoslovakia: Jan Švankmajer's *The Flat* and Věra Chytilová's *Daisies*

Alfred Thomas

In 1920 Otto Dix painted a street scene of Prague in which two legless men are seen in front of a shop window displaying artificial limbs and corsets. One of the men propels himself with sticks, his torso propped on a movable platform. Clearly visible next to the platform is a collage of a pamphlet with the words "Juden raus!" This grotesque scene, in which the mutilated veterans become indistinguishable from the inanimate objects on sale behind them, reminds us of the terrible human cost of war both now and then. In the same year Prague became a successful stop on the Dadaist tour of Richard Huelsenbeck, Johannes Baader and Raoul Hausmann. A year later Hausmann, Kurt Schwitters and Hannah Höch made an appearance in the Czech capital. In June 1926 Schwitters held two "Evenings of the Grotesque" and in the same year attended the opening of his one-man exhibition in Prague (Bydžovská 2002: 85–6). In spite of these high-profile appearances, Dada never made the profound impact on modern Czech culture that Surrealism did. When André Breton visited the Czech capital in March, 1935, and paid homage to its home-grown Surrealist movement, the event left a lasting impression that would survive not only the 1930s but also the wartime Nazi occupation of Czechoslovakia and the Communist regime that succeeded it (Sayer 2002: 90).

If Prague was second only to Paris as the leading centre of Surrealism, why does it fail to appear on the map of international Dada except as brief visits by particular individuals? The reason for the Czechs' failure to invest in a movement that took Europe by storm in the years 1916 to 1924 lies within the complex geo-political situation of central Europe after the Great War. Following the collapse of the Austro-Hungarian Empire in 1918 and the formation of the new state of Czechoslovakia in the same year, Czech artists and intellectuals to some extent benefited from the events which brought catastrophe to Germany and Austria. The new state of Czechoslovakia became one of the most stable and successful democracies in central Europe between the wars. Its president, the moderate T.G. Masaryk, was a relativist who tolerated many shades of political opinion, including a left-wing intelligentsia unashamedly (and naively) enthusiastic about the October Revolution of 1917. The political and cultural freedom enjoyed by the Czech Left meant that it did not share the bitterness and cynicism of its German counterpart. Where the German avant-garde favored the extreme artistic modes of Expressionism and Dada, the Czechs preferred the more gentle creed of Poetism, a movement based on a simple enjoyment of everyday life which rapidly gave way to the French-inspired tenets of Surrealism with its emphasis on the subjective and unconscious life of the artist rather than the objective and politicized tenets of *Neue Sachlichkeit*.

Given the powerful and pervasive influence of Surrealism on Czech culture both before and following the Second World War and the close – at times indistinguishable – affinities between Surrealism and Dada in the 1920s, it would be inaccurate to dismiss the significance of Dada in Czech culture altogether. In this essay I shall argue that Dada came into its own in that country following the rise to power of the Communists in February 1948. Just as in post-1918 Germany Dada served a powerful political role as an anti-establishment response to the Weimar Republic, so in post-Stalinist Czechoslovakia Dada provided an artistic antidote to the monopoly of the state in the sphere of the arts. The anti-realist strain in Surrealism and Dada made these movements especially appropriate and effective vehicles of counter-cultural resistance to the official doctrine of socialist realism in the Soviet satellite states of central Europe. The particularly important tradition of Surrealism in pre-war Czechoslovakia enabled post-war artists to deploy earlier forms of subjectivity in order to address issues of political and artistic freedom in an indirect, allegorical fashion.

I shall try to demonstrate the pervasive influence of Dada on two important Czech filmmakers of the post-war era by focusing on two examples of their work from the 1960s: Jan Švankmajer's short *Byt* [The Flat], made in 1968, and Věra Chytilová's full-length 1966 film *Sedmikrásky* [Daisies]. I shall argue that these films – in many ways so different from each other in style, technique and theme – one a black-and-white Kafkaesque portrayal of a man trapped in a nightmarish apartment full of malevolent objects, the other a colourful picaresque adventure of two anarchic young women refusing to acknowledge any limitations on their personal freedom – share a subversive resistance to aesthetic and political conformity typical of Dada. Reflecting the fate of a small nation trapped between the great powers, the films exemplify the ability of Dada to articulate an artistic language of defiance and subversion as well as the ultimate recognition that art can provide no metaphysical or political transcendence.

The Artist and Society in Communist Eastern Europe

In comparing Czech culture with its western European counterpart, it is important to bear in mind the very different social role expected of Czech writers and artists since the nineteenth-century National Revival. For example, existentialism acquired a particularly heightened political significance when it was transposed from France, its home of origin in the late 1930s, to the postwar conditions of the Soviet satellite states in the post-war period. Exemplary in this regard is Jiří Weil's Holocaust novel *Život s hvězdou* [Life with a Star] published in 1949 (Weil 1991). An autobiographical account of a Czech Jew who goes into hiding in Prague for the duration of the Second World War, the novel was condemned by the Communist authorities for its alleged "pernicious existentialism" even though the novel betrays few, if any, of the hallmark features of French existentialism. On the contrary, it might be argued that *Life with a Star* is fundamentally Czech in the emphasis it places on the importance of communitarian values and collective identity. These characteristics are notably absent from Albert Camus' early existentialist story "La mort dans l'âme" [Death in the Soul] from the 1937 collection *L'Envers et l'endroit* [The Wrong Side and the Right Side], a first-person account of a foreigner's lonely sojourn in Prague (Camus 1958). Where Weil finds human solidarity and cause for hope even in the most tragic circumstances of genocide, Camus' story is unremittingly pessimistic in its sense of human alienation and the absurd conditions of existence.

Since Czech artists are invariably concerned with the collective rather than the individual, it follows that their art is to a larger extent motivated by political rather than personal considerations. It has sometimes been maintained, rather lamely by Czech critics, that dissident culture in the Communist era of the 1960s was strictly anti-ideological and exclusively concerned with the private self. In fact nothing could be further from the truth: dissident art in a totalitarian system is invariably engaged in a collective struggle for power with the state and serves as a counter-discourse to the official discourse of the state. In the case of the Soviet satellites the official artistic discourse was socialist realism; but by the late 1950s this aesthetic had run out of steam and had to contend with a vibrant counter culture consisting of existentialism, Surrealism and, as I hope to demonstrate, Dada.

The focus on artistic subjectivity so often deployed in dissident art – and Švankmajer's films are exemplary here – is not an expression of political neutrality but, rather, a way of addressing the problem of political freedom by artistic means. Václav Havel's play *Vyrozumění* [The Memorandum] (1968) is indebted to the absurdist drama of Ionesco and Beckett but it is also a brilliant political satire on the failure of Communist discourse (allegorized as a bureaucratic language known as ptydepe) to supplant human language as a means of universal communication and absolute truth. The discursive struggle between ptydepe and human – or perhaps more accurately – humanist language and the latter's ultimate vindication allegorizes the larger conflict between the state and the individual (artist), a conflict in which Havel ultimately prevailed after the fall of Communism in 1989 and his own meteoric – not to say absurdist – rise to power as president of a new democratic Czechoslovakia in the same year. As we shall see, Švankmajer and Chytilová similarly use absurdist elements drawn from western existentialism to critique and subvert the ideological and aesthetic tenets of socialist realism.

Jan Švankmajer's *The Flat*

With its dream-like quality, its sense of claustrophobia, and its existentialist evocation of life as a nightmarish trap or prison, Švankmajer's thirteen-minute short *The Flat* (1968) exhibits many of the salient features of Surrealism. The sequence of the man dressed in a black suit and bowler hat moving slowly through the flat while stroking a live hen is a clear reference to the similarly dressed character in René Clair's *Entr'acte* (1924). The picture of the naked woman with a punctured breast and face recalls the preoccupation with female nudity in the work of Man Ray and other Surrealists. But the series of slapstick confrontations between the inhabitant of the flat and the resistance of the space and its artifacts to any form of domestication recalls not only the absurdist tenets of existentialism but also the self-consciousness of Dada. The protagonist endures one humiliation after another: when he looks in the mirror, he cannot see his own reflection; when he tries to get up from a chair, his jacket is mysteriously nailed to his seat; when he attempts to drink beer, the glass shrinks into a tiny shot glass only to magnify into a large tankard after he places it back on the table; when he tries to eat soup, his spoon is riddled with holes; when he tries to eat a meal of potatoes, dogs appear from a wardrobe, gobble them up, and jump back into the wardrobe; when he lies down, his bed dissolves into a pile of wood-shavings and he collapses onto the floor.

In many ways these malevolent tricks evoke the Theatre of the Absurd in which the human subject is doomed to suffer in a world entirely inimical to his well-being. This is, of course, the fate of Beckett's tragic-comic duo in *Waiting for Godot* (1952). Conversely, we can look at the confrontation of the man and the malevolent objects in the flat less in terms of an individual wishing – and failing – to find fulfilment in domestic routine than in terms of art's resistance to bourgeois (and hence political) conformity and the representational limits placed upon by it a socialist realist aesthetic. If we see the flat – and the artifacts within it – as a metaphor for the artistic process, we might argue that the film witnesses to Dada's resistance to all forms of political and aesthetic appropriation. Objects remain obdurately objects, independent of human mediation and subjectivity, their materiality unaffected by illusionism. This is particularly true of the mirror through which the man tries to see his own reflection. The mirror refuses to cooperate by reproducing the back of his head as seen from the perspective of the camera. Mirrors were a key component of Dada artists' critique of art, since they corresponded to the ultimate illusionism of the portrait:

> The picture as window onto another world was something of a mainstay in the
> Dada artists' critique of art, for which they substituted everything but the
> kitchen sink—including broken windows and blacked-out ones, doors to
> nowhere, and anti-illusionist pictures running the gamut from greeting card- and
> bulletin-board-like artworks to ersatz carpenter's benches. (Blythe and Powers
> 2006: 22)

Philippe Soupault's framed mirror known as *Portrait of an Unknown* was exhibited at the Salon Dada in Paris in June 1921. Now lost, the mirror highlighted the correspondence between portraits and mirrors in western art stretching back to Jan Van Eyck's *Arnolfini Marriage Portrait* and Diego Velazquez's *Las Meninas* in which the incorporated motif of the mirror self-consciously points to the act of portraiture itself. Soupault's mirror-as-exhibit may be said to represent the end-point of this long tradition of western illusionism.

Emblematic of the film's resistance to socialist realism is the uncanny ending when the protagonist tries to escape from the confines of the flat by breaking through a door frame behind which he comes face to face with a stone slab covered with engraved messages and names, presumably those of the previous inhabitants of the flat. On one level, this stark ending recalls the world of Kafka's fiction, in particular the parable "Vor dem Gericht" [Before the Law] where the nameless plaintiff waits and dies without gaining access to meaning and justice. But the door-frame and the opaque stone slab behind it also recall the anti-representational aesthetic of Dada, such as Marcel Duchamp's *Fresh Widow* (1920), a small replica of a typical French window (emblematic of bourgeois domesticity) that the artist commissioned from a carpenter in New York. The wood casement is painted turquoise-green but the glass panels are covered with shiny black leather. By insisting that there can be no transparent medium onto a representational world beyond the frame, Duchamp was rejecting the illusionist principles on which all western art has been based since Alberti's foundational Renaissance treatise on painting *De Pictura* [On Painting] (1435–36) (Blythe and Powers 2006: 9). The stone slab confronted by Švankmajer's protagonist is at once a *memento mori* in resembling a grave stone onto which the character dutifully inscribes his own name and – like Duchamp's window frame – a reminder of the aesthetic limitations of realism. If it is an uncanny emblem of our mortality, the slab is equally an assertion of the artist's autonomy and art's self-sufficient opacity, foiling the traditional assumption that it will provide a window onto an external reality and a transcendental politics.

The critical trend has been to interpret Švankmajer's film purely in terms of a negative theology and a doomed ontology: man is born to live and die without relief from his earthly prison. And of course, given the fact that it was made in 1968, the same year as the Warsaw Pact invasion of Czechoslovakia, the film inevitably invites a topical interpretation as a bleak metaphor of totalitarian oppression and the individual's fate within such a prison-like system. But the film equally entails a diametrically opposite political reading: the literal dead-end faced by the protagonist is – metaphorically speaking – also the dead-end of socialist realism. It is important to recall here that Lenin, always inimical to the avant-garde, regarded the nineteenth-century realism of Tolstoy as the apotheosis to which proletarian art should aspire.

If the preceding slapstick sequences in *The Flat* present experience as absurd, they equally highlight the comic futility of socialist realism to control and define that experience. Perhaps an even more apt Dadaist parallel to Švankmajer's stone wall covered with the names of the flat's previous inhabitants is Francis Picabia's *L'Oeil Cacodylate* [The Cacodylic Eye] (1921), which consists of personally inscribed sentiments of sympathy to the artist who was suffering from a severe eye complaint. Like Duchamp's French window, Picabia's two-dimensional canvas rejects all possibility of illusionist representation. Not only is it thoroughly anti-illusionist, it also brings high art closer to the world of everyday life in resembling an office card that circulates and is signed by the workers in sympathy with a sick or bereaved colleague (Blythe and Powers 2006: 15).

The ending of Švankmajer's film suggests a similar rejection of the transcendental aspirations of western realism. In the context of communist Czechoslovakia such a repudiation of traditional forms of realism amounts to far more than an abstract denial of illusionism; it also demonstrates in a radically political gesture the inability of socialist realism to redefine experience and the failure of Soviet Communism to transform social reality. Far from being a film about the inability of the individual to break out of an oppressive political system, *The Flat* should perhaps be read in opposite terms as a witness to the failure of any form of political attempt to limit the freedom of the artist.

Věra Chytilová's *Daisies*

The most significant manifestation of Dada in post-war Czech culture is, without doubt, Věra Chytilová's anarchic proto-feminist film *Daisies* (1966), made only two years prior to the invasion of Czechoslovakia in August 1968. Highly significant in this regard is the opening credit sequence of wheels turning on an industrial machine and alternating with shots of an aerial bombardment, the latter repeated right at the end of the film. The intervening antics of the two automaton-like young women act out the absurdist and fatalist mood suggested by these sequences of industrial mechanization and wartime destruction.

There has been a great deal of speculation concerning the representation of the two female protagonists and the fate that befalls them. Chytilová herself has claimed that the girls' deaths are a punishment for their selfish and irresponsible behaviour. But in her article "Dolls in Fragments: Daises as Feminist Allegory", Bliss Cua Lim (2001) argues that such a punitive stance is belied by the anarchic elements within the film itself and that the girls' doll-like comportment constitutes a feminist critique of rather than a reinforcement of patriarchal values. In harmony with this feminist revisionist reading, I would like to suggest that the two girls' anarchic disruption of patriarchal norms of behaviour allegorizes the political resistance of the 1960s Czechoslovak reform movement to the strictures of the Soviet leadership until "socialism with a human face" was abruptly and tragically brought to an end by the Warsaw Pact invasion of August 1968. Correspondingly, the old men whom the girls exploit allegorize the leaders of the Communist establishment, both in Czechoslovakia itself and in the Soviet Union. The violent deaths of the girls, intercut with sequences of falling bombs, can be read as the fate of the small-nation in its futile attempt to subvert super-power hegemony. The girls' symbolic role as a defiant, reformist Czechoslovakia rehearses in modern form the symbolization of woman-as-nation characteristic of nineteenth-century Czech revivalism.

Dolls and marionettes have long served as metaphors of female enslavement and bourgeois domesticity. Bliss Cua Lim cites various examples from feminist literature. But dolls are also a significant part of the repertoire of Dada, for example, the dolls and marionettes of Hannah Höch and Sophie Taeuber. Höch's *Dada Puppen* [Dada

Dolls], marionettes of Hannah Höch and Sophie Taeuber. Höch's *Dada Puppen* [Dada Dolls] (1916), which were exhibited at the Berlin Dada Fair in 1920, are recognizably female with skirts and breast nipples made out of beads (Dickerman 2006: 142). Dada's critique of the patriarchal treatment of women as sexual and domestic automata was an integral feature of the movement's anti-establishment and anti-military posture. Only two years after the Dada Fair and in the same year that the Great War ended women finally were given the vote in Britain and Germany, followed by the United States two years later.

The ambiguous tension in the portrayal of the girls is prefigured in the opening scene where they are seen dressed in bathing suits and seated on a wooden boardwalk at a beach resort. Moving with stiff and angular doll-like gestures, their staccato dialogue initiates their feminist defiance of bourgeois convention as well as their disregard for all moral values:

> Marie 1: A virgin! I'm like a virgin, aren't I? I'm a virgin.
> Marie 2: Uh-huh.
> Marie 1: You understand?
> Marie 2: Nobody understands anything.
> Marie 1: Nobody understands us!
> Marie 2: Everything's being spoiled in this world.
> Marie 1: Everything?
> Marie 2: Everything…
> Marie 1: In this world.
> Marie 2: You know, if everything's spoiled…
> Marie 1: (drumroll). Well?
> Marie 2: We'll—
> Marie 1: Be spoiled—
> Marie 2: Too---
> Marie 1: Us too.
> Marie 2: Right?
> Marie 1: Does it matter?
> Marie 2: It doesn't matter.

This dialogue serves as a kind of nihilistic manifesto for the rest of the film. As such as it recalls Dada's obsession with manifestos as exemplified by Picabia's "cannibal manifesto" read out by Breton in 1920:

> DADA, as for it, it smells of nothing, it is nothing, nothing, nothing
> It is like your hopes: nothing
> Like your heaven: nothing
> Like your politicians; nothing
> Like your artists: nothing.

The next scene in the film begins as Marie I pushes Marie II into a brightly coloured, flowery meadow. In a setting akin to the Garden of Eden, the girls dance around an ornate artificial-looking apple tree to the elegant strains of renaissance music. This reenactment of prelapsarian bliss is significant in lacking its key patriarchal protagonist: God and his human surrogate Adam. Supplanting the Biblical role assigned to Adam, who eats of the fruit and then offers it to Eve, the girls proceed to pluck ripe apples from the tree and begin to eat them, signaling their initiation into a series of post-edenic gustatory antics. Unlike Eve, who in the Biblical myth is assigned a purely passive and punitive role after the Fall, the girls are endowed with their own disruptive agency: they, rather than men, will determine the direction and shape of the ensuing narrative. As the proto-text for all subsequent narratives of transgressive women, the Eden myth is introduced at the very outset of the film only to be subverted.

Fundamental to this feminist re-scripting of patriarchal narrative is the reversal of standard linear and logical narrative. Like Dada art, the film dispenses with Cartesian logic by stringing together in a non-sequitur fashion random and mutually disconnected scenes. As the film progresses, linear live-action sequences of humans interacting are increasingly displaced and supplanted by speeded-up shots of collages and assemblages of flowers, fruit and butterflies. The influence of Surrealism is evident here in the Arcimboldo-esque blurring of human and mineral, animation and still-life. But Dadaist techniques are also apparent in the breakdown of illusionism and the rapid alternation between colour and black-and-white. Max Ernst's painting *Two Children are threatened by a Nightingale* (1924) inserts three human grisaille figures into a framed colour canvas. The effect of this tension between colour and monochrome in the painting – as in the film – is to enhance the illusory nature of realism, although they operate in opposite terms to each other: in Ernst's canvas the grisaille figures undermine the realistic perspective associated with colour landscape. By contrast the black-and-white sequences in the film are identified with the neo-realist and *cinema vérité* techniques favored by directors of the Czechoslovak New Wave such as Jiří Menzel, while colour is identified with still-life compositions such as shots of green apples, red roses, and butterflies. There is also a gendered opposition in the use of black-and-white versus colour. The former tends to dominate in the scenes where the girls are placed in "realistic" social settings such as interacting with men in restaurants or with other women in public bathrooms, whereas as colour predominates in the autonomous all-female space of the girls' bedroom.

The walls of the bedroom are especially significant in resembling Dada paintings and collages. In one scene a wall is filled entirely with the phone numbers of men whom the girls have picked up and discarded in a typical reversal of normative heterosexual roles. The wall recalls Picabia's *The Cacodylic Eye* discussed earlier. In another bedroom scene the girls' own disembodied heads and arms are inserted into the patterns on the walls as they enact a parody of the Surrealist practice of using reified images of female body parts for collages. Chytilová may have been familiar with Toyen's painting *After the Performance* (1943) with its headless female body suspended upside down (Bischof 1987: 40). This sequence also recalls Yoko Ono's film *Cut-Piece* (1965) based on a series of one-woman performances during which members of the audience are invited on to the stage to snip pieces from the performer's dress. Important in Toyen's painting and Ono's and Chytilová's film is the subversive way in which women are at once the artist of the composition and the composition itself.

As if to initiate such feminist revisionism of standard male-centered practice, one of the girls removes her crown of daisies from her head and casts it into a pond. Just as Švankmajer draws upon Karel Jaromír's Erben's nineteenth-century Czech folktale as the source for his film *Otesánek* [Little Otík] (1989), so does Chytilová here reprise nineteenth-century proto-feminist responses to Erben's patriarchal ballads in which women are cast in the punitive role of transgressors against societal norms. The throwing of the daisy crown into the water, for example, recalls the scene in Božena Němcová's story "Wild Bára" (1856) where Bára and her friend Elška cast wreaths into the river on St. John's Eve in order to discover what their fate will be and whom they will marry (Thomas 2007: 68).. But Chytilová's citation of this folkloric motif takes the feminist re-scripting of Erben's ballad "Christmas Eve" one stage further: if Bára and her friend are endowed with subjective agency by making their fates follow the direction of the wreaths, Chytilová's heroines exhibit absolute indifference to their fate by ignoring the daisy crown in the water.

Anarchic indifference to heterosexual decorum is reinforced in the next scene which takes places in the elegant surroundings of a high-class restaurant in Prague. Marie II is having a dinner date with an older man. As Herbert Read (1991: 228) suggests in his analysis of this scene, there is an implication here of sexual services rendered in exchange for an elegant dinner. This expectation, however, is summarily disrupted by the intervention of Marie I who usurps the role of older man by taking the initiative while he assumes the passive role normally assigned to the young woman in such situations. Asked by the waiter whether she will be dining, Marie I sets the subversive tone of the scene by responding: "And drinking". She proceeds to order food in a seigneurial tone ("Do you have snails? Do you have rabbit?") and, when the courses arrive, devours them in reverse order and in an unconventional fashion: a cream-filled dessert is eaten decorously with a knife and fork, whereas the soup is drunk straight from the bowl without a spoon and the whole chicken is dismantled and eaten by hand. In the same spirit of parody Marie I assumes complete control by dominating the conversation and asking the older man the kind of inappropriate questions usually reserved to men in this situation: "Do you have any little ones?" – "How old are you?" – "Do you smoke?"

Following the restaurant scene, the girls again subvert and invert normative gender roles by suddenly announcing that the man's train will be leaving in 40 minutes. The next scene shows the hapless figure being rushed along the station platform by the girls. In an attempt to speak to Marie II alone, the man asks Marie I to buy him a newspaper. Offering an ironic bow, Marie I goes off to buy a whole pile of reading matter with the implication that reading is *all* that the man will be doing. Meanwhile Marie II explains to the man that she had to tell her "sister" (as she styles Marie I) that he was her boyfriend's uncle, a ruse intended to get rid of the man without having sex with him. The man and Marie II get on the train while Marie I remains on the platform. But as the train departs in a cloud of smoke, Marie II re-emerges from the other side of the carriage.

The entire scene reprises in parodic form the conventional patriarchal narrative of a playboy bidding goodbye to his mistress as she returns to her provincial home. (This cliché scenario is familiar from Milan Kundera's novel *The Unbearable Lightness of Being* (1985) in which Tereza, having spent the night with Tomáš in Prague, returns by train to her provincial hometown.) In the film, this narrative convention is repeated several times with a series of increasingly old and ugly men cast in the inverted role of the compliant young woman. In one such scene Marie II asks the fifth man: "How old is your old woman?" We then see the man waving goodbye from the train window as tears stream down his face. Standing on the platform, Marie II waves a scarf as she feigns tears of regret.

If the scenes analyzed so far invert conventional gender roles, the next scene is even more subversive in parodying the standard heterosexual dyad of the married man and woman going out on a date. The girls show up at a night club where they wreak drunken havoc. Usurping the real performers of the evening – a bearded man in a tuxedo and a woman in a 1920s-style dress – they emerge through heavy satin curtains under a spotlight as if making an appearance on stage. When the two performers come out they are forced to push their way past the girls to achieve the spotlight on the stage. The girls then take their places behind a high parapet which makes them look like figures in a Punch and Judy show. Indeed, their doll-like movements bear out this impression as they walk precariously along the parapet which separates them from a bourgeois older couple seated below them. Stealing the limelight, the drunken girls perform mischievous antics such as drinking the lady's wine glass or stroking the man's bald head with their boas. The scene ends with the forced ejection of the drunken girls from the club. As Herbert Read points out, the girls' expulsion from the nightclub anticipated the film establishment's devastating criticism and outright rejection of the film when it first appeared in 1966.

In the next scene we see Marie II lying on her bed and surrounded by green apples in what resembles an artistic composition. Marie I comes in and, detecting the smell of gas, turns off the valve. "Who is going to pay for this?" she asks the supine Marie II, then walks up to the open window and laughingly adds: "You forgot to close the window". When the phone rings, Marie I says: "Don't answer it!" but picks up the receiver herself and announces in an official voice: "Rehabilitation Centre. Die, die, die!" In what is manifestly a retort to a long history of the clinical classification of women as inherently predisposed to mental instability, this scene at once re-cites and subverts the pathologized status of women in western society. The reference to gas in this scene recalls the celebrated suicide of the American poet Sylvia Plath in London in 1963. When the girls literally play with fire in their apartment by setting coloured streamers alight one recalls the self-immolation of the student Jan Palach in a public square following the Soviet invasion of Prague in August 1968. Although *Daisies* was made prior to this tragic event, a sense of despair pervades the entire film, a reminder that the exuberant experiment of "socialism with a human face" symbolized by the girls' antics was destined to come to an abrupt and violent end. This sense of foreboding increases as the film progresses.

Throughout the film eating serves as one of its major preoccupations, a surrogate for sex and an act of defiance in a culture which defines women exclusively in terms of their bodies and their physical appearance. The film shows the girls eating on several occasions. To the sound of a boyfriend's plaintive and cliché-filled phone call ("You don't belong to this century"), the girls roast and devour various forms of phallic food (sausages, pickles, bananas), which they hold with surgical forceps and snip with large scissors in a ritualistic parody of giving birthing. But here the act of giving birth is reversed: instead of men performing the gynecological act on women's bodies, the girls perform it on men in the symbolic form of phallic food. Not only does this scene set the birthing function in reverse, it also exploits male Freudian anxieties of castration and impotence. As if in revenge for the consumer-status of women's bodies, symbolized by the boyfriend's large butterfly collection, the girls turn men's bodies into reified and inanimate objects of consumption.

In spite of – or perhaps because of their unrelenting anarchism – a sense of nihilistic anxiety increases as the film progresses. In the country sequence the gardener seems to ignore the girls' appeals for attention; and the workers riding their bicycles to (or from) work also fail to notice them. Marie I is worried by the fact that none of these men notice her, reinforcing the fact that she cannot imagine her identity outside the narrow matrix of heterosexual desire. In achieving their goal of a world without men, the girls become invisible to themselves as well as to the men they shun. The fear of being overlooked correlates with the geopolitical anxieties witnessed by the aerial bombardments which frame the entire film: just as the girls become increasingly invisible as they gradually achieve their desired goal of freedom from male constraint, so too the small nation

Czechoslovakia risks being ignored by the West as it deviates from the political conformity imposed by the Soviet Union.

The film culminates in a bizarre scene where the girls enter a deserted banquet hall and begin to eat the delicacies laid out on the tables. In what Herbert Read (1991: 233) calls "the spirit of a Dada happening", the scene shows the girls' gluttonously devouring the food and destroying the exquisite arrangement of dishes. Once again they parody established gender roles by walking up and down the table draped in curtains in a mock enactment of a fashion-show cat-walk. As if being punished for their wanton destructiveness, the girls are next shown floating in the dark waters of a river just as – as Read points out – pre-modern witches suffered punishment by drowning. But this expectation of punishment is rapidly dispelled when the girls reemerge into the banqueting hall dressed in pieces of newspaper strapped tightly to their bodies with string. Mocking the redemptive ending of patriarchal narratives which inserts wayward women back into their dutiful domestic roles as wives and mothers, the girls waddle around and declare: "We won't be spoiled anymore. We'll be diligent. We'll be happy!" They proceed to clean up the mess in a parody of uxorial diligence, placing broken bits of crockery together in what resembles a Dada still-life. Finally, the girls lie down next to each other on the table in an apparent gesture of resignation and surrender to the inevitable fate they must suffer. Their dialogue concludes as it by began in the Dadaist spirit of negation and nihilism:

> "Are we pretending?"
> "No, we are really and truly happy".
> "Does it matter?"
> "It doesn't matter".

In spite of – perhaps even because of – its subversive exuberance, the film offers no alternative to the nihilistic negation of traditional gender and sexual roles. In the opening dialogue cited earlier, one of the girls asserts that she is a virgin before donning the floral crown traditionally associated in folklore culture with marriage. In repudiating patriarchal and heterosexual values, the women choose to remain virgins rather than defining their gender and sexual identity in alternative ways, styling themselves as sisters rather than, say, as lovers. The sense of nihilism implicit in this ultimate acceptance of hetero-normative relations correlates with the imagery of violent destruction with which the film both begins and ends. The film offers no way out of its own sexual and political impasse: women will always be subordinated to male power – the film appears to conclude – just as small nations will always be oppressed by the great powers. In the final scene of the film an enormous chandelier comes crashing down onto the women below, anticipating the bombs falling on the buildings in the final shot. In this sense the ending of the film is not so very different from the no-exit conclusion of *The Flat*. Both films allegorize the political dilemma of a country experimenting with a middle way ("socialism with a human face") and trapped between two political extremes.

As we have seen, the western movements of Dada and Surrealism were particularly well suited to the needs of dissident art in Communist Czechoslovakia. But what is Dada's relevance to post-Communist reality? Does Dada have any relevance to today's capitalist globalization? Švankmajer's short *The Death of Stalin in Bohemia* (1990), made soon after the end of Communism in Czechoslovakia, provides a cynical response to these questions. The bust of Stalin which is repeatedly extracted like a monstrous, screaming baby from the body politic is finally repainted with the national colours of the Czechoslovak flag, thereby undermining the teleological optimism provided by the film's title: there is no death to Stalinism in Bohemia, merely a constant reinvention of the practices of power in different guises. Like the bust of Stalin, global capitalism cunningly feigns the local colours of Czech nationalism in order to exercise its supreme authority. Švankmajer's *Little Otík* offers a similarly jaundiced perspective on post-Communist reality, the eponymous gargantuan and all-devouring tree-stump serving as an allegory of rampant and uncontrolled capitalism. A visit to today's Prague reveals not only the quantum leap from Stalinism to unbridled capitalism but the affinities between these systems in allowing no resistance to or deviation from its practices. In these post-Communist films the Dadaist principles of defiance and subversion continue to play a creative and dynamic role in allowing the artist to resist total appropriation by the forces of the marketplace. In today's global and neo-imperial reality Dada art – as exemplified by the two films discussed in this paper – provides an important – perhaps even a unique – opportunity for counter-cultural resistance to power.

Bibliography

Benson, Timothy O. (ed.). 2002. *Central European Avant-Gardes: Exchange and Transformation, 1910–1930*. Cambridge, MA: MIT Press.

Blythe, Sarah Ganz and Edward D. Powers. 2006. *Looking at Dada*. New York: MOMA.

Bydžovská, Lenka. 2002. "Prague" in Benson 2002: 82–9.

Camus, Albert. 1970. "Death in the Soul" in *Lyrical and Critical Essays* (tr. E.C. Kennedy, ed. P. Thody). New York: Vintage: 40–51.

Dickerman, Leah. 2006. *DADA*. Washington: National Gallery of Art.

Kundera, Milan. 1985. *Nesnesitelná lehkost bytí*. Toronto: '68 Publishers. *The Unbearable Lightness of Being* [1987] (tr. M.H. Helm). New York: Harper Collins.

Lim, Bliss Cua, 2001. "Dolls in Fragments: Daisies as Feminist Allegory" in *Camera Obscura* 16(2): 3777.

Read, Herbert. 1991. "Dada and Structuralism in Chytilová's *Daisies*" in *Cross Currents* 10: 223–34.

Sayer, Derek. 2002. "Surrealities" in Benson 2002: 90–107.

Thomas, Alfred. 2007. *The Bohemian Body. Gender and Sexuality in Modern Czech Culture*. Madison, WI: University of Wisconsin Press.

Weil, Jiří. 1999. *Život s hvězdou*. Prague: Lidové noviny; *Life with a Star* (tr. R. Klímová with R. Schloss). Harmondsworth: Penguin.

Chapter 16

The Importance of Talking Nonsense: Tzara, Ideology, and Dada in the 21st Century

Stephen Forcer

> Pour faire un poème Dadaïste.
> Prenez un journal.
> Prenez des ciseaux.
> Choisissez dans ce journal un article ayant la longueur que vous comptez donner à votre poème.
> Découpez l'article.
> Découpez ensuite avec soin chacun des mots qui forment cet article et mettez-les dans un sac.
> Agitez doucement.
> Sortez ensuite chaque coupure l'une après l'autre.
> Copiez consciencieusement dans l'ordre où elles ont quitté le sac.
> Le poème vous ressemblera.
> Et vous voilà un écrivain infiniment original et d'une sensibilité charmante, encore qu'incomprise du vulgaire. (Tzara 1975: 382)

Tzara's recipe for Dada poetry remains one of his most well-known published pronouncements. Other famous Tzaraisms come to mind: "DADA doute de tout. Dada est tatou. Tout est Dada"; "La pensée se fait dans la bouche"; "Dada ne signifie rien" (Tzara 1975: 381, 379, 360). Over 90 years after the first *Dada soirée* at the Cabaret Voltaire in Zurich, Tzara still speaks to us as arguably the most popularly recognisable figurehead for Dada: but this Tzara is more often than not one made up of sound-bites or aphorisms – a sort of *papier mâché* Tzara strangely reminiscent of Dada montage in which human figures are bound up by newspaper headlines or even wholly constructed out of fragmented printed language – and not read closely as the producer of a heterogeneous six-volume *Œuvres complètes* who remained active until his death in 1963, nearly 40 years after the totemic *Sept manifestes Dada* (1924).

In this chapter I want to use Tzara – and the ways in which he is remembered and read – as the starting point for a discussion about actually reading Dada textuality beyond gesture and quotable quotation. I will begin by summarising extended research I have conducted elsewhere in order to show ways in which it is possible to read Tzara's Dada poetry in its own terms as polyvalent text, and as more or simply other than an extension or creative embodiment of Dada axioms and manifestoes. I will then consider some of the ways in which Tzara's Dada manifestos speak to a reader coming upon them now, many decades after the highly particular socio-historical context within which they were produced. The chapter as a whole will call for an open-ended approach to Dadaist production, for a flexible mode of reading that is prepared to think about Dada not only as time-specific performance – as symptom, reaction and gesture within a particular period of modern history – but also as an extraordinarily mobile, multi-faceted and long-lived fund of meaning, ideas, and (despite Tzara's ludic protestations to the contrary) ideology. I shall in turn argue that Dada retains a striking relevance to a range of modern phenomena, ranging from the mass news media and the rhetoric of international politics to the day-to-day business of simply getting by.

Let us then begin by looking at Tzara's early Dada poetry, and in particular those elements that look like nonsense words.[1] To take an example, in "Pélamide" from *Vingt-cinq poèmes* (1918) the vowel sounds of non-conventional elements mimic and morph into the phonology of actual words from the French language: "ambran bran bran et rendre centre des quatre / beng bong beng bang" (Tzara 1975: 102). Elsewhere, the opening of Tzara's 1917 poem "Le Géant blanc lépreux du paysage" offers a more extended foray into seemingly nonsensical phonographic play, which is here offered within a fantastical scene of biological process and action:

> le sel se groupe en constellation d'oiseaux sur la tumeur de ouate
> dans ses poumons les astéries et les punaises se balancent
> les microbes se cristallisent en palmiers de muscles balançoires
> bonjour sans cigarette tzantzantza ganga
> bouzdouc zdouc nfoùnfa mbaah mbaah nfoùnfa
> macrocystis perifera embrasser les bateaux chirurgien des bateaux
> cicatrice humide propre. (Tzara 1975: 87)

A certain amount of critical thought has been devoted to the general characteristics of Tzara's nonsensical elements, and most commentators seem to agree that they are, as René Lacôte and Georges Haldas (1952: 20) have said, "inventés". Other critics have stressed the link between Tzara's poems and Dada's origins as performance. G. F. Browning (1979: 63, 68, 78), for instance, sees units such as "beng bong beng" and "mbaah mbaah" as a nostalgic homage to the *bruitisme* of the Cabaret Voltaire, recalling the days when Tzara and his collaborators would pepper their stage performances with mock-African chanting. Mary Ann Caws has also mentioned the idea of Tzara's nonsense as imitative of non-European languages: "Tzara speaks of undergoing a severe psychological crisis around 1916 and then of trying to efface the sentimental from his poems. For this purpose, he incorporates into the poems sounds, scraps of pseudo-language, and phrases resembling African dialects" (Tzara 1973: 23-4). However, I want to argue that, although a purge of the sentimental may indeed have been Tzara's intention, the psycho-textuality of the poems themselves has other ideas.

To begin demonstrating this I should first of all deal with the word "nonsense": for, when working with the sorts of verbal formations used by Tzara, "glossolalia" seems to be a more useful and specific term in that it describes an often disquieting stylistic performance in which the poet appears to be speaking in tongues, and which features verbal compounds that may or may not be related to existing words from French or other languages. The notion of glossolalia also relates helpfully to the various oratory figures that Tzara evokes and mimics in his texts, and who also spout various sorts of difficult or apparently nonsensical verbiage, from dictators and Catholic priests to medicine men and babbling babies.

To take an individual glossolalic element as an example, the unit "bouzdouc" from the start of line 5 of 'Le Géant' reveals under close analysis a dense and multi-levelled signifying play. Firstly, bouzdouc contains Tzara's signature letter "z", which comes to function as a cipher for Tzara's name and sense of self. For example, "Danse caoutchouc verre" from *Vingt-cinq poèmes* introduces a certain "monsieur [sic] / tzacatzac" (Tzara 1975: 111); in "Le Géant" the repetition of the distinctive combination t-z-a in "tzantzantza" offers an early suggestion that the poem is in some way bound up with issues of personal identity and selfhood. Also connected to identity and selfhood is the letter "b", another common character in the glossolalic compounds of "Le Géant". One clue as to this frequency comes later on in the poem: "berthe mon éducation ma queue est froide et monochromatique nfoua / loua la" (Tzara 1975: 87). In Tzara's aborted autobiography *Faites vos jeux* (1924) "berthe" turns out to be Berthe Hughes – an Anglo-French girl with whom he had an abortive sexual encounter around 1916 – and who apparently aroused in Tzara conflicting currents of (self-)loathing, misplaced pride and incomprehension. There in turn seems to be a sense in which "Le Géant" refers to the two participants not just at low resolution through "berthe" and the unit "tza", but also fragments distinctive individual characters from their names and scatters them throughout other parts of the poem's verbal terrain. I have already said that the Tzarian "z" skitters through the text, ghosting in and out of words both conventional and not – so too the figure and name of Berthe offers a compelling context for the abundant "b's, stated and restated in "balancent", "balançoire", "bonjour", "bouzdouc", "mbaah", "bateaux" and so on. Thus at the end of the poem Tzara babbles baby-like as he over-determines the start of Berthe's name but without being able to name her in full: "nfoùnda nbabàba nfoùnda tata / nbabàba".

Also significant in these parting lines is the presence of "tata". For although it often is said that Dadaist nonsense resembles or sounds like an African language, many of the words used by Tzara do in fact check out against a Swahili dictionary.[2] "Tata", for instance, means "confusion" in Swahili, and therefore fits with an immediately previous boast from the poet that the reader is basically an imbecile and cannot understand the poem: "[le lecteur] est mince idiot sale il ne comprend pas mes vers il crie" (Tzara 1975: 88). Moreover, in its close proximity to "nbababa" and the stammered, abortive naming of Berthe, "tata" also relates to Tzara's admitted inability to understand Berthe, which he describes in *Faites vos jeux* as transforming into "[une] férocité qui sauve quand on ne comprend pas" (Tzara 1975: 283). So in "tata / nbabàba" we find both a phonographic fragment of Berthe as a problematic love object and the confusion she instilled in Tzara, but recoded into a word from Swahili.

It is against this backdrop of loathing and Tzara's contradictory desire to both expel Berthe and understand her that we may see a further function in "bouzdouc". For as in Freudian dreamwork there is more than a sense here of a verbal condensation, of different existing words being squashed into a new and unrecognisable form. Prominent among such existing words in French is "bouc", evoking both a male goat and an unclean or lewd individual, and suggestive of the figure of speech "bouc émissaire". Etymologically describing a goat chased out into the wilderness by Jewish communities, "bouc émissaire" is a telling suggestion from within a supposedly nonsensical formation: Tzara was born to Jewish parents and in 1915 was sent by them to study in Switzerland, if not a wilderness at least a place that Tzara describes in a 1920 letter to Francis Picabia as a form of exile and "une tumeur où Dieu a craché quelque lacs" (Sanouillet 1993: 532). Beyond "bouc" other French words are half-contained or hinted at by "bouzdouc". There is "bouse", for instance, meaning "bovine excrement", which fits with Dada's scatological iconography and which would later find its way into the lexis of Tzara's *L'Homme approximatif* (1931) (Tzara 1977: 88). There is "boucan", an indistinct but deafening hullabaloo of noise and shouts, and which recalls the mêlée of performance Dadaism. There is "boucanier", harbouring within "Le Géant" 's nautical lexis of boats, starfish and seaweed. As we have seen there is also "bouc", a cognate of the eponymous leper, what with its connotations of uncleanness and sexual impropriety. All of which leaves the oft-quoted remarks about Dada poetry being pulled out of a hat looking somewhat simplistic as a context for actually reading the poem: rather, when read close to, 'Le Géant' reveals itself as a rich and multi-levelled poetic exercise in fragmented experience, selfhood and language, figuring Tzara himself as the "Géant blanc lépreux" as he struggles to come to terms with competing currents of sexual desire, self-loathing and confusion. So too textual features that may appear to be "scraps" or "pseudo-language" are nonetheless invested with extremely powerful and intimate affective currents. Moreover, this is wholly in keeping with the semantic characteristics of work by a range of other Dadaists.[3]

To an extent, then, Tzara has been a victim of his own propaganda. That is, he joyfully tells us that Dada poetry is simply plucked out of a hat at random – and with surprising readiness literary scholarship has more often than not taken him at his word.[4] Instead, and as Johanna Malt (2004) has done recently with Surrealism, researchers may have much more to gain by reading Dada literature outside of or against essences such as authorial "intention" or a seductive and continued – but limiting, I would argue – tendency for bio-historical accounts. In Tzara's case the striking density of his poetry suggests that other areas of his Dada work may be ripe for review. In order to give a suggestion of this potential, I will now move into the second section of the discussion: in the same way that Tzara's poetic glossolalia carries strong affective and personal charge – as well as its unexpectedly complex signifying potential – so too there is scope for reading his Dada prose more closely and beyond the qualities of gesture, provocation and shock.

To begin this, it is worth noting that for all the raucous claims to anti-ideology and nihilism made both by and on behalf of Dada its origins within a period of epic human failure mean that it inevitably does assume a considerable degree of ideological drive. For example, as Lee Harwood (2005: 121) has said in a very useful discussion, "[t]he protests and works of the Dadaists were for them the one sane answer any artist could make to a world apparently gone insane. A feeling that absurdity and confusion must be carried further and further until everything breaks down into a silence from which a new vision can be constructed". Harwood's point about silence and breakdown is an important one, suggesting as it does that Dada's apparent nonsense is also a trajectory towards the cessation of language, a necessarily bizarre half-way house between conventional discourse and silence. He quotes Hugo Ball (*Zur Kritik der deutschen Intelligenz* 1919): "Perhaps it is necessary to have resolutely, forcibly produced chaos before an entirely new edifice can be built on a changed basis of belief". The mêlée and confusion of Dada performance and text would seem to be a crucial part of Ball's "forcibly produced chaos", aspiring to a situation in which conventional discourse is not simply written over, but rather arrested, torn up and atomized before anything new can be constructed.

So one could argue that Dada style is in itself "ideological", representing the point of breakdown that comes between the silence mentioned by Harwood and the well behaved institution of conventional language – an institution which is, moreover, complicit with and intrinsic to government, industry, the middle classes and other human systems that had not only failed to prevent the particular idiocy of the First World War but in many ways actively encouraged it and profited from it economically. In Tzara's case, the epic failure of war contrasts with his emphasis on the immutable value and vitality of human life. His "Dada Manifesto 1918", for instance, concludes with the following impassioned lines: "Liberté: DADA DADA DADA, hurlement des douleurs crispées, entrelacement des contraires et de toutes les contradictions, des grotesques, des inconséquences: LA VIE" (Tzara 1975: 367). Within this concern for life there is further stress on the personal, individual and unknowable aspects of human existence, and on Dada as a response to the basic question of how to live better. For example, in the 1922 text "Conférence sur Dada", Tzara writes that

> Dada est un état d'esprit. C'est pour cela qu'il se transforme suivant les races et les événements. Dada s'applique à tout, et pourtant il n'est rien, il est le point où le oui et le non se rencontrent, non pas solennellement dans les châteaux des philosophies humaines, mais tout simplement au coin des rues comme les chiens et les sauterelles. (Tzara 1975: 424)

Despite Dada's popular reputation for nihilism and anti-ideology, as elsewhere there nevertheless emerges here a clear set of basic positive tenets. For whatever else Dada may be, and however bizarrely this may be expressed, it aspires to a fundamental improvement in the human condition, an improvement which in many ways values detail over size and scope. Beyond its obvious disgust at the mechanized massacre of the First World War,[5] Dada is about a basic access to autonomy and equality, cherishing the small and the seemingly irrelevant parts of life, and respecting the day-to-day of human existence: "non pas solennellement dans les châteux [...] mais tout simplement au coin des rues".[6] This is why, when Tzara happily announced the death of Dadaism in 1922, he concluded: "[Dada] ne combat même plus car il sait que cela n'a pas d'importance; ce qui intéresse un Dadaïste, c'est sa propre façon de vivre" (1975: 423–4). Or, as Micheline Tison-Braun (1977: 7) has said, "Toujours à mi-chemin du désespoir et de l'utopie, la révolte Dada implique une conception positive de ce que l'homme et la vie *devraient* être (emphasis in original)". So in this general, life-affirming sense Dada is both of its time and outside of it, asserting its own necessity through disgust at its own present, but also looking to a new and better way of life in which Dada is no longer active. In other words, and to borrow from Bernard Noël, Dada could be described as "nostalgique d'un avenir dont il ne fera plus partie".[7]

It is this open-ended attitude to the future which seems to help make for Dada's general appeal to us as readers and politico-ideological subjects in the 21st century. For while cultural historians have rightly stressed the absolutely fundamental links between the avant-garde and its own historical moment, there remains in Dada itself a fundamentally pan-human quality, an appetite for substantive interpersonal contact across the human cosmos, that reaches out both to other nationalities and classes from its own time, and to generations both past and future. Recourse to Tzara's texts confirms that Dada speaks to us not only about a base sharing of human subjectivity but also about a specific set of values and concepts that underpin the political and personal discourses of our own time. For instance, in his important work *Le Surréalisme et l'après-guerre* (1947) Tzara casts the following look back on Dada:

> Dada naquit d'une exigence morale, d'une volonté implacable d'atteindre à un absolu moral, du sentiment profond que l'homme au centre de toutes les créations de l'esprit, affirmait sa prééminence sur les notions appauvries de la substance humaine, sur les choses mortes et les biens mal acquis. [...] Honneur, Patrie, Morale, Famille, Art, Religion, Liberté, Fraternité, que sais-je, autant de notions répondant à des nécessités humaines, dont il ne subsistait que de squelettiques conventions, car elles étaient vides de leur contenu initial. (Tzara 1982: 65)

Striking here is the extent to which the "notions appauvries" mentioned by Tzara still occupy a place within popular, political and ideological discourse. Indeed, "liberté" and "patrie" stand out as notions that are deployed and appealed to again and again within 21st-century political discourse in general and the so called " 'so-called' war on terror" in particular. For instance, let us consider the word "freedom" as used in two separate speeches given by Tony Blair and George W. Bush. Blair's 2003 speech to the US Congress – the first from a British Prime Minister since Margaret Thatcher in 1985 – registered 24 uses of "free" or "freedom".[8] A speech of similar length by Bush contained 51 such references.[9] Perhaps aware of the abundant repetition, both speakers (or their scriptwriters) used the word "liberty" to break up the flow a little: references to this synonym total 6 and 16 respectively. It is perhaps rather easy to go for such sources and individuals (though Dada would probably say that by default political figureheads are there to be attacked) but next to the 75 uses or cognates of "free" in two appearances by leaders of the "free world" (whatever that is) Tzara's point about the essential divestment or emptiness of traditional notions does seem to describe the continuing way in which certain values or ideas are so over-determined by political discourse as to be little more than rhetorical tics or buzz-words wrung dry of any real meaning, and raising more questions than they answer. What "freedom", for example? At whose expense? In whose favour? And so on and so forth. In the fetishised repetition of a word like "freedom" one might also say that there is an echo here of repeated Dadaist glossolalia, of "mbaah mbaah nbababa", or the childish game of saying a word so many times that one becomes disoriented from its original meaning. So too the idea of a mantra-chanting figurehead is reminiscent of the bishops mumbling away absurdly in Luis Buñuel's *L'Age d'or* (1930). At the same time, it is important to note that Tzara again proposes an antidote to the problems he perceives in the emptiness of traditional notions, and that his alternative again lies with his fundamental belief and trust in "les créations de l'esprit", in the assertion of human vitality, creativity and personality over inherited, imposed and homogenising "values", values that must be regarded with particular care and suspicion when mobilised by political figures. Not that Tzara only has negative or hostile lessons to give concerning politics. There is in his Dada manifestos, for instance, a timely emphasis on the inevitably of self-contradiction, as if in the end to speak is in itself to contradict oneself, whether speech involves an individual person or a collected body or organisation. In the UK at least, the acceptance of contradiction is an instructive counterpoint to the apparent party political anxiety to stay on-message and to avoid disagreement or even – sin of all sins – the admission that one was wrong or that language might be a flawed vehicle for the transport of ideas.

In the same way that Tzara's Dada texts embrace contradiction, so too Tzara's handling of Dada as a phenomenon exhibits an ideological sense of its own self-termination, a willingness and indeed desire to accept one's own shelf-life. In notable contrast to Breton and Surrealism, Tzara always had a marked sense of his own cultural mortality, and was refreshingly open about the need to adapt to changing climates, to call time when a movement or idea had reached the end of its useful life, and to not carry on at all costs or to equate success with historical longevity. Indeed, in encouraging us to adopt a sense of our own mortality, as both individuals and as national or historical entities, there is in Tzara's Dada more than a pre-echo of Valéry's famous remarks in "La Crise de l'esprit": "Nous autres, civilisations, nous savons maintenant que nous sommes mortelles [...]

Et nous voyons maintenant que l'abîme de l'histoire est assez grand pour tout le monde. Nous sentons qu'une civilisation a la même fragilité qu'une vie" (Valéry 1957: 988). Like Valéry, Dada deplores the First World War, its epic loss of life and the cultural generations that will never be – but in word and deed Dada asserts the importance of embracing the abîme when it is time to do so. And it makes such assertions in the firm belief that the inherent vitality and goodness of the human spirit will re-emerge from disaster and despair, with marked emphasis on optimism, affection and love along the way: as Tzara says in his "Manifeste de Monsieur Antipyrine", with a degree of mocking but also candour, "je vous aime tant, je vous assure et je vous adore" (Tzara 1975: 358).

So to begin concluding, when talking of the extent to which Dada can or cannot be said to exist outside of its own time-frame I would perhaps stress the need to distinguish between, on the one hand, attempts to continue or revive Dada as a practice (as in neo-Dada) and, on the other, Dada as a living spirit, as an extraordinarily rich and heterogeneous fund of ideas born out of a response to a fundamentally twentieth-century set of failures, stimuli, provocations and aspirations. In turn, Dada connects with a range of other major currents in early twentieth-century thought, discovery and ideology: with linguistics and the relationships between signifier and signified; with psychoanalysis and the irrepressible vitality of the human mind *avant la lettre* of Surrealist attempts to extend Freud's work into art and literature; and with Heisenberg and the notion of doubt, itself formalised into the uncertainty principle in 1922 (the same year that Tzara proclaimed the end of Dada). Undeniably, Dada's emergence and vitality meshed themselves into the density and complexities of the movement's own present. At the same time, Dada resolutely was and remains a phenomenon that has within its view a range of possible human futures, in terms both of an ideal world (or at least one that is vastly improved) and of a planet plagued by idiocy. So Dada still speaks to us – and not just in quotable aphorisms – functioning in general as a call to critical thinking and in particular as a response to specific manifestations of human stupidity in the modern world: a world where war has emphatically not gone away and remains at the centre of global political agendas, where politics is more than ever characterised by point scoring, sound-bites and quotable statistics, where we find both large-scale famine and the spectaclurisation of a single man wilfully going without food suspended in a Perspex box opposite Tower Bridge,[10] and where world leaders measure the success of their presidency by the fish they have caught.[11] As both ideology and as literature Dada asks us think again about the textual richness that can be mobilised within seemingly nonsensical cultural practice, and about the legitimate guises genuine nonsense is often found to be wearing in the world outside Dada's own ludic complexity.

Notes

[1] The extended analysis underpinning the following discussion of nonsense words is presented in Forcer (2006: 10–28).

[2] Glossolalic elements in "Le Géant" were checked against The Internet Living Swahili Dictionary provided by the Kamusi Project, Yale University http://www.yale.edu/swahili/ [accessed 14 January 2007].

[3] For example, at the "Eggs Laid by Tigers" conference, Roger Cardinal discussed the way in which the letter "N" features in Schwitters' collages as a solitary and fragmented cipher for Norway, to which Schwitters fled in 1937. As with Tzara, in Schwitters' work the potential for meaning and intensity actually increases as language is broken down. Cardinal made his remarks on Norway in a moving paper entitled " 'Sch... Sprechen Sie Merz?' On reading Kurt Schwitters" (8 July 2006).

[4] See Henri Béhar: "A l'exception de quelques formules particulièrement violentes, je me demande si quelqu'un a jamais lu, ce qui s'appelle LIRE, l'œuvre Dadaïste de Tzara, et cherché à en dégager la portée doublement révolutionnaire, sur le plan intellectuel comme sur le plan esthétique". "Introduction" (Tzara 1996: 5).

[5] See, for example, the "Manifeste de Monsieur Antipyrine", in *Sept manifestes Dada* (Tzara 1975: 35–78).

[6] For a reading of how this spirit is remobilized in other French experimental work, see Foster 2007.

[7] See volume 1 of the present edition.

[8] Address to joint meeting of US Congress, 17 July 2003. Transcript available at http://news.bbc.co.uk/2/hi/uk_news/politics/3076253.stm [accessed 12 June 2008].

[9] Remarks by the President at the 20th Anniversary of the National Endowment for Democracy, 6 November 2003. Transcript available at http://www.whitehouse.gov/news/releases/2003/11/20031106-2.html [accessed 12 June 2008].

[10] One feels it would be a revealing but probably depressing exercise to calculate the respective TV media hours devoted in 2003 to world famine on the one hand and, on the other, to the 44 days of self-imposed starvation spent by David Blaine by the River Thames.

[11] "Landing a big fish: as good as it gets for Bush", *The Guardian* (8 May 2006).

Bibliography

Browning, Gordon Frederick. 1979. *Tristan Tzara: The Genesis of the Dada Poem or from Dada to Aa*. Stuttgart: Heinz.

Forcer, Stephen. 2006. *Modernist Song: The Poetry of Tristan Tzara*. Oxford: Legenda.

——. 2007. "Ceci n'est pas une transmission: Dada and Surrealism in work by Jean-Luc Godard and Anne-Marie Miéville" in I. McNeill and B. Stephens (eds). *Transmissions: Essays in French Literature, Thought, and Culture*. Bern: Peter Lang: 179–97.

Harwood, Lee. 2005. *Chanson Dada: Tristan Tzara*. Boston, Mass.: Black Widow Press.

Lacôte, René and Georges Haldas. 1952. *Tristan Tzara*. Paris: Seghers.

Malt, Johanna. 2004. *Obscure Objects of Desire: Surrealism, Fetishism, Politics*. Oxford: Oxford University Press.

Sanouillet, Michel. 1993. *Dada à Paris*. Paris: Flammarion.

Tzara, Tristan. 1973. *Approximate Man and Other Writings* (tr. and ed. M.A. Caws). Detroit: Wayne State University Press.

——. 1975. *Œuvres complètes I* (ed. H. Béhar). Paris: Flammarion.

——. 1977. *Œuvres complètes II* (ed. H. Béhar). Paris: Flammarion.

——. 1982. *Œuvres complètes V* (ed. H. Béhar). Paris: Flammarion.

——. 1996. *Dada est tatou. Tout est Dada* (ed. H. Béhar). Paris: Flammarion.

Valéry, Paul. 1957. *Œuvres I*. Paris: Gallimard (Collection la Pléiade).

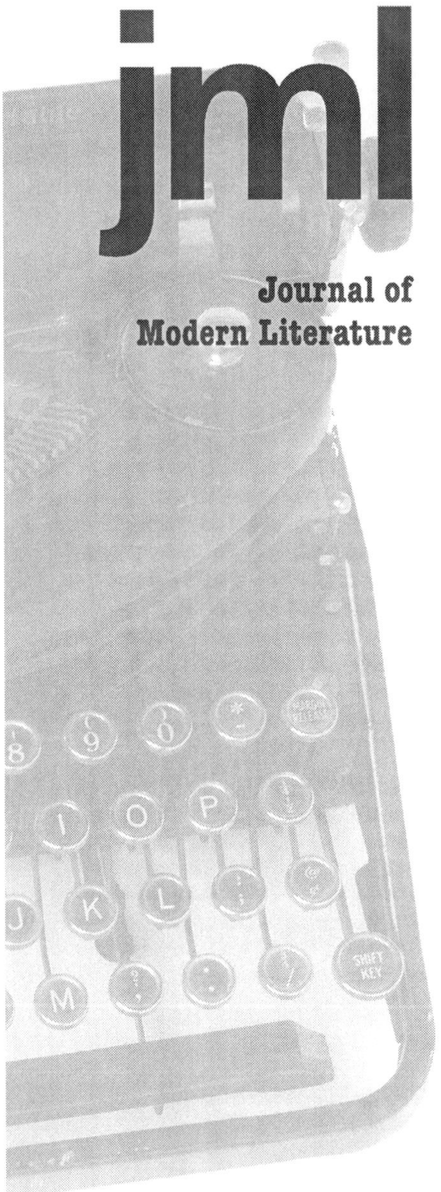

EDITED BY PAULA MARANTZ COHEN, RACHEL BLAU DUPLESSIS, JEAN-MICHEL RABATÉ, ROBERT CASERIO, AND DANIEL T. O'HARA

More than three decades after its founding, *jml* remains the most important scholarly serial in the field and is widely recognized as such. It emphasizes scholarly studies of literature in all languages, as well as related arts and cultural artifacts, from 1900 to the present. *Jml* is international in its scope; recent contributors include scholars from Australia, England, France, Italy, Nigeria, Saudi Arabia, South Africa, and Spain.

PUBLISHED QUARTERLY
eISSN 1529-1464
pISSN 0022-281X

Available in electronic, combined electronic & print, and print formats

SUBSCRIBE http://www.jstor.org/r/iupress

For more information on Indiana University Press
http://www.iupress.indiana.edu

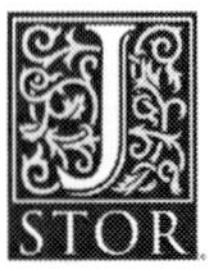

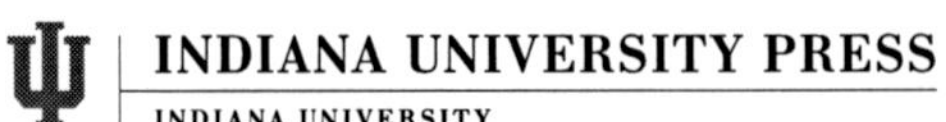
INDIANA UNIVERSITY PRESS
INDIANA UNIVERSITY

IUP/*Journals*

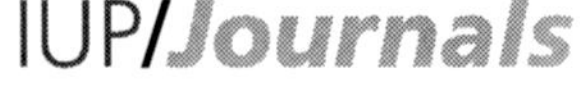
601 North Morton Street, Bloomington, Indiana 47404-3797 USA

Samuel Beckett and Pain

Edited by
Mariko Hori Tanaka,
Yoshiki Tajiri, and Michiko Tsushima

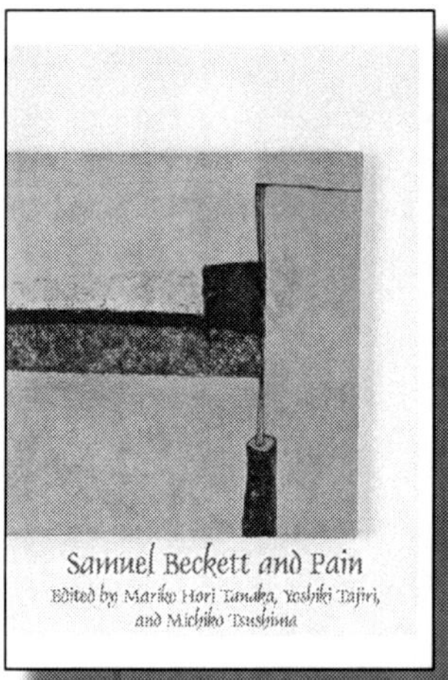

Samuel Beckett and Pain is a collection of ten essays which explores the theme of pain in Beckett's works. Experiencing both physical and psychological pain in the course of his life, Beckett found suffering in human life inevitable, accepted it as a source of inspiration in his writings, and probed it to gain deeper insight into the difficult and emotionally demanding processes of artistic creation, practice and performance. Acknowledging the recent developments in the study of pain in literature and culture, this volume explores various aspects of pain in Beckett's works, a subject which has been heretofore only sporadically noted. The topics discussed include Beckett's aesthetics and pain, pain as loss and trauma, pain in relation to palliation, pain at the experience of the limit, pain as archive, and pain as part of everyday life and language. This volume is characterized by its plural, interdisciplinary perspectives covering the fields of literature, theatre, art, philosophy, and psychoanalysis. By suggesting more diverse paths in Beckett studies, the authors hope to make a lasting contribution to contemporary literary studies and other relevant fields.

Amsterdam/New York, NY
2012. 247 pp.
(Faux Titre 372)
Paper €50,-/US$65,-
E-Book €45,-/US$59,-
ISBN: 978-90-420-3523-2
ISBN: 978-94-012-0798-0

USA/Canada:
248 East 44th Street, 2nd floor,
New York, NY 10017, USA.
Call Toll-free (US only): T: 1-800-225-3998
F: 1-800-853-3881

All other countries:
Tijnmuiden 7, 1046 AK Amsterdam, The Netherlands
Tel. +31-20-611 48 21 Fax +31-20-447 29 79
Please note that the exchange rate is subject to fluctuations

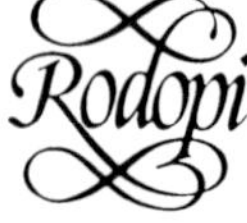

9 789042 035898